Selected Essays by
Fukuzawa Yukichi

SOAS Studies in Modern and Contemporary Japan

SERIES EDITOR:
Christopher Gerteis (SOAS, University of London, UK)

EDITORIAL BOARD:
Stephen Dodd (SOAS, University of London, UK)
Andrew Gerstle (SOAS, University of London, UK)
Janet Hunter (London School of Economics, UK)
Barak Kushner (University of Cambridge, UK)
Helen Macnaughtan (SOAS, University of London, UK)
Aaron W Moore (University of Edinburgh, UK)
Timon Screech (SOAS, University of London, UK)
Naoko Shimazu (NUS-Yale College, Singapore)

Published in association with the Japan Research Centre at the School of Oriental and African Studies, University of London, UK.

SOAS Studies in Modern and Contemporary Japan features scholarly books on modern and contemporary Japan, showcasing new research monographs as well as translations of scholarship not previously available in English. Its goal is to ensure that current, high quality research on Japan, its history, politics and culture, is made available to an English speaking audience.

Published:
Women and Democracy in Cold War Japan, Jan Bardsley
Christianity and Imperialism in Modern Japan, Emily Anderson
The China Problem in Postwar Japan, Robert Hoppens
Media, Propaganda and Politics in 20th Century Japan, The Asahi Shimbun Company (translated by Barak Kushner)
Contemporary Sino-Japanese Relations on Screen, Griseldis Kirsch
Debating Otaku in Contemporary Japan, edited by Patrick W. Galbraith, Thiam Huat Kam and Björn-Ole Kamm
Politics and Power in 20th-Century Japan, Mikuriya Takashi and Nakamura Takafusa (translated by Timothy S. George)
Japanese Taiwan, edited by Andrew Morris
Japan's Postwar Military and Civil Society, Tomoyuki Sasaki
The History of Japanese Psychology, Brian J. McVeigh
Postwar Emigration to South America from Japan and the Ryukyu Islands, Pedro Iacobelli
The Uses of Literature in Modern Japan, Sari Kawana
Post-Fascist Japan, Laura Hein
Mass Media, Consumerism and National Identity in Postwar Japan, Martyn David Smith
Japan's Occupation of Java in the Second World War, Ethan Mark
Gathering for Tea in Modern Japan, Taka Oshikiri
Engineering Asia, Hiromi Mizuno, Aaron S. Moore and John DiMoia

Forthcoming:
Kenkoku University and the Experience of Pan-Asianism, Yuka Hiruma Kishida
Automobility and the City in Japan and Britain, c. 1955–1990, Simon Gunn and Susan Townsend

Selected Essays by Fukuzawa Yukichi

On Government

Introduction and Commentaries by
Albert M. Craig

Translations by
Teruko Craig

BLOOMSBURY ACADEMIC
Bloomsbury Publishing Plc
50 Bedford Square, London, WC1B 3DP, UK
1385 Broadway, New York, NY 10018, USA
29 Earlsfort Terrace, Dublin 2, Ireland

BLOOMSBURY, BLOOMSBURY ACADEMIC and the
Diana logo are trademarks of Bloomsbury Publishing Plc

First published in Great Britain 2019
This paperback edition published in 2021

Introduction and Editorial Content © Albert M. Craig, 2019
English Translation © Teruko Craig, 2019

Albert M. Craig has asserted his right under the Copyright,
Designs and Patents Act, 1988, to be identified as Editor of this work.

For legal purposes the Acknowledgments on p. xi
constitute an extension of this copyright page.

In association with the Fukuzawa Memorial Center for
Modern Japanese Studies, KEIO University.

Cover image: Yukichi Fukuzawa, circa 1890 in Japan.
(© The Asahi Shimbun/Getty Images)

All rights reserved. No part of this publication may be reproduced or transmitted
in any form or by any means, electronic or mechanical, including photocopying,
recording, or any information storage or retrieval system, without prior permission
in writing from the publishers.

Bloomsbury Publishing Plc does not have any control over, or responsibility for, any
third-party websites referred to or in this book. All internet addresses given in this
book were correct at the time of going to press. The author and publisher regret any
inconvenience caused if addresses have changed or sites have ceased to exist, but
can accept no responsibility for any such changes.

A catalogue record for this book is available from the British Library.

A catalog record for this book is available from the Library of Congress.

ISBN:	HB:	978-1-3500-9661-5
	PB:	978-1-3501-9245-4
	ePDF:	978-1-3500-9662-2
	eBook:	978-1-3500-9663-9

Series: SOAS Studies in Modern and Contemporary Japan

Typeset by Integra Software Services Pvt. Ltd.

To find out more about our authors and books visit www.bloomsbury.com
and sign up for our newsletters.

For our children and grandchildren

Contents

Foreword	viii
Acknowledgments	xi
Part 1　General Introduction	1
1　The Progress of Civilization and the Stages of Government	3
2　Fukuzawa's Politics	19
Part 2　Fukuzawa's Essays in Translation	27
3　The Division of Power (*Bunkenron*), 1877	29
4　On a National Assembly (*Kokkairon*), 1879	77
5　The Trend of the Times (*Jiji taiseiron*), 1882	109
6　Revering the Emperor (*Sonnōron*), 1888	133
7　The Future Course of the Diet (*Kokkai no zento*), 1892	167
Notes	209
Index	219

Foreword

In East Asia, Japan was the first to become a modern nation. In the late nineteenth century, it broke with past history, took in learning and institutions from the West, and catapulted ahead. One day it had been a land of samurai, daimyo, and castle towns, with a culture totally unlike that of the West. The next day it had factories, trains, universities, political parties, a constitution, and a parliament. What strange alchemy had produced this rapid transformation?

Of those who could read Western books during the last years of the Tokugawa era (1600–1868), and who understood how the West saw itself and the challenge it posed to Japan, none was more influential than Fukuzawa Yukichi (1835–1901). His writings on the important issues of the day were widely read; his *Collected Works* come to twenty-one volumes. This book presents five essays he wrote between 1876 and 1890. All concern, directly or indirectly, the transition to representative government in Japan.

Fukuzawa was from Nakatsu, a middling-sized feudal domain in northwest Kyushu. He was a samurai, a member of the ruling 5 or 6 percent of the population, but his family ranked near the bottom rung of that class. His father died when he was one and the family was poor, so he entered school late. At school, he studied the typical curriculum of Confucian classics and Chinese history. By his own account, he was slower than most during the morning reading exercises but excelled in the afternoon debates on the interpretations of the texts.

At age twenty, two years after Commodore Perry "opened" Japan in 1853, on his older brother's advice, he went to Nagasaki to study Dutch and gunnery. This was followed by two years of intensive study at the renowned school of Ogata Kōan in Osaka, which taught Western medicine. In addition to reading Dutch books on medicine, he performed a few chemical experiments. In his autobiography, he recounts his years at the school as a time of unbridled freedom.

After completing his medical studies in 1857, he was ordered by his domain to open a school at its second Edo estate to teach Dutch to its young samurai. While in Edo, he visited the nearby treaty port of Yokohama and, becoming convinced of the greater utility of English, he switched to the study of that language. He subsequently persuaded a high official of the first bakufu mission to the West to take him on as a servant. In that capacity, he traveled on the *Kanrin-maru* to San Francisco in 1860 and spent two months there. On returning to Japan, his linguistic talents were recognized, and he was appointed to the corps of translators at the Gaikokugata, the bakufu office that handled relations with foreign powers. He worked there from 1859 to 1868. The precision he brought to his early translations, in part at least, reflects the skill he had achieved in translating diplomatic documents. The post also gave him a first-hand view of Japan's relations with Western powers.

Fukuzawa traveled abroad two more times: to Europe in 1862, and to the United States in 1867. On both occasions, though still of low status, he went as an official interpreter for the missions. During his second trip to the United States in 1867, he somehow incurred the wrath of the mission's leader, and on his return, he was suspended from his job at the Gaikokugata. After some months, the suspension was lifted and he returned to work, but he resigned after the fall of the Tokugawa shogunate and the Meiji Restoration in 1868. In a letter to a friend, he confided that he had had enough of government service and that in the future he would support himself by translating Western works. The number of translations he made during the next three years was prodigious.

Fukuzawa's translations of Western works and his original writings set him apart from other samurai. But it remains unclear what ambition, what inner drive, what intellectual curiosity, prompted him to begin translating. His first work, in 1864, was a Chinese–English phrasebook into which he inserted Japanese readings; he had bought the phrasebook in San Francisco in 1860. He next translated articles from treaty port newspapers and distributed these to bakufu officials.

His first full-length work, which established his reputation as the preeminent interpreter of the West, was the three volumes of *Conditions in the West* (*Seiyō jijō*), published in 1866, 1868, and 1870. The first and third volumes (called volumes I and II, respectively, in the Japanese editions) contained histories of the Netherlands, the United States, England, Russia, and France, together with materials on their governments, finances, and military. These were mainly translations from American and British gazetteers, encyclopedias, and school histories. The second volume (called *Gaihen* or supplementary volume) was largely a translation of chapters from *Political Economy* by the British writer John Hill Burton. During the early years following the Restoration in 1868, Fukuzawa published two more books that became best sellers of the day: *An Invitation to Learning* (*Gakumon no susume*, 1872–6) and *An Outline of Theories of Civilization* (*Bunmeiron no gairyaku*, 1875). Both works spelled out prescriptions to strengthen Japan that were based on Fukuzawa's understanding of the changes that had produced the industrial West.

During the 1870s, Fukuzawa continued to read English-language books on the history of the modern West, wrote essays recommending changes in Japan, and taught at his school, which eventually developed into Keiō University. Early on, he was critical of the newly formed Japanese political parties, and held their leaders in low regard; he felt that Japan was not ready to adopt the elective government system of the modern West. But in the face of rebellions by ex-samurai in 1876, he changed his mind and came out in favor of elective assemblies at the prefectural level. In 1879, he took a giant step further and strongly advocated a national assembly.

Through the years, Fukuzawa modified his views in accord with Japan's progress. To interpret historical change, he sought out different explanations and models. Eventually, he arrived at three models:

1. Early on, when he wrote *Conditions in the West* and *An Outline of Theories of Civilization*, he thought that the historical spirit moved slowly and that the progress of civilization occurred over centuries. This was his first model of history.
2. In 1879, he propounded a new model that stressed technology and rapid historical change. In England and elsewhere, the steam engine, telegraph, postal system, and printing had led to revolutions in transportation and communications, and these in turn had led to fundamental changes in thought and social relations. Even the advanced nations of Europe had reached civilization only after 1800. In short, what was modern was recent; important changes could occur within decades. Japan, he thought, was not that far behind the leading countries of the West. This was his second model.
3. While the second model explained much, Fukuzawa came to feel that this, too, was inadequate in that it placed too great an emphasis on external forces. So, in 1890, soon after the opening of the Diet, he put forth the sketch of an entirely new model that explained Japan's historical readiness for parliamentary government. The model was based on developments in Japan's own society prior to 1868, changes that had European parallels but were indigenous to Japan. Over the course of two hundred and fifty years of Tokugawa rule, he asserted that the balance between institutions in Tokugawa society had produced a kind of indigenous self-rule and individual independence. This spirit of independence would make the new parliamentary institution succeed.

Acknowledgments

Our debts are many. First we would like to thank Iwatani Jūrō and the staff at the Fukuzawa Yukichi Memorial Center at Keiō University for their hospitality during our stay in the spring of 2013. Nishikawa Naoko at the Center patiently answered our questions and arranged meetings with scholars in the field, including, among others, Anzai Toshimitsu, Hiraishi Naoaki, Karube Tadashi, and Matsuda Kōichirō.

In the United States, we owe thanks to Mitani Hiroshi for his insightful comments, to Phyllis Birnbaum for technical advice and suggestions on points of style, to Andrew Gordon for thoughtfully expediting the publication of the book, and to the Harvard-Yenching Institute for a subvention.

Part One

General Introduction

1

The Progress of Civilization and the Stages of Government

Japan might have advanced from a form of feudal monarchy to a more centralized form of monarchy, but it had yet to achieve civilization and was not yet ready to become a parliamentary state. This was Fukuzawa's judgment during the first eleven years following the Meiji Restoration. He had many reasons: the people's educational level was low, the imprint of the feudal past was still strong, and the necessary institutions for an elective system were not in place. He accepted the general proposition that representative government accorded with the basics of human nature; Western history had demonstrated this to be true. He described Western parliamentary systems in exemplary terms in both his translations and original writings, and he wanted such a system for Japan. He also associated the strong military power of the Western nations with their parliamentary systems, but felt that Japan was still unprepared for such a system. A turning point came in 1876, when he came out in favor of local assemblies, and in 1879, he advocated a national assembly.

Why did Fukuzawa change his mind? As history, eleven years is brief. Had Japanese society, still constrained by traditional practices, really changed sufficiently to adopt so Western an institution as a parliament?

Fukuzawa viewed the changes in his own society in terms of history. Early on he had been schooled in Chinese history. He had then studied Western history, both of Europe and the United States. He had learned from the latter that Western scholars had two ways of casting their own history: one focused on civilization, the other on government.

The progress of civilization

Put simply, a "civilization" consists of the totality of systems, ideas, institutions, and feelings of a people. Civilization is what society is to the sociologist, or culture to the anthropologist. Fukuzawa compared civilization to an ocean into which various rivers flow, or a drama in which the several actors fulfill their designated roles. European historians of the nineteenth century saw the development of human civilization as a panorama stretching from the earliest stage of primitive savagery to barbarism, continuing through a half-civilized stage, and finally, to civilization and enlightenment. It is not surprising that Fukuzawa should have picked up the Western idea of civilization and applied it to Japan, since most of the books he translated used the concept of civilization as their framework.

In his *An Outline of Theories of Civilization*, Fukuzawa stresses the point that civilization should not be sought in externals, such as stone buildings or iron bridges; what matters is the spirit (*seishin*) that animates a people. He explains that "spirit" is formless and difficult to describe.

> When it [civilization] is nourished, it grows to embrace the myriad things of the earth; if repressed or restrained, its external manifestations will also vanish. It is in constant motion, advancing or retreating, waxing or waning. It may seem a will o'-the-wisp or an apparition, but if we look at its real manifestations within present-day Asia and Europe, we can clearly see it is not illusory.

He continues:

> Let us now call this "the spirit of a people" (*ikkoku jinmin no kifū*). In respect to time, we call it "the trend of the times" (*jisei*). In reference to persons, it may be called "human sentiments" (*jinshin*). In regard to the nation as a whole, it may be called "a nation's ways" (*kokuzoku*) or "national opinion" (*kokuron*). These things are what is meant by the spirit of civilization. And it is this spirit that differentiates the manners and customs of Asia and Europe. Hence the spirit of a civilization can also be described as the sentiments and customs of a people.[1]

To understand how a civilization changes and progresses, Fukuzawa drew on books by the popular American geographers Samuel Augustus Mitchell and Sarah Cornell, the British writers John Hill Burton and Thomas Buckle, and the French historian François Guizot (in English translation). In *An Outline of Theories of Civilization*, he twice translated a simple sketch of civilization's progress from Mitchell's high school geography text, *New School Geography*. The theories presented by these authors vary in emphasis and detail, but they can all be traced back to the ideas of Adam Smith and other early thinkers of the Scottish Enlightenment, or, in the case of Guizot, to the writings of A. J. R. Turgot in France.

In his lectures and writings, Smith held that all peoples were originally in the "savage" state. They gathered and hunted and often engaged in warfare with other savage tribes. Some savages then domesticated animals and advanced to the state of "barbarism." Following their flocks, they gained a more dependable source of food. Then came the discovery of agriculture, and the development of a "half-civilized" state, with cities, commerce, and literacy. From this intermediate stage, certain Western nations advanced further, developing machine industry and science, reaching higher levels of literacy, and eventually adopting representative government to attain a "civilized" stage. Nineteenth-century writers later added a further "enlightened" stage to describe the advanced state of their own civilization.

The stages were seen as applicable to all peoples of the world. Fukuzawa accepted this view and applied the schema to Japan. He recognized Japan's cultural borrowing from China in ancient times and maintained that it had been half-civilized from that time through the Tokugawa years. That is to say, prior to the Meiji Restoration, Japan had cities, commerce, a degree of literacy, and agriculture, but lacked the science, machine technology, and parliamentary institutions found in the advanced nations of the West.

In his early three-volume *Conditions in the West*, Fukuzawa made clear that it had taken Western nations hundreds of years to advance from one stage to the next. He wanted Japan to change along similar lines, though he never specified an exact timetable. In the event, Japan's advance turned out to be far more rapid than he had imagined possible. This was partly because its historical situation was so markedly different. The West had been the pathfinder; it had found its way forward by trial and error, and in recent centuries had never encountered a civilization more advanced than its own. In contrast, Japan, suddenly exposed to the most advanced nations of the West, was able to deliberately pick and choose. That it was already half-civilized when it encountered the West made the swift transition possible.

In *An Outline of Theories of Civilization*, Fukuzawa described the psychological impact of Japan's encounter with the West. The sudden encounter caused "violent upheavals" in men's minds, the repercussions so complex as to "almost defy imagination." "Contemporary Japanese culture is undergoing a transformation in essence, like the transformation of fire into water." Going from one state to the other, "it is just as if a person had led two lives in a single body, or as if a single person possessed two bodies."[2]

The shock of exposure to a very different civilization, which Fukuzawa, who had studied the West, experienced more keenly than most of his compatriots, prepared the Japanese for the overthrow of Tokugawa rule and the series of revolutionary actions taken by the new post-Restoration government. Though initially taken aback by the turn of events, Fukuzawa came to approve of the pace of change. For Japan to survive as an independent nation, he increasingly felt that a swift transition was necessary.

Feudal government, West and East

A government is merely one component of a civilization—there is no double helix—and since it is a smaller topic than civilization, it is easier to address.

As noted, Fukuzawa translated histories of the Netherlands and England in the first volume of *Conditions in the West*, and histories of Russia and France in the third. For sources he used entries in encyclopedias and gazetteers or national history textbooks. In doing so, he discerned a common pattern: an advance from medieval "feudalism" to some form of monarchy, and then (Russia excepted) to "representative government." He also treated the United States in the first volume, but he found its history "irregular": it had not experienced feudalism or monarchy, but had piggybacked the history of England.[3]

Fukuzawa never attempted a point-to-point correlation between the stage of a nation's civilization and its form of government. He recognized that a nation's government could sometimes be ahead or behind other dimensions of its civilization. He nevertheless assumed a rough correlation: as a nation's civilization advanced, it would progress from feudalism to monarchy, and then, after entering the stage of civilization and enlightenment, it would advance further to adopt some form of representative government.

Such a view was standard in the West during most of the nineteenth century. Fukuzawa's adoption of the schema would have been unexceptional save for one crucial fact: he judged that Japan's society during the Tokugawa era—the society in which he was born and spent half of his life—was feudal; that is to say, it was roughly similar to the societies of medieval or late medieval Europe. Based on this similarity, he surmised that the future course of Japan's development would more or less replicate the European pattern: it would first advance to centralized rule, and then, in time, to some form of representative government. This grasp of a parallel inner dynamic working within Japan shaped his political thought from the 1870s through the 1880s.

Thus, if we can clarify Fukuzawa's notion of feudalism and his understanding of the transition to monarchy, the intellectual foundation of his later writings in which he recommended an advance to constitutional government will become clear. In short, a careful consideration of the schema of government will provide a context for the essays in this book.

Feudalism is, of course, an abstraction. The German feudal system differed from that of France; the French system, from that of England. One can debate how many points of similarity are required to call all of these systems "feudal." If we add Japan's past to the list of feudal histories, the range becomes even greater. Given the differences in culture, this is inevitable. But what concerns us here is that during the decade after the Restoration, Fukuzawa looked at the similarities and saw both medieval Europe and Tokugawa Japan as feudal, as somewhat dissimilar members of the same category. Only two decades later would he alter this judgment.

Fukuzawa's understanding of feudalism had two layers. The first was Chinese. As a youth, Fukuzawa had read the Chinese classics—*Zuo zhuan, Shiji, Hanshu,* and others—as part of his schooling. In these books, he came across the term *fengjian* (read *hōken* in Japanese), which Chinese historians used to describe the decentralized system of rule during the Zhou dynasty (1122–221 BC). (The complementary term used to describe the centralized, bureaucratic rule of most succeeding dynasties was *junxian* [read *gunken* in Japanese]. Fukuzawa avoided this term because China, despite its centralized government, was then a weak Asian nation.)

Tokugawa historians, educated in Chinese learning, had applied the term *hōken* to their own partially decentralized society. Just as early Zhou kings had assigned lands to their vassal-lords, so had Tokugawa Ieyasu, the first Tokugawa shogun, assigned fiefs to his vassal-daimyo. They, in turn, had given fiefs or stipends to their samurai vassals. Some Tokugawa historians pointed out the shortcomings of *hōken* society, which had led to its demise in China. Most, however, argued that Ieyasu had in some measure recreated in Japan an ideal society, similar to the early Zhou society so praised by the Confucian sages.[4]

The second layer was Western. In 1866, when Fukuzawa began translating Western texts for the first volume of *Conditions in the West*, he used books he had purchased in London in 1862 or obtained from the library at the Gaikokugata. The major challenge he faced in translating these texts was to find equivalents or approximations for the terms he encountered. He first encountered the term feudal in a brief history of the Netherlands in *Lippincott's Pronouncing Gazetteer*. The passage reads: "Soon after this [establishment of an empire by Charlemagne], the whole country was parceled out into small principalities, in accordance with the feudal spirit of the age."[5] To translate the last phrase, Fukuzawa plucked the term *hōken* from his Chinese and Japanese readings and used it for the Western term feudal. "The feudal spirit of the age" became *jidai no hōken no fū*.⁶

In applying the Sino-Japanese term *hōken* to a medieval European society, Fukuzawa was not solely maintaining that European society had been decentralized. He was also claiming, as we shall see, that medieval Europe had a great number of institutions and practices that closely resembled those of Japan. This was the discovery that would guide his judgments for more than a decade. In short, post-medieval Europe could serve as the model for the future development of Japan.

By using approximately equivalent Japanese terms, Fukuzawa was able to translate a wide range of Western feudal terms with considerable accuracy. On the whole, they are apt. It is the sheer number of such terms—I ask for the reader's patience—that convinces us of the feudal (or at least semi-feudal) character of Tokugawa society.

To start with, *shokō* was a term Fukuzawa often used in *Conditions in the West*. In Tokugawa times, the term referred to "the collectivity of daimyo" or the "various lords." *A Dictionary, Geographical, Statistical, and Historical of the Various Countries, Places, and Principal Natural Objects in the World*, by John Ramsey McCulloch, one of Fukuzawa's sources for English history, states that the Anglo-Saxons divided the land between the various lords. Fukuzawa translates the phrase various lords as "great lords" or *daishokō*. Elsewhere in *Conditions in the West*, Fukuzawa uses *shokō* almost interchangeably with nobles (*kizoku*) and great nobles (*daikizoku*), terms also used by Tokugawa historians but less frequently.

In the same passage, McCulloch writes of the division of "land." For land, Fukuzawa uses *ryōchi*. In Tokugawa Japan, *ryōchi* usually referred to daimyo domains or, possibly, to the fiefs of higher-ranking samurai. That is to say, Fukuzawa understood that the term land in the McCulloch passage meant fiefs, and so in translating it, he used the more precise Japanese term *ryōchi*. *Seroku* (hereditary stipends or fiefs) was another frequently used Tokugawa term. McCulloch states that after the Norman conquest, "a new order began and the land was divided into 60,000 knights' fees or estates (*seroku*)." The notion of hereditary estates is essential to any definition of feudalism, and Fukuzawa sometimes uses *seroku* as an alternate term for feudal. Thus, in translating the phrase "feudality existed among the Saxons as well as the Normans," he used *seroku no hō* for feudality.⁷

The McCulloch passage continues: "the greater part of the territory of England became the property of the Norman knights." Fukuzawa understood that in this context the neutral term property referred to fiefs, and translated it as *saichi*, a Tokugawa term for the smaller fiefs held by middle-ranking samurai. Knights becomes *bushin*, or military vassals. McCulloch lists the "development of the feudal system" as one of the principal historical changes of the years between 1066 and 1272. In translating this, Fukuzawa joined his two terms for feudalism, *hōken* and *seroku*, into a single combined term, *hōken seroku no hō*.[8]

Baishin was the Tokugawa term for rear vassal. (Fukuzawa himself was a *baishin* in that he was the vassal of the Nakatsu daimyo, who, in turn, was the vassal of the shogun.) McCulloch writes that the English king Edward I (1272–1307) issued a statute prohibiting his feudal lords from "increasing the number of their vassals by subinfeudation." Fukuzawa translates vassals in this sentence as *baishin*, since the vassals of the vassal-lords were rear vassals vis-à-vis King Edward. He accurately translates subinfeudation as "newly awarded fiefs" (*arata ni seroku o atauru*).[9] Time and time again, he grasped what he read of Western institutions in terms of the corresponding Tokugawa institutions.

Kerai and *rōnin* were two more common Tokugawa terms, the first referring to retainers and the second to masterless samurai. Fukuzawa used these terms to translate the following passage from McCulloch. "And when dismissed from service (*rōnin suru koto areba*) ... they [the retainers (*kerai*)] generally supported themselves by theft and robbery."[10] The translation is apt because the social situations in England and Japan were similar.

For Fukuzawa, feudalism continued to be a serious topic even after the Restoration since the daimyo domains were not abolished until 1871. The third volume of *Conditions in the West* (1870) deals with Russia and France. In translating the history of Tsarist Russia, he often uses the word *shizoku*, an early Meiji term for samurai, for the lower-ranking strelitzes. He renders boyars as *kizoku* (nobles) or *kokunai no shizoku* (the domestic military class).[11]

For the long section on France, Fukuzawa used passages from W. C. Taylor's *History of France and Normandy* (in Pinnock's School Series) and the entry on French history in the *New American Cyclopaedia*. In describing the origins of feudalism, Taylor treats of "the old German custom" by which early chiefs bestowed "an ornamented battle-axe or a fine warhorse" to favored warriors. Later, in place of such favors, the Frankish kings of Gaul distributed a part of their domains to their vassals. Taylor states that, at first, the benefices (*saichi*) were for a single generation.

But when he [the Frankish king] consented to alienate for ever portions more or less considerable of his domain (*hōken seroku no ikioi o nashi*), he soon found it impossible to repair his prodigalities. When the leudes [vassals] could obtain no more from the king, they began to desert him; an independent aristocracy (*seroku no kizoku*) was formed, which daily increased in power as the royal authority became less.[12]

Fukuzawa uses the Japanese verb *kakkyo shite* to describe the autonomy of the feudal lords. In Taylor's *History of France and Normandy*, once the feudal lords were established in their domains as independent or semi-independent rulers, French history became the story of the balance between feudal lords and royal power, a balance that shifted over the centuries in favor of the kings.

Westerners' view of Japanese feudalism

Westerners who lived in Japan before and after the Restoration also saw the country as feudal, as akin to the medieval society of Europe. Could Fukuzawa have been influenced by their views? There is little direct evidence. If he was, it was probably by articles he translated from Western newspapers published in Japan and not through personal contacts; his reading ability was superb, but his spoken English, by all accounts, was poor.

The following passages from books by foreigners resident in Japan suggest the kind of view that often appeared in these newspapers. (Of course, Fukuzawa did not read these books; many are of a later date.)

The British diplomat Sir Rutherford Alcock wrote:

To traverse Europe, and the whole breadth of Asia, and find the living embodiment of a state of society which existed many centuries ago in the West, but has long since passed utterly away ... is certainly a novel condition ... It is therefore with deliberate fore-thought, and in order that the reader may more fully realize this oriental phase of feudalism, such as our ancestors knew it in the time of the Plantagenets, that I would pray him to keep the stereoscopic tube to his eye, and shut out all preconceived views, and all surrounding objects, which speak of a later age and a different race. We are going back to the twelfth century in Europe, for there alone shall we find the counterpart, in many essential particulars, of Japan as it is.[13]

A description by the American educator William Griffis of his samurai pupils conveys the immediacy of first-hand experience:

All were bare-headed, with the top-knot, cue, and shaven mid-scalp, most of them with bare feet on their clogs, and with their characteristic dress, swagger, fierce looks, bare skin exposed at the scalp, neck, arms, calves, and feet, with their murderous swords in their belts, they impressed on my memory a picture of feudalism I shall never forget.[14]

C. H. Eden, a British traveler and writer, emphasized the role of the daimyo. Though his knowledge of Japan was partly secondhand, the following passage reflects a view prevalent among foreigners in pre-Restoration Japan:

If the Mikado be but a phantom and the Tycoon a prisoner in his own palace, who are the real governors of Japan? These are the Daimios, the great nobles or princes, the real owners of Japan, ruling their subjects with a power that knows little check save their own arbitrary will. Like our own early barons, these Daimios are followed by hosts of armed retainers, Japanese counterparts of the swash-bucklers of old England. These Daimios are worshipped by the populace as beings of a superior order, whom even to look upon is a stretch of daring never ventured on by a humble *bourgeois*.[15]

Years after his arrival in Japan in 1876, the German doctor Edwin Baelz, who was intimately acquainted with Japan and had treated the ailments of its government leaders, wrote to his family in Germany about the transformation he had witnessed:

To understand the situation you have to realize that less than ten years ago the Japanese were living under conditions like those of our chivalric age and the feudal system of the Middle Ages, with its monasteries, guilds, Church Universal, and so on; but that betwixt night and morning, one might almost say, and with one great leap, Japan is trying to traverse the stages of five centuries of European development ...[16]

These Western residents experienced the shock of recognition; with their own eyes they had witnessed what they had only read about in history books. Or so they thought. If Fukuzawa came across such opinions in English-language newspapers, he may well have been persuaded to see Tokugawa society as similar to that of late feudal Europe.

But Fukuzawa differed from Western observers in one vital respect: Westerners saw the workings of Tokugawa feudalism and thought, "How fascinating!" Fukuzawa saw the same and thought, "How awful that we are so backward." For him, the concept of feudal summed up all of Japan's weaknesses in confronting the West.

Monarchy, the second stage of government

In Fukuzawa's schema of the progression of governments, monarchy follows feudalism. Consider France. One of his texts, the *New American Cyclopaedia* entry on France, recounts that the first step toward a centralized government in France occurred during the twelfth-century reign of Louis VI, a king of "uncommon ability."

> Louis VI [1108–37], a king of unsurpassed activity and bravery, forced a great many of the nobles into submission (*ōi ni kizoku no ken o seishitari*), and to this end more than once availed himself of the support he found among either the clergy or the people of the cities. The latter, whose material and moral condition had greatly improved during the previous century, were then vindicating their municipal liberties, and willingly entered into an alliance with the king against their feudal masters.[17]

In the third volume of *Conditions in the West*, Fukuzawa translates "activity and bravery" as "wisdom and bravery." He omits the reference to the clergy. For that matter, whenever he could, he downplayed the influence of religion in history. He changes "people of the cities" to "people" (*minsho*), and describes them as "aiding" (*tasuke*) the king rather than entering into an alliance with him. For Fukuzawa, the word alliance smacked too much of a relation between equals. "Municipal liberties" became "unfettered liberties."[18]

The same entry next comments on Louis IX, the thirteenth-century king who established "a high court of justice, which was to supersede gradually all feudal jurisdiction." This, it declared, was a mighty addition "to the efficiency of royal power." Fukuzawa renders the last sentence as: "Royal power became a hundred times greater than in the past." Then, in the fifteenth century, after the expulsion of the English, French kings resumed their "traditional policy of enlarging the royal domains and consolidating the royal power by the destruction of the feudal nobility" (*hōken seroku no ken o seishi*). None was more zealous in pursuit of this great goal than "the crafty and tyrannical Louis XI [1461–83]," during whose rule "numberless nobles of every rank were delivered to the executioner" (*kizoku o koroshi*).[19]

At this point, for a more complete interpretation of the factors affecting the demise of feudalism, Fukuzawa turned from the *New American Cyclopedia* to Taylor's *History of France and Normandy*.

> The wars in this reign show us that the spirit of chivalry was fast declining (*hōken seroku no kizoku sekijitsu no kaoiro nashi*). Firearms were gradually superseding the

use of the bow, and cavalry, which had been hitherto the most important part of an army, was, by the new system of warfare, considerably diminished in value. These changes in the art of war had a considerable influence on the political condition of society: for the knights and small proprietors (*seroku no ie ni umareshi bushi*), who had hitherto possessed great influence by the importance of their services, sunk all at once when these were performed by hired soldiers. The authority of the feudal aristocracy was thus destroyed. In England it was transferred to the members of the House of Commons ... but in France it centered on the crown, and thus the government became an absolute monarchy (*ikkun shinsai no seifu*).[20]

Then, after a time, Cardinal Richelieu [1585–1642] steps onto the stage of French history. To do justice to the cardinal's role, Fukuzawa turned from his two principal texts, the *New American Cyclopaedia* entry on France and Taylor's *History of France and Normandy*, to the *New American Cyclopaedia* entry on Richelieu. The entry credits Richelieu with having brought about the "extinction of the last remains of feudalism, and the full subjection of the high nobility to the royal power." To his translation Fukuzawa adds the sentence: "The old evil (*kyūhei*) of feudalism was first ended at this time." *Kyūhei* was a term frequently used in the early Meiji era to denigrate "bad" customs of the previous era.[21]

The sections on France, we note, were published in 1870, just as Japan was undergoing an extremely rapid centralization. This was one year after the return of domain registers, one year after daimyo were appointed as governors, and one year before the abolition of the daimyo domains. In presenting French history, Fukuzawa surely must have had the conditions of his own country in mind.

Whitewashing European monarchy

Fukuzawa understood his texts thoroughly. He translated accurately, with wit and verve. In contrast, the original texts he used were often dull and contained long passages that added little to the story. Fukuzawa ruthlessly excised these passages. He wanted to give his Japanese readers a picture of the West that was faithful, yet simple and easy to grasp. He wanted to give them an understanding of history that could provide a basis for action to strengthen Japan. Japan had been weak under Tokugawa feudalism; monarchy would strengthen it. Fukuzawa understood, of course, that Tokugawa rule was already partially centralized, but he favored a swift transition to full centralization. To make this goal attractive to his readers, to make the model of Europe appealing, he sometimes removed the warts, so to speak, from the faces of European monarchs. Consider his handling of English monarchs.[22]

In *Elements of General History*, Alexander Tytler describes William II (r. 1087–1100), son of William the Conqueror, as follows: "He inherited the vices, without any of the virtues, of his father. His reign is distinguished by no event of importance, and after the defeat of a conspiracy at the outset, presents nothing but a dull career of unresisted despotism." Fukuzawa sums up the passage: "During William II's reign, there was no event of importance."[23]

Fukuzawa also prettied up accounts of other kings. According to Tytler, Henry I (r. 1100–1135), after the death of his predecessor, seized the crown of England, and "with most criminal ambition" invaded "his brother's dominions of Normandy." Fukuzawa usually follows the Tytler text closely, but in this instance, he deletes Henry I's "criminal ambition." Or, to pick other examples, McCulloch describes the later years of Edward II (r. 1307–27) as follows: "The rest of Edward's reign was occupied by a lengthened struggle in support of his favourites against the barons and his queen." Tytler describes the queen as a "vicious adulteress" who sided with the barons. Fukuzawa omits the fact that Edward II had favorites and Tytler's description of the queen.[24]

Writing of Henry IV (r. 1399–1413), Fukuzawa again used the works of McCulloch and Tytler. The two books agree that Henry IV wrested the throne from King Richard II. According to McCulloch, Henry IV is Richard II's cousin and a "usurping monarch": "Richard II was dethroned in 1399 by Henry of Bolingbroke, his cousin, and murdered shortly afterwards." According to Tytler, Henry IV is Richard II's uncle, who "rose in open rebellion, and compelled Richard ... to resign the crown. The Parliament confirmed his deposition and he was soon after privately assassinated." Fukuzawa writes simply: "In 1399, the king's uncle, Henry of Lancaster, raised troops, dethroned Richard (*Richarudo o haishite*), and established himself as king. This was Henry IV." *Haishite* means "abolish" or "put aside." It is considerably weaker than "murder" or "assassination."[25]

The cleanup of Henry VIII (r. 1509–47) required more strenuous effort. According to McCulloch:

> The great event for which the reign of Henry VIII. is memorable was the Reformation. The event was, to some extent, accelerated by his passions. Unable to procure from the see of Rome a consent to his divorce from his wife, Catherine of Aragon, Henry involved the kingdom in a rupture with the pope, and assumed the title of Head of the Church ... At the commencement of his reign Henry was popular; but his passions were violent and, being unrestrained in their indulgence, he came to be the most sanguinary tyrant that ever ruled England.[26]

Fukuzawa cuts McCulloch's description of Henry VIII's passions. Instead, he writes that Henry VIII wished to divorce his wife "for a certain reason" (*yue arite*). This suggests the possibility that the queen was somehow in the wrong. He renders "unable to procure … a consent" as "did not receive a consent" (*yurushi o ezu*), suggesting that Rome was being unreasonable. After all, who was the pope to deny the wishes of a king! The last sentence in which the king is branded a tyrant is excised altogether.[27]

Similarly, Fukuzawa altered the account of Henry VIII's daughter, Elizabeth I (r. 1558–1603). The McCulloch text comments that Catholic plots "explain and in part palliate," but "never can justify the execution of Mary [Queen of Scots], which will always remain a dark blot on the character of Elizabeth and her advisors." Fukuzawa deletes Mary's execution. He also deletes McCulloch's description of Elizabeth I's last years, which were "darkened by intrigues of the court" and by "the rebellion of her favourite Essex."[28]

For Fukuzawa, the most delicate topic in European history was regicide. Loath to tell his compatriots that Europeans sometimes killed their kings, he passed over the murders of Richard I, Richard II, Edward II, and Mary, Queen of Scots. In his treatment of the English Revolution, too, he sidesteps. McCulloch writes:

> Charles soon afterwards fell into the hands of the army and after a variety of intrigues and negotiations between that body and the parliament and the king, he was condemned and executed by a warrant of judges nominated by parliament on the 30th Jan. 1649. A republican government was next formed, styled the Commonwealth of England, which ended in the Protectorate of Cromwell.[29]

Fukuzawa takes out the fact that Charles I "fell into the hands of the army," and omits the "intrigues and negotiations," the king's execution, and Parliament's involvement in the deed. He writes simply: "In 1649, by a decision (*teigi*) of Parliament, the position of king was abolished (*kokuō no kurai o haishite*) and a republican government was formed."[30]

In the passages describing the English Revolution, Fukuzawa mentions but downplays McCulloch's long discussion of the role of religion; his focus is rather on the struggle between the king and Parliament. For Fukuzawa, nineteenth-century England was the epitome of an advanced and powerful Western state, and in many ways his model for Japan. He did not want to tell his readers that, as recently as the seventeenth century, the English had killed their king in a struggle over religion.

Fifty years of revolution ended in 1688, when the Convention Parliament, according to McCulloch, "declared that James had abdicated the crown, and raised our great deliverer [William III] and his consort Mary to the throne." Fukuzawa's translation makes William the king but does not mention Mary.[31]

One may well ask, was Fukuzawa's whitewash of European kings deliberate? Could it not have been random? Fukuzawa deleted huge amounts of miscellaneous, uninteresting materials from his English sources, even stripping critical passages to the bone. Was the whitewash not simply the byproduct of these cuts? In a few instances, this may have been the case, but not all of his cuts are random: the changes run uniformly in a single direction and are more systematic than can be explained by inadvertent omissions.

A related question is whether Fukuzawa's cleanup of Western monarchs was only a small part of a general cleanup of the West that was intended to make his Japanese readers more open to reform on Western lines. A few deliberate changes of this kind can be found here and there. For example, McCulloch described the reign of George II (1727–60) as follows:

> Moral and orderly habits, on the whole, characterised the period: the violence of earlier times had disappeared, and the peculiar vices attending on great wealth and manufacturing industry had scarcely, as yet, begun to prevail.[32]

Fukuzawa keeps "moral and orderly habits" (*fūzoku bunmei ni omomuki reigi o omonji*) and the disappearance of the "violence of earlier times," but he deletes entirely "the peculiar vices attending on great wealth and manufacturing." Great wealth and manufacturing were just what he wanted for Japan! When he visited England in 1862, he immediately grasped the connection between British factories and British naval power in East Asian waters.[33]

In the second supplementary volume of *Conditions in the West*, Fukuzawa drew heavily on Burton's *Political Economy for Use in Schools and Private Instruction*. At one point Burton writes:

> In the progress of civilization, a system called the law of nations, or international law, has been devised, and though there be no authority compelling nations to submit to it, yet it has some influence over them, since they make enemies by infringing or overlooking it.[34]

In his translation, Fukuzawa mentions the lack of a compelling authority, but then adds, "Yet if a country breaks this law, it will without fail (*kanarazu*) make enemies, so of all the countries, none disobeys it." There is a huge difference between "some" and "all," and between "some influence" and "without fail."

Such instances are rare, however. Fukuzawa cleaned up general conditions only occasionally, but he cleaned up monarchs systematically.

Representative government, the third stage

To recapitulate, the pattern that Fukuzawa found in European history was a gradual development from feudalism to monarchy and then to representative government. He felt that the feudalism of Europe closely resembled that of Japan. He effortlessly applied the extensive vocabulary of Japanese feudalism to the institutions of medieval Europe, and depicted monarchy as arising from within feudalism. Monarchs struggled with feudal lords, and on winning, consolidated their power. When he wrote the first volume of *Conditions in the West*, he must have judged that Europe was ahead of Japan, and that Henry VIII was more powerful than the Tokugawa shogun, whose power depended on feudal vassalage as well as the apparatus of the bakufu.

Fukuzawa recognized that the third stage of representative government was missing from Japan. Still, Japan had been like Europe in having feudalism, and during the late Tokugawa era and after 1868, Japan was like Europe in developing a centralized monarchy. That some form of representative government—perhaps in combination with monarchy, as in Britain—would follow in Japan, he did not doubt. This would take time, and until 1879, Fukuzawa never specified a date.

But Fukuzawa was also an educator; he felt he had a mission to guide his countrymen. To prepare them, they had to be taught how representative government worked in the advanced nations of the West, particularly in England, the United States, and France. They had to become familiar with the ideas and principles that undergirded those governments.

1. The first volume of *Conditions in the West* (1866) contains a short account of American history, which includes a complete translation of the Declaration of Independence. The section on American government that follows includes a partial translation of the United States Constitution, together with a description of the workings of Congress. Fukuzawa felt that actual documents could be useful, even though American history lacked feudalism and was less relevant to Japan. There is also a chapter with an extremely brief history of the Netherlands that treats its progress from feudal to representative government. The much longer chapter on English history traces the evolution of the British government from its origins, through the Magna Carta, to its nineteenth-century Parliament. The section on British government also describes relations between the monarch, the House of Lords, and the House of Commons.

2. The second volume of *Conditions in the West* (1868) contains a translation of half of the chapters of Burton's *Political Economy*, which describes the human predisposition toward civilization, the rights of freedom and equality, and the duties these rights entail. It also discusses the British Parliament and the educational system that sustains it.
3. The third volume of *Conditions in the West* (1870) begins with a translation of "Of the Absolute Rights of Individuals," a chapter taken from an abridgment of Sir William Blackstone's *Commentaries on the Laws of England*.[35] The chapter defines human rights in the fashion of John Locke. Other chapters in the third volume examine the histories, governments, military, and finances of Russia and France. The very detailed account of French history traces the progression from feudalism to monarchy to representative government, and includes a description of the origins of the French National Assembly and its workings.
4. Two other early translations should also be mentioned: *All the Countries of the World* (*Sekai kunizukushi*), published in 1869. Partially based on Mitchell's *New School Geography*, Philadelphia, 1860, it contains descriptions of Western parliaments. *A Discussion of the British Parliament* (*Eikoku gijiin-dan*), published two years later, was partially based on Dorothea Beale's *The Student's Textbook of English and General History*, London, 1857.
5. Fukuzawa's two major original works (which contain some translations) of the 1872–6 period are *An Encouragement of Learning* (*Gakumon no susume*) and *An Outline of Theories of Civilization* (*Bunmeiron no gairyaku*). They discuss types of governments and their relation to civilization, and present representative government as the form of government appropriate to the civilized stage of history.

In sum, Fukuzawa wanted Japan to progress to representative government.

2

Fukuzawa's Politics

Fukuzawa wrote an autobiography, and consequently we know more about his life during the years before and after the Meiji Restoration than we do about the lives of any other historical figure of that period. The autobiography is detailed; for that era, there is no other like it. He vividly recounts his feelings, decisions, and the events of his life during a time when Japan was undergoing epochal changes. Nevertheless, it must be read with a measure of caution, since he wrote it in 1897, four years before his death, and tells his story as he wanted his readers to remember him. He glosses over the fact that he was a firm supporter of the Tokugawa bakufu, the losing side in the Restoration struggles.[1]

Despite the autobiography, it is difficult to ascertain Fukuzawa's thoughts on specific political issues in Japan prior to 1866. A samurai of his rank did not presume to express political opinions, and on the whole he did not. We know little of what he talked about with other young samurai at the domain school, or with his fellow students at Ogata Kōan's medical school in Osaka. What he recounts in his autobiography holds our interest, but it is mainly apolitical. We also do not know, except by inference, how his views changed after his 1860 voyage to San Francisco. The English-language phrase book—his first publication—gives us no clues. We have only an imperfect idea of what he discussed with other scholars of Dutch learning in Edo in 1858 and 1859, or what he talked about with junior officials at the bakufu foreign ministry. His travel diary of 1862 indicates the breadth of his interests during his travel in Europe, but none of his thoughts about the politics in Japan at that time.

Fukuzawa's philosophy poses the same problems. As a samurai youth, he received the standard education in Confucian philosophy. He probably abandoned the Confucian ideas of *yin* and *yang* and the five elements while studying Dutch medicine at the Ogata school during the 1850s. Years later, in 1875, he would write bitterly that while the Japanese were expounding on yin and yang and the five elements, the Westerners were discovering the sixty-element atomic chart. But the Ogata medical school offered little in the fields of philosophy, politics, or ethics. Despite the passages in his autobiography expressing disdain for all Chinese learning, he probably did not discard his Confucian political ideas until he began to digest Western philosophical writings in the late 1860s. Some Confucian notions can still be found in *Conditions in the West*.[2]

Thus, we can only surmise how Fukuzawa's political views changed. As a low-ranking vassal of the Nakatsu daimyo and as a translator at the Gaikokugata, he was of too low a status to voice opinions. Also, he was cautious by temperament. We can only guess what he thought from chance remarks in his early translations. Certainly, he was loyal to the bakufu and its policies, wholeheartedly in favor of Western studies, and confident of his ability to read English. But on the specific political issues of the day, we must use the general to arrive at the particular.

The political situation in 1866 was complex. Japan was like a circus with 300 rings, some large, some small, with each domain containing a different configuration of forces. Central controls over the daimyo had frayed since Commodore Perry's visits in 1853 and 1854. The system of alternate years' attendance at Edo had also broken down. The shoguns' blood-kin daimyo and the numerous small collateral daimyo—those who had been vassals before 1600—still strongly supported the bakufu and, in so doing, hoped to buttress their own power. But many of these domains were economically weak. In contrast, a handful of the larger "outside" daimyo—those who had become vassals only after 1600, acted with growing autonomy, even petitioning for rule by a council of daimyo composed of themselves. Of these, Chōshū, and later Satsuma, were openly hostile toward the bakufu. Following considerable provocation, the bakufu launched a military expedition against Chōshū in 1864, and after an internal war in the domain restored the anti-bakufu faction to power, it mounted a second expedition in 1866. Needless to say, opinion within the bakufu foreign ministry was united in favor of these expeditions and Fukuzawa concurred.

The year 1866 marked a critical turning point in Fukuzawa's life in three respects. First, it was the year in which he was promoted to be a direct vassal of the shogun and given a larger personal stipend. This was a clear recognition of his talent. Miyazaki Fumiko, who has studied the Kaiseijo, a bakufu office similar to the Gaikokugata, has shown that during the years from 1862 to 1866, a sizable number of rear vassal employees of that office were made direct vassals to prevent their recall for service to their domains. She suggests the same thing happened at the Gaikokugata. As it happened, in both offices the most able of those adept in foreign languages were domain samurai, not direct bakufu retainers.³ Fukuzawa was one of those chosen. As a direct vassal of the shogun, Fukuzawa for the first time had sufficient status to express opinions.

Second, 1866 was the year the first volume of *Conditions in the West* was published. The subjects Fukuzawa chose give us some indication of his thoughts at the time.

Third, in the seventh month of the same year, Fukuzawa presented a memorial to the bakufu in which he urged the total subjugation of Chōshū. More significantly, he stated explicitly that the time had come for Japan to advance from a Tokugawa-style feudal monarchy to a more centralized state. The memorial not only spells out his political ideas but also reveals his special skill in applying the historical development of other nations to Japan.

1. Comparing the Chōshū rebels to the Taiping rebels in China, Fukuzawa writes, "To punish vassals who anger both heaven and man is right in both name and fact."
2. To crush the rebels, he urges the bakufu to hire foreign troops, whose up-to-date weapons would counter those purchased by Chōshū from foreign merchants. Fukuzawa's willingness to use foreign troops makes clear that, in 1866, his attention was still focused on the bakufu's domestic enemies and not on the threat to Japan from Western powers.
3. He links the suppression of the hostile domain with the system of government prevailing in Japan. "If any daimyo objects [to the suppression of Chōshū], direct your banners against them, and with one blow display your glory and change the entire Japanese feudal system (*hōken no goseido o goippen*)."
4. Fukuzawa's rationale is totally realistic and cuts through the swirl of ideological arguments raging at the time in Japan:

Principle (*meigi*) is determined by military power. When [Akechi] Mitsuhide murdered Nobunaga [in 1582], the emperor immediately named him shogun. And when Hideyoshi vanquished Mitsuhide, the country became his. The emperor recognized Hideyoshi, and no one questioned his right to rule. All of this was brought about by military might. Today, the Chōshū rebels are battling the bakufu army. If, by any chance, they win, they will march on Kyoto, change their name from "enemy of the court" to "champion of the emperor," and scheme to give the name of "enemy of the court" to the bakufu army. Names such as "enemy of the court" and "champion of the emperor" sound ever so fine, yet such designations are determined by military strength. Imperial rescripts are like papal bulls issued in Rome; they merely legitimize existing military power.⁴

Together with the memorial, he submitted a partial draft of the first volume of *Conditions in the West*.

Another indication of Fukuzawa's thoughts in 1866 is a letter he wrote three months after the memorial to a Keiō student studying in England. In it, he unequivocally asserts the need for a "shogunal monarchy" (*taikun no monaruki*). He makes no mention of the emperor. In proposing the shogun as monarch, he no doubt envisioned a strong central government that would build on the bakufu's "open the country" policy. As noted earlier, several politically active domains at the time were calling for a council of daimyo to deliberate on national policy. In the letter, Fukuzawa stoutly maintains that such a council of regional interests would only impede Japan's progress toward "civilization and enlightenment."[5]

As it was, the second bakufu expedition against Chōshū failed. Early in 1868, Chōshū and Satsuma, with the support of Tosa and Saga, seized the court and proclaimed the Meiji Restoration. Using rifles purchased from Western merchants in Japan, they then defeated a numerically superior bakufu army in a fierce battle at Toba-Fushimi. The battle decided the day: the last shogun resigned, and the bakufu, which had ruled for more than two and a half centuries, collapsed.

In the early months after the Restoration, Fukuzawa felt that a government put together by the forces that had overthrown the bakufu would only end in disaster. He viewed the new leaders as "snakes and scorpions"—fanatics who had launched the "expel the barbarian" movement, violated the treaties, and assassinated foreigners and bakufu officials. Fearing the worst, Fukuzawa resigned as a vassal of the shogun and retired to the confines of his school. He wrote to a friend: "I have had my fill of service as a vassal. From now on, it is my intention to throw away my pair of swords and go through life as a book-reading commoner." He confided that he would make a living by doing translations for money. He would charge one gold *ryō* a page for military matters, physics, geography, chemistry, and newspaper articles, and 1.3 *ryō* for theoretical writings on politics, economics, international law, and military systems.[6]

To Fukuzawa's astonishment, and contrary to their actions before the Restoration, the samurai leaders of the new Meiji government acted with vision and cool judgment. Responsible for Japan's future, they redefined their goals: rather than expelling the barbarians, they upheld the treaties. Borrowing Western technologies, they laid telegraph lines the length of Japan, improved ports and bridges, and began the construction of railways. Several times they offered Fukuzawa a position in the government or as a teacher at a government school. He wrote to a friend that he had accepted an offer and would possibly be sent to teach in some other part of Japan, but in the end, for reasons unknown, nothing came of the offer and he remained in Tokyo.[7]

During the first three years, the new government leaders destroyed the old feudal system and created a highly centralized state. The 1868 Charter Oath proclaimed that "Deliberative assemblies shall be widely established and all matters decided by public discussion." It also declared that: "Knowledge shall be sought throughout the world so as to strengthen the foundations of imperial rule." The Oath was indicative of the new government's direction, but it cannot be taken at face value, since it was issued to shore up the government at a time when its existence was still precarious.

More important were the steps that followed. The Edict for Domain Offices (*Hanji shokusei*) of 12/1868 ordered all domains to simplify and standardize their offices. In so doing, the government assumed an authority over the domains that the bakufu had never possessed. The Return of the Domain Registers (*hanseki hōkan*) in 7/1869 made the daimyo governors of their former domains and at least, in theory, responsible to the central government. Then, in the seventh month of 1871, after two years of uncertainty, both the daimyo domains and their daimyo governors were abolished in a single stroke and prefectures were established in their place. During the reform, the government made every effort to appear even-handed. A former bakufu samurai was appointed as the new governor of Yamaguchi (the former Chōshū). Elsewhere, able men from domains other than their own were appointed governors. Only in Kagoshima prefecture, the former Satsuma, which was most resistant to change, was a domain samurai named as the governor.

In making these changes, the Meiji government always acted within the limits of its military strength. The victory at Toba-Fushimi had established its power. The Return of the Domain Registers in 1869 was based on assumptions about the strength and loyalties of the armies of Satsuma and Chōshū. The two years that elapsed between 1869 and the abolition of the domains in 1871 was a period of hesitancy. Nevertheless, small military reforms were carried out: the French army was taken as a model, the domains were required to maintain troops, and garrisons were established throughout the country. The abolition of the domains in 1871 was a gamble that worked.

After the abolition of the domains, many key members of the Meiji government went on a mission abroad; its ostensible purpose was the revision of the "unequal treaties" of 1858. Although the treaties were not revised, the mission afforded its members—among them the noble Iwakura Tomomi, Kido Takayoshi, Ōkubo Toshimichi, Itō Hirobumi, and Yamagata Aritomo—a first-hand look at the West. During these years, Fukuzawa was occupied with translations, other writings, and his school. But he doubtless believed that the leaders would form impressions similar to those he had gleaned during his own earlier travels abroad.

While the mission was abroad, the stay-at-home officials in Tokyo passed a law providing for a conscript army no longer dependent on samurai. Also, to give employment to former samurai and to bring glory to Japan, the stay-at-home government planned an expedition against Korea. But when the Iwakura mission returned in 1873, its leaders quashed the expedition as too dangerous; the Western powers, they feared, might use the expedition as a pretext to move against Japan.

Saigō Takamori of Satsuma, Itagaki Taisuke of Tosa, and other stay-at-home officials who had advocated the expedition against Korea, thereupon quit the government. The next year, Itagaki and eight others abruptly changed their bellicose positions and petitioned the government for the immediate establishment of an elective national assembly. They secretly hoped that a national assembly would help them regain authority. The government, however, ignored their petition; only too aware of the gap between Japan and the West, and of Japan's financial weaknesses, the government, instead, carried out two great reforms. Fukuzawa approved of the reforms, as he did of most of the actions taken by the Meiji government.

The first reform dealt with the land system. The cultivators of land during the Tokugawa era had been more than serfs but less than free farmers. In most domains, though not all, the farmer's "ownership" of the land he cultivated was recognized in fact, if not in theory. The land tax reform of 1873–6 gave the cultivators a clear legal title to their lands for the first time. The reform also made land taxes more equitable: some taxes were lowered, others were raised, and taxes on non-paddy lands increased. In general, the tax rate remained much higher than comparable rates in Europe. When some farmers rose in protest, in December 1876, the government cut land taxes by 16.7 percent across the board. (The tax dropped from 3 percent of the value of the land as determined by the reform to 2.5 percent.) This move, in combination with an unexpected inflation that raised the price of rice, led to growing prosperity in rural Japan. (Tenant farmers, to be sure, lost out.) Revolts continued in some areas even after the reduction in taxes, but they were usually small in scale and quickly suppressed. The overall consequence of the reform was to end the quasi-feudal character of land tenure in Japan.

The second reform, from 1873 to 1876, disestablished the samurai class. The abolition by fiat of a ruling social class was a huge change, with few parallels in the histories of other nations. Samurai stipends, already reduced, were cut further and converted to government bonds. Inflation caused the bonds to drop in value. As a result, former samurai not in the government or army became impoverished and restive.

During this early Meiji period, while remaining outside of government, Fukuzawa was active. He taught at and managed his Keiō Academy. He set up an enterprise to publish his writings, which later became the Keiō University Press. Above all, he wrote constantly, with an eye to forwarding the progressive actions of the government, and adding criticisms from time to time.

Part Two

Fukuzawa's Essays in Translation

Introduction: The Later Essays

To recapitulate, by 1875, Fukuzawa had written a number of accurate and eminently readable histories of the Western nations that were most involved with Japan. The three volumes of *Conditions in the West* were vastly superior to any other account available in Japan at the time. More significantly, in his writings of the mid-1870s, Fukuzawa had made European history relevant by locating Japan along the European path of historical development: Tokugawa Japan had been feudal, sharing common features with late medieval Europe, and post-Restoration Japan was monarchic, resembling to a degree the centralized monarchies of Europe. Fukuzawa firmly believed that Japan would one day advance further and become a parliamentary state like the most advanced nations of Europe.

Yet, in 1875, when he reviewed in his mind the early Meiji developments sketched earlier, he felt that Japan's further advance to representative government lay somewhere in the future. To be sure, the previous year a few ex-samurai had submitted a memorial calling for the immediate establishment of a national assembly. But in Fukuzawa's eyes, they were both self-serving and irresponsible, and he largely ignored them. The majority of Japanese, on whom any assembly would depend, were still politically backward and lacking in independence and individualism. Japanese institutions were unbalanced at every level, tilted toward the next higher level of power. Also, Japan lacked science, machine industry, and institutions of higher learning. Given the magnitude of these shortcomings, representative assemblies would not work. Only in natural products and scenery, he wrote despairingly, could Japan compare with the West. He therefore remained adamantly opposed to all demands for a national assembly.

3

The Division of Power
(*Bunkenron*), 1877

Introduction

In 1876, Fukuzawa's opposition to representative institutions in Japan changed. Toward the end of that year, he wrote the essay translated here, "The Division of Power."¹ In it he proposed that elective local assemblies be established and given a small portion of the central government's power. This is a clear break with his previous stance. We know the approximate date of the essay, since he mentions it by name in a letter he wrote to a friend, Yamaguchi Hiroe, on December 20, 1876. However, the essay was not published until a year later, in November 1877. We do not know whether he rewrote it before publication since no copy exists of the 1876 draft. He confided in the letter that he feared the essay might run afoul of publication regulations, a consideration that may account for the delay in publication.² But in comparison with essays printed in the radical people's rights newspapers at the time, the essay will strike a reader today as extremely mild and inoffensive.³ Fukuzawa may also have feared that the essay, if published immediately, would help the political parties, which he held in low regard. He may also have felt it prudent to wait for the country to recover political stability after the sweeping reforms of the previous three years.

When Fukuzawa wrote this essay, the immediate problem facing the government was samurai revolts. Two years earlier, former samurai had rebelled against the government of Saga, a domain with a supporting role in the Restoration. Late in 1876, rebellions broke out in Hagi (the former castle town of Chōshū), Kumamoto, and Fukuoka. That is to say, the spate of uprisings all occurred in the southwestern domains that had been active in the Restoration.

Roman numerals indicate Fukuzawa's marginal notes; Arabic numerals indicate endnotes to the Commentary and Translation.

Samurai from these areas had expected rewards but instead had suffered losses of livelihood and status. In Fukuzawa's judgment, the rebellions threatened to destroy the progress made since the Restoration and render Japan vulnerable to rapacious foreign powers.

To mollify samurai discontent, Fukuzawa proposed elective local assemblies, which, he expected, would be largely composed of samurai. His proposal is prescient in two respects. First, it addressed the issue of samurai revolts prior to the Satsuma Rebellion, which would begin the following year in January and continue until September. Much larger than previous uprisings and drawing support from thousands of Kyushu samurai, the rebellion almost amounted to a civil war. Its leader, Saigō Takamori, had been one of the top three leaders after the Restoration, but, as noted, had left the government in 1873 when his plan for an expedition against Korea was rejected.

Second, in proposing the establishment of local assemblies, Fukuzawa anticipated, and possibly influenced, the government's own plan for such institutions. In March 1878, barely five months after the essay's publication, Ōkubo Toshimichi, the leading figure in the government, proposed what later became known as the "Three New Laws." The first law was to reestablish villages and counties—the traditional units of rural administration—in place of the "artificial" large and small districts (*ku*) that had been used to push through the land tax reform. The second law, which echoed Fukuzawa's recommendation, was to establish prefectural assemblies. The third law provided for local taxes to finance the assemblies. Although Ōkubo was assassinated two months later, in May 1878, his proposals were enacted in July.

Translation

This book is a record of idle conversations I had with my colleagues at Keiō from time to time and contains nothing out of the ordinary. Nibbling roasted nuts and sipping tea, we talked about culture, discussed science, and covered a wide variety of subjects. Indeed, after we dispersed, in moments of quiet recollection, I would often wonder what we had talked about that evening. We met merely for the pleasure of each other's company, and our conversations would hardly cause anyone to raise objections. Still, in the course of our desultory talks, we touched on such matters as national power, randomly bringing in scholarly and political issues and referring to universal as well as present-day theories on the nature of power. If others heard about our conversations, they might possibly misinterpret what we said, and for this reason I have decided to put several of our talks on the centralization and division of political power into some sort of logical sequence and publish them as a book. The author is to be considered no more than a recorder of these casual conversations.[4]

November 1877
Fukuzawa Yukichi

Coal emits heat when it is burned, and when that heat comes into contact with water, the water turns into steam, which propels ships and trains. Thus, the power or force that propels steamships and locomotives is steam, and because it is generated by fired coal, we can say the power that moves steamships and trains is contained within coal. Coal itself was formed from vegetation that grew on the earth millions of years ago, and since the vegetation was nurtured by the warmth and light of the sun, we can say the source of power presently contained in coal is the sun that shone millions of years ago.[i]

Now, in this world, power cannot emerge from nothing, nor can something that exists be destroyed and reduced to nothing. In the same way, matter cannot be created or destroyed. We talk about a physical object or power being destroyed, but this does not mean that it has actually been reduced to nothing; the object has simply changed its outward form. In the case of a physical object, we say it has been transformed. Oil, for example, is transformed into gas, and tobacco into smoke and ash. In the case of physical power, we also say it has been transformed. Steam power is such an example.

The functioning of the human mind and body is also a kind of power. It cannot emerge from nothing and acquire form, nor can it be destroyed and reduced to nothing. In course of time, it merely changes form. For example, reading books is a function of the human mind. Reading Chinese books is not the same as reading Western-language books, yet people who have studied books in Chinese learn to read Western books in no time. Again, people skilled in understanding Western books have no trouble reading and grasping the meaning of Chinese books, even though they have never seen them before. This proves that the power to read books is never destroyed. Merchants who undertake a new business are usually successful, whereas members of the former samurai class invariably fail when they put their hand to business. This proves that the power to conduct business is not something that is suddenly acquired. Similar examples are too numerous to mention, so I shall next discuss conditions in Japan today.

I shall put aside the ancient past and discuss the period from the first years of the Tokugawa bakufu until the Kaei year period [1848–53], when people who participated in state affairs were always limited to the samurai class. Farmers, artisans, and merchants followed the guidance of samurai and merely attended to their own physical well-being. To be sure, there were literate farmers and merchants who took pleasure in studying and reading literature, but as far as politics was concerned, they were content to leave everything to samurai and to gaze up at them from their lowly position. The three lower classes merely led physical lives, as it were, and not political lives.

Samurai were different; even the lowliest foot soldier with a meager stipend of ten bales of rice performed military service so long as he was worthy of the name of samurai. And what did military service mean? It meant the readiness to die in battle when a political incident threatened the security of his lord and master's house and endangered society. In other words, the samurai's duty was to give up his life for the sake of the domain. A samurai held this conviction all his life and not for a moment was allowed to forget it. Soldiers conscripted today were, until recently, ordinary farmers and unconcerned about politics. Now, as members of the military, they will have to pay attention to national affairs.

What was true for a lowly foot soldier was even more so for a higher-ranking samurai. Not only was he obliged to fight in battle, he had to take part in government, if not directly, at the very least, to discuss it as a bystander. A samurai had to discuss politics, argue politics, rejoice or grieve over the state of politics; reading was for the sake of politics, the pursuit of learning and the military arts was for the sake of national affairs; his name and honor hinged on politics, so too did the reputation of his family. In sum, a samurai's life was grounded in the country's political affairs, and without exception, the two million people living in four hundred thousand samurai households—men and women, young and old—took part in political discussions.

One hears that people in the United States hold so-called **political ideas** and that everyone is concerned with public affairs, but I daresay their interest is not as intense as it was among the samurai class in Japan.[5]

Of course, customs differ between the East and the West: in Japan, people speak of fealty to lord and master, death in battle, the cultivation of military and literary arts, and a warrior's correct demeanor; in the United States, people speak of the abiding principle of patriotism, upholding the honor of the national flag, the merits and demerits of the Constitution, and regional assemblies. In intent and purpose, the customs of the two countries are completely different, but in their heartfelt concern for the nation's affairs, they are undeniably the same.[ii]

Samurai in Japan nurtured their interest in politics over hundreds of years, and in the course of transmitting what they learned from generation to generation, they developed a certain spirit that set them apart from the other classes, as if they belonged to a different race. They functioned in two ways: one, to maintain their physical lives, the other, to maintain their political lives. The life of the three lower classes was simple, the life of the samurai class, complex. The former functioned for personal purposes, the latter, for both personal and official purposes. And because the function of samurai educated and nurtured in this manner still exists as a kind of power that controls Japanese society, that function cannot be destroyed suddenly, even in a crisis; only its form can change. In this immense world, it is an incontrovertible truth that a power of whatever kind can never be reduced to nothing.

The opening of relations with foreign countries in 1854 was a momentous event, unprecedented in our country. When a society changes, the forces in society necessarily change, the purpose of learning changes, the conduct of business changes, and even more notably, systems of belief show signs of change. There is nothing that is not subject to change, and the most rapid and vigorous transformation takes place in politics. Such a change was the swift overthrow of the Tokugawa bakufu, which had maintained peace unchallenged for two hundred and fifty odd years, and the abolition of three hundred feudal domains. What accounted for these political changes? Changes in commerce and trade are far-reaching but by nature confined to the physical side of life; they concern only the three lower classes and so the social perturbations are correspondingly small. In comparison, politics, the self-appointed function of the samurai class, exerts a far greater power. It thus stands to reason that a sudden change instigated by this power produces immediate and sweeping results.

There is no question that recent political reforms are the result of the power of *shizoku*, the former samurai class. But did this power suddenly emerge in the 1850s? Most certainly not! The opening of the country at the time was a critical event, but power is not suddenly created because of a single event; only the form changes because of that event. The recent political reforms stem from samurai power, but that power was not created anew; this was only a different form of the particular power held by samurai since ancient times. Which is to say, the aforementioned ethos, of fealty to lord and master, readiness to die in battle, correct demeanor, and cultivation of military and literary arts, was transformed to serve other purposes: the furtherance of civilization and enlightenment, progress and reform. Unimpeded, this transformation made Japan what it is today.

Recent political reforms were thus effected by the transformed power of *shizoku*. But this does not mean that the power of the entire body of *shizoku* was transformed at once, or that everyone gained positions in which they could exercise that power. To illustrate my point, I shall divide *shizoku* into three categories.

Category One: *Shizoku* who overthrew the Tokugawa bakufu, formed the new government, advocated programs to advance so-called civilization and enlightenment, and now occupy government office.[iii] This category also includes those not directly connected with the government but holding influential jobs in the private sphere. To attain these positions and wield power, observing the correct order of things in this world was of utmost importance; needless to say, men in this category acted in the proper fashion to secure social peace and stability. In times of military turmoil, their bold and forceful action frequently caught people by surprise, and with the passage of time and wisdom of hindsight, it has become increasingly clear that many of these acts should not be repeated. Some people will claim to be cautious and circumspect in approaching matters, but from an objective viewpoint they are really against any kind of change.[iv]

Category Two: *Shizoku* whose power was transformed and who embraced the ideas of civilization and enlightenment but were unable to attain positions in which they could fully exercise that power, or obtained office but subsequently lost it. That is to say, men who sought office but were unsuccessful, or achieved office but were dismissed; men who missed the opportunity to start a business venture, or started one but failed; men who succeeded to their satisfaction but are dissatisfied because they have no part in politics. *Shizoku* in this category embraced the ideas of civilization of their own volition, and as the first to do so, have nothing to regret or be ashamed of, but unable to gain a position in which they could realize their ambitions, they cannot help but be dissatisfied. Or should we say they are dissatisfied in spirit and unhappy with their station in life? Or perhaps say they are satisfied in one part of their hearts but dissatisfied in another?

Taken together, these men are what we now call popular rightists. Among them are scholars and professional critics who are respected widely and whose influence is by no means negligible. On the very lowest tier of these popular rightists are *shizoku* who mistakenly turned in their government stipends early on. As a group, popular rightists lack practical experience and see things only from the sidelines, so their arguments are almost always simple and straightforward. But simple and straightforward arguments can often be persuasive. One such example would be the argument to restore imperial rule and expel foreigners that stirred up society at the end of the Tokugawa era. It is not without reason, then, that the argument for popular rights is influential today.

Category Three: *Shizoku* who continue to uphold the spirit distinctive to the samurai class and whose function remains unchanged; that is to say, men who cling to outmoded customs and dislike change of any kind. They are not necessarily unhappy with the Restoration or the new government, but they would prefer to preserve the form and structure of traditional politics in Japan. In general, men in this category are incapable of keeping up with the changing times and lack mental acumen, but in no sense are they listless or ineffectual. They constitute about 70 or 80 percent of *shizoku*, and though the dregs are beneath notice, some are influential and upstanding, and many are admirable for their zeal in cultivating the inner self.[v]

It is a given that mindless power is always found in people with moral conviction. Thus, even if men in this category lack mental acumen, they possess an abundance of energy, which makes for a force to be reckoned with. It is quite possible that they have changed their minds and know the way to progress and enlightenment but have yet to find the right moment to act, or, having tried, were led astray and were subsequently disappointed. Disaffected to begin with, they look at society and find nothing satisfactory. They scrutinize in particular their fellow *shizoku* in the first and second categories and find a multitude of shortcomings. Saying this or that is wrong, they see only the bad points and none of the good; they become further estranged and unwilling to meet the others halfway.

The four hundred thousand *shizoku* who make up the politicians in Japan can thus be divided into three categories, according to their views. The first and second are for progress and reform, the third, for maintaining the status quo. Needless to say, commoners in the three lower classes are connected to politics indirectly and constitute a base of power, but discussing politics and worrying about its state goes against their true colors. Farmers, artisans, and tradesmen have never taken part in national affairs. Therefore, the proximate cause for the country's peace or disorder must be attributed to the former samurai class. This has been the case ever since the Restoration, with progressives squarely opposed to conservatives, peace and order when they are merely dissatisfied, and turbulence and disorder when they threaten to take up arms. Splitting into factions and arguing endlessly about politics has never been admired. Yet, it can also provide an excellent opportunity for people to express their opinions boldly and sharpen their eyes in observing the actions of others, which, in turn, helps to restrain and even out excessive political power. Nevertheless, forming factions and secretly resenting others, or heedlessly resorting to arms to give vent to resentment, can only be to the detriment of the factions themselves and to the country.

Of the several military uprisings since the Restoration, the most conspicuous have been those by the irregular militia (*kiheitai*) in Chōshū, former samurai in Saga, and this year, in Kumamoto and Hagi. The uprisings in Chōshū and Saga have already been suppressed by the military, and those in Kumamoto and Hagi will doubtless meet the same fate. Some critics condemn these samurai rebels, saying they are obtuse and stubborn, incapable of adjusting to changing conditions, reckless and violent, harmful to the peace and stability of the country. They say we should ridicule their folly, abhor their violence, and rejoice when the government seizes the right moment to crush them. Others argue that no matter how troublesome, uprisings by *shizoku* are inevitably quashed, and so, just as the ground hardens after the rain has stopped, each uprising strengthens the foundation of the government and serves as a welcome opportunity to issue regulations that further civilization.

The second view would appear to be simple and lucid but, to my mind, it does not explain the situation adequately. In a country with an established government, people who defy its laws are traitors. Traitors must be extirpated by armed force; without question, this is the meet and proper way of government.

But it must also be said that law-abiding people can become traitors on the spur of the moment, and so, no matter how disaffected or ill-willed these people are, they should be treated by the government as good citizens as long as they do not express their feelings openly. If, on the other hand, they are unable to restrain their feelings and act on them, they are traitors from that very moment and guilty in the eyes of the law. The term traitor is defined by existing laws, and in discussing each case, scholars will have to examine the reasons a person became a traitor, the procedure by which he is punished, and the possible repercussions of that procedure. The critics who condemn the rebels focus solely on the external events of the uprising from the day of its outbreak to its suppression, and ignore the background causes and the course of developments. They are like a person who catches a cold, takes medicine to induce sweat and immediately recovers, but on catching a cold again, however irksome, takes another dose of medicine and thinks this is enough. The person is completely ignorant of the workings of the human body. Had he known how to take proper care of his health, he would have paid more attention to even a slight cold. And this is what I mean when I say these critics fail to examine the circumstances thoroughly.

I shall next discuss what I consider the reasons for these rebellions. As mentioned earlier, the country was long maintained by the four hundred thousand samurai who handled all its affairs. The question is, what was the basic factor that enabled them to do this? It was not trade and commerce, manufacturing, religion, or scholarship, but rather their spirit of loyalty and military bravery. From ages past, samurai in Japan did not believe in gods or Buddhas, spend their time in scholarly pursuits, or deign to engage in trade.[vi]

Instead, they sought honor and fame through loyalty to lord and master and acts of military bravery. True, not a few samurai aspired to learning, but this, too, was no more than a way to strengthen traditional virtues. Japan was founded, as it were, on the principles of loyalty to master and to military valor, and the country's rise and fall determined by whether these virtues were properly honored.

Since the opening of the country, however, the purpose of trade and commerce has changed and methods of academic inquiry have been reformed. In consequence, the two fields have gained in prominence; loyalty and military valor are no longer considered sufficient to maintain the country. To keep up with the times, *shizoku* in the first and second category have already abandoned old customs and practices, while those in the third category still look in vain for vestiges of the virtues they consider the foundation of the country. For conservatives, the disappearance of loyalty and military valor is tantamount to the disappearance of the country's whole purpose as a nation. They are like someone looking in vain for a person wearing a black robe but this person has, in the meantime, taken it off. They are Japanese, but can no longer find Japan, a country that used to wear a black robe. Progressives for their part have cast off their old robes, but have yet to decide whether to wear new ones, or look as though they have discarded the old robes and are wearing new ones. White in the morning and black in the evening, now white, now black, the frequent changes make it difficult to single them out as a target. They know in general what the old Japan should abandon and are determined to do what is required, but they have still to discover what the new Japan should be.

Conservatives seek to preserve the old but are unsuccessful; progressives seek the new but are also unsuccessful. Both fail to find what they seek, and because they seek a different object, they naturally differ in their motives. Or worse, unable to find what they seek, they look for it in each other, as if the other side is concealing it and, growing ever more suspicious, they begin to view each other as enemies. Critics see conservatives refusing to keep up with the times and dismiss them as eccentrics, whereas I see the conservatives' attitude as an unavoidable part of human behavior. From times past, men of the samurai class have regarded themselves as politicians concerned with affairs of state, so even though they might be misinterpreting a situation, would they have any reason to remain silent if they thought the country's future was at stake?

Let us say someone in the United States proposes a sweeping reform in government and a constitution modeled on that in France. The change may in fact be beneficial, but would the people remain silent? In my opinion, they would most certainly not. *Shizoku* in Japan are just like Americans in their sincere concern for national affairs; they would never be indifferent to changes in the country's affairs or fight endlessly like the ancient Chinese kingdoms of Wu and Yue. Progressives and conservatives view each other as enemies and clash because the function of one has changed and the function of the other has yet to change; it is as if a cart heading west has collided with a cart heading east. This difference, then, is the remote cause for the conflict between progressives and conservatives.[vii]

Remote causes alone do not explain events; there are always a number of proximate causes. I shall list these in order.

One: Soon after the Restoration, samurai were stripped of their hereditary stipends and left without any means of support. It is a given that people will be tempted to rebel when they are mired in poverty.

Two: Samurai can somehow endure poverty; what they cannot endure is the loss of their pride as samurai. At one time, they had exclusive control over the country's military and civil affairs and presided over the three lower classes as if they were the lords and masters of the realm. Now, with their political prerogatives suddenly taken away, their military duties handed over to a standing army of conscripted soldiers, and government office open to men of talent from all four classes, they are left without what distinguished them as a privileged class. Think of a carpenter with a steady job who is as skilled as ever but is suddenly told not to report for work. He not only forfeits future earnings, his pride is wounded, and he cannot help resenting his employer. If this is the case with a worker, how much more so is it with a samurai! The loss of wages hurts the body; the loss of pride hurts the human heart. Mental pain is far greater than physical pain.

Three: It is difficult enough for merchants to change the way they handle business dealings. This is to say nothing of *shizoku*, who traditionally know how to consume but not to labor and have been suddenly forced to take up farming or trade. The only way they know how to make a living is by working for the government, but jobs are already filled, so they cannot help being disgruntled.

Four: By nature, ordinary mortals will blame others rather than themselves. *Shizoku* are not base in conduct, but judged from a scholar's detached point of view, they are mediocre and not above envying those in a superior position. They look at the world of government officials and see how they live in spacious mansions, wear elegant clothes, dine on fine food. What officials spend on a lavish banquet could easily buy a year's worth of food and clothes for a poor *shizoku* family. Even the lowliest official earns more than anyone in the three lower classes. And it is not as though these officials are particularly talented or competent; in fact, they are much the same as the rest of former samurai, who cannot help being envious.

In former times, when hereditary rule by high-ranking samurai was the norm, the immense gap between a minister with an income of three thousand *koku* [seven thousand five hundred bales of rice] and a foot soldier with a stipend of ten bales of rice was accepted as part of the natural order of things.[6] This is not the case today. Disgruntled *shizoku* know in their hearts that the system of hereditary rule has been abolished and that one no longer looks into a person's family origins. People should be able to obtain jobs commensurate with their talents: all the bureaucrats in the treasury should be competent in mathematics, and naval officers, skilled in navigation; the fifteen ranks in government posts should be strictly assigned according to fifteen grades of talent. Yet, more often than not, the facts belie this principle. Men skilled in horsemanship serve as naval officers; experts in the military arts are appointed as regional bureaucrats; men not necessarily adept in numbers work for the accounting office; officials in charge of looking after indigent *shizoku* are themselves frequently bankrupt. Given the present situation, they say, even I could work for the government. They conclude that getting a job is purely a matter of luck, and can only seethe with resentment at the unfairness of life.

Five: Owing to the convenience of the modern postal system and publication of books and newspapers, *shizoku* in the countryside are able to obtain a wide variety of information about developments in Tokyo very quickly. Even more effective are steamships and rickshaws.[viii] The improvement in land transportation is unprecedented, and the number of Japanese traveling to Tokyo many times over what it was in the past. Visiting peasants, artisans, and tradesmen are astonished by the hustle and bustle of the city, which reminds them of the crowds of pilgrims that throng Ise Shrine. But to *shizoku* from the countryside, who, by habit, are concerned with the nation's political affairs, the crowds hardly suggest pilgrims at Ise. To the contrary, they see the prosperity in Tokyo and immediately compare it with the dismal condition in the countryside. They gaze at the lofty Western-style buildings that dot the city, see the elegant horse-drawn carriages, and, regardless of who owns them, are angered by what they consider unseemly extravagance. A former samurai happens to go for an audience at the home of a famous high-ranking personage. He asks the attendant about his master's antecedents, and is surprised to learn that he is from the same village, and in fact was an impoverished student to whom he once lent money. Poor before, now rich and powerful, the change in the man's circumstances not only takes the former samurai by surprise but also makes him, a mere mortal, jealous and resentful.

Once in a while, a thoughtful and farsighted visitor will set aside his personal feelings and turn his attention to government finances. He will be dismayed by the amount of debt owed to foreign countries, appalled by the enormous sums of paper currency and public bonds issued, astonished by the large number of ministries and bureaucrats, alarmed by the figures for fixed expenditures. The same visitor from the countryside takes a look at the buildings constructed in the last decade and is amazed to hear that one cost 500,000 yen, another, 300,000, this cost 100,000 and that, 50,000. He quickly totes up the figures in his head and arrives at a total of millions and millions of yen. To his mind, a Western-style structure is completely unnecessary. To protect against fire, a traditional earthen warehouse would do just as well; it requires neither material from abroad nor foreign workers; there is nothing wrong with using Japanese materials and hiring Japanese workers. If Western materials are absolutely necessary, one can always get by with a minimum and build a simple Western-style structure. As for office buildings, if they were built in the traditional Japanese style, at least two-thirds of the monies would be saved, and there would be no need to float bonds abroad and pay interest. He thinks that if he, and others like him, were in government, they would certainly do things differently. Although an outsider, he plans what he would do if he were in office, talks about it to one person, who passes it along to ten others, and as a result, many secretly feel frustrated like someone trying to "scratch his itching foot through his shoe."

Twenty years earlier, when transportation was still hazardous and only an occasional report was delivered by a courier, *shizoku* in the countryside would not have known that the Tokugawa bakufu built Hama Palace, repaired Zōjōji temple in Shiba, Kan'eiji temple in Ueno, and otherwise used hundreds and thousands of forced loans to adorn the city of Edo with new structures. They would have been completely uninterested in what the government did. This is no longer the case. The change is due to political reforms, of course, but increased convenience in communication and transportation, together with the dissemination of books and newspapers, has played a significant role.

Six: Life in the countryside is simple and plain, life in the cities, elegant and extravagant. Virtue is found in simple living and dissipation accompanies extravagance. The great majority of conservative *shizoku* lives in the countryside and keeps to its traditional frugal ways, while those for progress and reform usually live in cities or frequently travel there and naturally adopt wasteful habits, with not a few becoming quite dissolute. Licentious behavior was just as rampant during the age of feudal lords and bakufu bannermen, but such behavior was confined to private quarters, well-mannered in the way of court nobles, and never obtrusive. Samurai were free to hold entertainments and parties at home but forbidden to attend plays in the city. On occasion, life in the inner quarters was indescribably decadent, but since the residents were sealed off from the outer world by bolted gates, there was little chance of ugly rumors leaking outside. A husband's decision to acquire a mistress was prompted by his carnal desires, but the transaction took the form of a ceremony in which his wife presented the woman as a gift. A mistress sometimes took advantage of her position and behaved high-handedly, but house retainers felt no compunction about regarding her as no better than a kitchen maid, and were never openly reprimanded by their masters for this. In short, the dissolute way of life was conducted with the utmost discretion and refinement.

The times have changed, however. Ever since freedom became a byword, educated gentlemen of high standing have set themselves free from the strictures of marriage, and expending their energy on parties and merrymaking, openly indulge in unrestrained licentious behavior. They brazenly take mistresses and hire geisha; geisha houses and drinking establishments prosper as never before. Behavior of this kind has been especially egregious since the last years of the Tokugawa era down to the present. The reality of immorality remains the same, but there is a huge difference in that what was formerly private is now out in the open, drawing people's attention and disturbing them. The authorities are aware of this but dismiss it, saying people have simply become more broad-minded and easy-going, which is nothing but a hollow excuse. Heroes or scholars may act courageously in an open and forthright manner, but if there is the faintest suspicion of lewdness, they will be accused immediately of bestial behavior. Moralists are ever on the alert to attack the conduct of others, and in this respect, heroes and scholars are the most vulnerable. At present, more than a few progressives have this weakness. Conservatives are always on the lookout.

Seven: The most immediate and influential cause of military uprisings is incitement by popular rightists in the second category of *shizoku*. My use of the word incitement may be inappropriate here, so I shall add a word of explanation: by incitement, I do not mean that popular rightists stir up people directly and encourage them to rebel but that they lend their implicit support. This is not with any clear intent, but unknowingly and by chance. Let us say a traveler is walking alone in the dark without a lantern and happens to see someone with a light. He does not ask the other traveler if he may walk with him, nor does the other traveler offer to share his light. The two continue to walk wordlessly, one following the other, who walks ahead completely unaware. The owner of the lantern is not knowingly helping the traveler but lighting his way by chance; if you saw the two, however, you would not think this was the case. And this is what I mean when I say popular rightists implicitly incite rebels.

When people are asked why they planned or instigated rebellions after the Restoration, they will give all manner of reasons: to restore direct imperial rule, to get rid of foreigners, to force the government to invade Korea, to reinstate the feudal system, to purge the sycophants surrounding the throne. Some will even claim that they had a dream or received a divine revelation. Yet when we look into the particulars behind these reasons, we find that the real cause is generally what I described earlier. Considering the number of remote and proximate causes, why has there been no [further] outbreaks? This is because even the most narrow-minded and unreasonable *shizoku* must first look at prevailing social conditions. And by social conditions I mean what scholars call public opinion.

At the time of the Restoration, the first task was to abolish the old, and people were still undecided as to what they should do anew. Men, both in official and private circles, held a diversity of ideas and were unable to agree; there seemed to be no such thing as public opinion. The only thing clear was that a new government had been formed in Japan and that it stood for progress and reform. The conservative *shizoku* mentioned earlier were at a complete loss; arms folded, they could only look on as spectators. The general direction of the government became clearer once the feudal domains were abolished, and the centralized prefecture system was put in place. This move displeased conservative *shizoku* even more, but there was little they could do; by then arguments for reform and progress had swept through society, and in the face of overwhelming public opinion in favor of such decisions, conservative samurai could do nothing to strengthen their ranks. As it was, they had not changed their function; [they] knew only what they themselves stood for and nothing about the position of others. By contrast, progressive *shizoku*, who at one time were conservative, knew both the old and the new, the respective merits and demerits of each side. The conservatives knew themselves but not their opponents, whereas the progressives knew themselves as well as their opponents. It goes without saying which side is stronger. Thus, if conservatives change their views and gradually join the progressives, they will be able to set their minds at rest. Otherwise, they will have to spend the rest of their lives disgruntled and eventually wither away.

But then, as society became more settled and disorder receded, the situation took an unexpected turn. People who called for popular rights emerged from among the progressives. They belong to the second category of *shizoku* I mentioned earlier. Their views are diametrically opposed to those held by conservatives, the two sides, as inimical as fire and water but alike in resenting *shizoku* in the first category, who proudly monopolize government office. They may not express their resentment openly, but neither do they show any sympathy. Needless to say, *shizoku* in the first and second categories are united in favoring reform.

If human beings were completely impartial and endowed with the wisdom of old age, there would be no room for bitterness. But impartiality and the wisdom born from experience are rarely found in this world. Mutually antagonistic, mutually suspicious, some people in Japan have become political enemies. *Shizoku* in the third category refuse to acknowledge *shizoku* in the second category as one of their kind and persist in regarding them as political enemies; yet at the same time, they implicitly support *shizoku* in that group because they similarly resent those in the first category. Or, if they do not actually support them, they believe in their hearts that *shizoku* in the second category will not deliberately harm their cause. In this respect, conservative *shizoku* are like the aforementioned traveler who sees another traveler with a lantern and silently follows him, trusting all the while that the owner will not object or deliberately extinguish the light. Hence, my statement that the proximate cause of recent military disturbances is incitement by popular rightists.

Eight: *Shizoku* in the countryside rely primarily on newspapers for information about conditions in society. People in Tokyo are able to see things for themselves, and not having to rely solely on newspapers, they read selectively; in contrast, *shizoku* in the countryside read newspapers avidly and believe every article, however mistaken or misleading. Also, because journalists are always boasting about their grave responsibility to report public opinion, these *shizoku* believe every word, and assuming that editorials and letters from readers truly represent public opinion, they judge the world accordingly and plot their future course of action. In brief, newspapers are powerless in Tokyo and powerful in the countryside. Scholars in Tokyo read newspapers; scholars in the countryside are swayed by newspapers.

More recently, however, journalists have frequently been punished for violating government regulations. An ordinary word or phrase that is blameless under any law will take on a completely different connotation when scrutinized in the larger context of the article. Construed as resentful or complaining, as wanting to speak out but held back, as impelled to cry but reluctant to utter a sound, their articles often deeply move the reader. One is reminded of a meek and pleasing young bride who does not know what her mother-in-law has in mind and wants to ask, but is afraid of offending her. Fretting by day and night and at her wit's end, she sits alone in her room, wiping her tears with her kimono sleeve. Sunk in despair, she is like a *kaidō* flower drooping in the spring rain; even the most hard-hearted ruffian would feel sorry for her. Journalists today are like the young bride and cleverly play on the sympathies of the reader; as a result, *shizoku* in the countryside put even greater trust in newspapers and follow the articles with single-minded devotion. Newspaper companies publish editorials that express different views, but their primary concern is not the content of the editorials but the number of sales. To win the loyalty of readers, journalists act just like the new bride, or in extreme cases, abandon their mild and pleasing prose style, and, fearless of fines or imprisonment, adopt a bellicose and abrasive tone and risk punishment in order to increase sales. Thus, journalists, too, indirectly incite military disturbances.

Nine: Government reforms since the Restoration have been based on the principle that the four classes possess equal rights. But habits ingrained for hundreds of years are not eliminated in one day. Even now, *shizoku* in the countryside act like samurai of old, and commoners look up to them as a matter of course. The government, too, presides over the country in full dignity, and just as they did during the Tokugawa past, commoners regard officials with fear and awe.[ix] Present laws are designed to deter officials from flaunting their authority, and the more discerning in the higher ranks heed these laws and seldom err, but regrettably enough, the countless petty officials who formerly served in the domains persist in their arrogant ways. Men of their ilk are pleased with themselves not only because they draw salaries from the government but also because the exalted status of "honorable official" gives them immense satisfaction.

A wise and experienced superior will try to restrain them, but he is hopelessly outnumbered. In Tokyo, one rarely comes across this kind of offensive behavior, but in the countryside, where government officials are few yet invested with great power, it is unavoidable. Regional officials are supposed to act in accordance with the law in dealing with *shizoku* of former domains. Also, under the law, *shizoku* and commoners are supposed to be treated alike. In the eyes of commoners, however, "honorable" prefecture officials are no different from honorable domain officials of old, with the happy exception that they are now more accessible. For *shizoku*, however, it is a different matter. Many regard these officials as no better than their equals; they look into their former domain and village affiliation, check their genealogy and past career, and, heedless of present-day relationships, use antiquated standards to compare their background with their own and secretly despise them.

During the Tokugawa era, low-ranking officials stationed in the provinces were extremely arrogant, but they were beyond the scrutiny of the bakufu in Edo and subject only to high officials who occasionally passed through. Today's prefecture office is neither distant nor inaccessible. Local *shizoku* are thoroughly conversant with its affairs, but are legally unable to enjoy the same social prestige as government officials. Indeed, in several instances, former domain ministers have been rebuked and forced to submit humbly to the lowest-ranking functionary. To *shizoku*, equal rights for all four classes does not mean that the lower three have been raised to their level so that they can approach the government together. To the contrary, they feel that both the government and three lower classes remain on the same level, while they have been dragged down, further removed from the government, and stripped of their distinctive honor and pride.

When I listed the proximate causes for military insurrections, I was far from suggesting that conservative *shizoku* act in a reasonable fashion. In fact, those who instigated rebellions were invariably the least intelligent and least discerning among them. Relying on brute force to foment trouble, putting their hopes on the wrong cause, inept in whatever they undertook, they failed to win popular support. Without any support or encouragement, they were completely isolated. Misjudging conditions in the country, they seem to have been deluded by what they thought was public opinion. People who turn against the government that governs them are enemies of the state. However inept they were, this is no reason to excuse them; they must be ruthlessly stamped out. Since the Restoration, every single rebel has been punished. If, by misfortune, someone rises up in the future, he will face the same fate. This is the meet and proper way of politics. Traitors who rebel only to be extirpated are like someone who falls ill but recovers. He is to be congratulated for recovering, but the illness itself is never a cause for celebration. Traitors to the country are an illness that afflicts the country. I shall examine next how the illness affects the vitality of the country.

The proximate causes for military uprisings are many and diverse, but the remote cause is none other than the clash between progressive and conservative elements. The former has already changed its function and the latter has yet to change. Despite the fact that one has changed and the other has not, if the two forces eventually come to blows and one is destroyed, will the power of the defeated force be reduced to nothing? Or will it perhaps change its form, move to the winning side, and bolster the winners even further?

Let me be more concrete and discuss the particulars. Government troops have suppressed rebels and peace has been restored. Yet, we can never tell when malcontents in the countryside will attempt another insurrection. For this reason, the military must be strengthened. Also, to thwart the rebels beforehand, stringent police laws must be enacted. In urban areas where large numbers of people congregate, and in former domains in the countryside where many *shizoku* live, the police force must be thoroughly organized; regional officials must be put on the alert and, over and above their regular duties to protect the people, keep a close watch on *shizoku* and take action when necessary. If the entire country is vigilant and prepared for contingencies, there is no need to worry about rebels. Should the people act unlawfully, the police will always know. Should the police fail to deter them and violence erupts, the regional garrison will be ready. Should the garrison be insufficiently armed, a telegram will instantly summon an army of several thousand, which will come by steamed-powered ships if not by rail. In the feudal past, every domain possessed a sizable amount of weapons and provisions and insurgents could use the castle precincts as a stronghold. Today, castles have been destroyed, and bows, arrows, and guns have been discarded. Temples and monasteries, as well as highway inns once used by traveling daimyo, have fallen into disrepair; even if a large rebel force were raised and provisions procured, their uprising would be like trying to cook rice without a big pot; a successful rebellion would be out of the question. Suppressing rebels will be easy; there is nothing to fear.

No matter how obtuse or stubborn, a former samurai will not pinch a flame once he is burned. He may attempt something, but after repeatedly failing, he will abandon his self-righteous indignation and in a moment of distraction, decide that rather than sacrificing his precious life to gain fame and honor, he would be better off drinking five cups of cheap sake and having a good night's sleep. Or, rather than arguing in vain about worldly affairs and losing all his money, he should be growing potatoes to satisfy his hunger. He thinks to himself, better to obtain real results than to seek fame, better to earn money than to educate his children. Having so decided, he will rush about the kitchen and die surrounded by jars of bean paste and salt; or he will fall into deep despair, and at an utter loss as to what to do, quietly wait for death. Ten years will pass, then twenty, and by the next generation, hardly a trace of the family's samurai antecedents will be left, the only items in the house, a pair of iron swords not worth taking to the pawn shop, a crested kimono bequeathed by a feudal lord and now lining an undergarment. When the elderly grandmother explains what these objects represent, the younger generation is dumbfounded. The samurai spirit has vanished, and the warrior class is no different from the lower three, perhaps even poorer and condemned to subsist on bran. Many *shizoku* have already married commoners and no longer constitute a distinct group; their craven attitude goes without saying. In the past, farmers and tradesmen cowered in awe of "honorable warrior families." Twenty or thirty years hence, the second generation of erstwhile samurai families will probably cower in awe of "honorable government officials," and parents will quiet a crying child by threatening to call a policeman.ˣ

When the spirit and energy of the former samurai class disappears forever, there will be no fear of another military disturbance. Free of the threat, the government will be more powerful and control the country with ease. Firmly established as the center of national power, the government will become stronger still, and as power generates even greater power, it will be the locus of military and financial power, attract increasing numbers of capable men, and foster commercial activity. With the forces of the entire country assembled in the capital, the capital will be Japan, and Japan will exist because of the capital.

Then, when we cast our gaze across the countryside, we will see villagers living in undisturbed peace, and though burdened with taxes, never wanting for food. They may complain loudly about their lot but in fact suffer little; as long as they pay their yearly taxes, they will have nothing to worry about. Busy enough minding family and home, will they have the time to pay attention to their village, much less their county or their prefecture? Or for that matter Japan? To villagers, Japan is Tokyo; what happens there is not their personal concern; let others be responsible for the nation's rise or fall; they are like visitors in their own country. Only very rarely will a villager of intelligence leave for the capital and shed memories of his birthplace, as he might toss out a pair of worn out straw sandals. Of course, there are cities of considerable size in the provinces. In cities like Hyōgo [Kobe], Shimonoseki, and Nagasaki, commerce and industry flourish, but the sole purpose of life for the inhabitants is, literally, to stay alive, work hard, and earn enough money so as to secure an easeful passage to the next world. They are physically alive, but when it comes to politics or national affairs, they are completely lifeless. They may accumulate immense riches, but it is as though each one has put his soul into a cashbox, ten rich men just like ten cashboxes, utterly incapable of holding serious opinions or discussions.

If present trends continue and no unexpected incident occurs, twenty or thirty years hence, the foundation of the government will be more solid, the people more settled in spirit, and the entire country reminiscent of a single domain in the Tokugawa past. During those years, when three hundred daimyo ruled their respective domains, each daimyo concentrated political power in the castle town, and residents submitted without a second thought. It was as if there were three hundred centers of power in Japan, with each maintaining order. Now, the multiple centers have been merged into one center, which not only maintains order as before but also has issued ordinances that open government office to all men of talent and that simplify procedures to prevent corrupt practices. Compared with the evils of hereditary rule, the advantages of the new system are too obvious to mention. Furthermore, as school education develops apace, the number of literate people will grow, the level of scholarship will rise, the arts will advance, manners will be more dignified and refined, and people will no longer be simple-hearted and naive. They may be accused of servility and cunning but never of crude and boorish behavior.

The strengthening of the government's foundation, the people's increasingly orderly behavior, the efflorescence of the arts and learning would seem a matter of rejoicing for both the government and the people.[xi] Yet, when I think ahead to the country's long-term good, I find in the midst of joy something that fills me with foreboding: the *shizoku* class has lost its spirit and vigor; commoners, who never had much to begin with, have no say in affairs of the state, which, to them, could just as well not exist. But whether *shizoku* or commoner, they are equally human beings who belong to one nation and should never be allowed to sink to the depths of apathy. Especially at a time when school education expands by the day and people are gaining knowledge, when hereditary privileges no longer hold in the public and private spheres, those with talent and learning will naturally not rest content to crawl about like insects. *Shizoku* and commoner alike will seek positions they think they deserve, but alas, jobs have already been taken over by the government. Could they engage in commerce or industry? For this, they must rely on government funds; as it is, the government has already started enterprises. Could they open up land for agriculture? The government has already done this. Explore mines? Again, the same problem. Found schools and teach? Unless sponsored by the government, they will not get funds, and unless they teach at government schools, they will not be paid. Write books or translate? They cannot compete with cheaper editions put out by the government. Establish popular assemblies in the countryside and hold discussions? At most, they will become a district head and have to submit meekly to a regional official's orders. Wherever they look, jobs are unavailable. Seek government employment, and every position is filled; go forward, and there is no seat to occupy; retreat, and there is no place to rest. Perhaps, the old saying is true that literacy is the beginning of grief and the poor are happiest when they are kept ignorant. Learning acquired after years of arduous study becomes the source of anguish.

A Western scholar of political economy has written that salaries for bureaucrats should be proportional to ability, and that high salaries attract men of superior quality, while low salaries attract men of inferior quality. His argument applies to his own country, where jobs are plentiful in the private sphere, but this certainly does not apply to Japan. Able men flock to the government, which already has a surplus, and even if it expands, there will always be too many applicants. In the years to come, the imbalance in supply and demand will inevitably lead to a lowering of salaries. And even then, a reduction of 20 percent, 30 percent, or as much as 50 percent, will not deter men of talent from seeking jobs in government.

Men of talent seek jobs in the private sphere but are unsuccessful; they seek jobs in government and again, are unsuccessful. Even the most benighted commoner knows that despotic rule by hereditary rulers is no longer permitted. The present government is not intentionally authoritarian; it simply cannot hire men endlessly or hand over the reins of power to the untutored masses. It has no choice but to exclude unqualified applicants from affairs of the state. Already, a distinction exists between those in power and those out of power, with the latter prevented from knowing what takes place inside the inner circle. Under the Tokugawa system, the inner circle of government was lofty and far removed; entering it was like ascending a ladder to heaven. No matter how competent or talented, those outside the circle did not presume to look inside and were content to let affairs take their natural course.

The situation is different now. To be sure, the inner circle of government is still lofty and distant, but since one can always gain entry by using the right approach, aspirants are reluctant to give up hope. The inner circle that determines state affairs can be likened to a celestial paradise. In days past, an iron gate barred entry; try as one might, one could not enter. Today, the gate has been replaced by a glass door through which one can peer but still not enter: the restriction is harder to bear. Faced with such a restriction, how will people act? When they were barred by an iron gate, they still lived in a dreamlike state of darkness and were honest and simple-hearted; now, barred by a glass door, they are half-awake and half-dreaming—an indeterminate state that is bound to negatively affect people's behavior in society. In fact, compared with the past, sentiments like envy and jealousy, sycophancy and deceit, have increased many times over, with truly deplorable consequences. (The foregoing section concerns moral conduct.)

It is a given in human affairs that as society advances, people become more extravagant and nothing seems to stop them. Teachings about virtue and frugality have little influence, admonitions by elders are seldom heeded, and ordinances meant to restrain such behavior have proven totally useless. An important principle of civilization is to refrain from crude and boorish behavior and to strive for elegance and refinement. But it is extremely difficult to distinguish between elegance and extravagance, since what some people deem extravagance is frequently open to question. In this immense and restive world, where people are easily swayed, there is little one can do about the propensity for extravagance. Yet if there is one thing that partially restrains this propensity, it can be found within us: the spirit of self-confidence. By this, I mean trusting in oneself and relying on oneself. For example, someone from a very wealthy family is not ashamed to wear shabby and threadbare clothes. The reason? Because he knows he can always rely on his family fortune. To give another, more edifying example, Yanhui, a high-ranking disciple of Confucius, was content to live in a congested back alley and beg for food like an itinerant monk because he firmly believed in his purpose in life. Or to give an example from Japan in the past, a samurai is poor, his family suffers from cold and hunger, he is hard pressed to pay his debts and barely scrapes by, yet he proudly hangs on to his treasured pair of swords because he knows he must live by the honored code of loyalty and military valor. The spirit of self-confidence is created by the public opinion that prevails at the time (or more specifically, by one's group), and if people are so minded, it will help restrain extravagance in this mundane world.

Nevertheless, when I think of future developments in Japan, I very much doubt that people excluded from state affairs will make firm decisions about what they will do next. Men in government, too, will still be wearing black and white robes interchangeably and remain undecided about their ultimate goals. With neither side possessing the spirit of self-confidence, the tendency to extravagance will become ever more pronounced. Even now, men purchase smoking pipes of gold, women wear sashes of brocade, scholars and educated gentlemen dress like actors, their wives adorn themselves like geisha. People compete in a show of finery and buy so-called civilized goods imported from the West. Be it a house, household article, clothing, food or drink, they take delight in whatever is novel, the costlier the better. Coveting this and that, they feverishly compete with one another to acquire these items. To this day, one can determine the wealth of the owner, the level of his intelligence or lack thereof, by the amount of Western goods in his house—a strange situation unheard of previously. Should this trend continue for the next twenty or thirty years, the waste in public and private monies will be fearful indeed. One can only despair for the country. (The foregoing section concerns extravagance.)

The authority of the central government is strong and unchallenged, the country offers a place of residence for the silent masses; men of ambition are excluded from government and at a loss as to their future direction. At such a time, if foreigners are permitted to travel and live in the interior of Japan, conditions in the country will change drastically. And by foreigners, I do not mean foreigners who will come in the future but those who are already here, and through long years of associating with the Japanese, know how to deal with us. In contrast, most Japanese have never laid eyes on foreigners and know nothing about them. One side is experienced, the other side, inexperienced and naive; the disparity in skill and knowledge is undeniable. The day the two sides come into greater contact, host and guest will reverse positions: inevitably, the Japanese will be under the control of foreigners, cheated in trade, and treated unfairly under existing treaties. Religious beliefs may also be affected, the system of marriage as well. Less significant, there will be issues concerning the hiring of foreign employees, hunting and bearing firearms. With cunning and deceitful visitors on one side, and on the other side, dull-witted and heedless country folk, the consequences of dealing with foreigners will be immense and manifold. The government will be indignant but helpless; when it tries to fix one thing, something else will blow up before a settlement is reached. No matter how it bestirs itself, no matter what strategy is employed, the government will be like a father trying to lead a hundred children by the hand.

A lawsuit between two Japanese will be easily resolved, but if a third party, a foreigner, testifies, negotiations will be needlessly drawn out. Or in a legal case between Japan and a foreign nation, Japan cannot hope for a favorable resolution under present conditions, regardless of existing regulations. Incidents that have occurred since the opening of ports bear this out. More galling, people will forget how they should act, and their spirit of patriotism will be as thin and fragile as a sheet of paper. To gain a moment's respite, even scholars and educated men may well rely on foreigners and go around looking pleased like the errand boys in service today.[xii]

Still more extreme, some misguided Japanese may secretly ask foreigners to help them oppose the country's laws, if only to give vent to their dissatisfaction. People have already lost money in commercial dealings, forfeited their legal rights in courtrooms, and even betrayed their country. I fear for Japan's independence; its loss would be the greatest of sorrows.

I have now listed the misfortunes that I imagine will befall us in the near future. Will critics say I am being overly cautious? But it is better to be overly cautious than to be insufficiently so. Even at the risk of being criticized, I am compelled to speak out my mind, and this, in no uncertain terms. How, then, can we solve these problems? Let me state that the only solution is to unite *shizoku*—the group that determines the rise or fall of Japan—and to have both progressives and conservatives move forward as one on the same path. How can this be done? I shall consider the ways.

Shall we restore the feudal system of hereditary stipends, entrust *shizoku* with their erstwhile military duties, and choose the talented and able among them to serve as civil bureaucrats in central government? That would be like *shizoku* from the former three hundred domains handling three hundred kinds of weapons; three hundred bureaucrats spouting three hundred arguments; three hundred men in one building making three hundred cooking stoves so they can eat together at one long **table**. In short, it will be like building a castle in the air.[xiii]

Or shall we appoint everyone in the *shizoku* class to government office? Once in this position, they would be able to work with those already in office to further the cause of progress and reform. But would this plan work? Even today, there are too many officials, some of whom are excessively zealous. Besides which, the government could not possibly support four hundred thousand men. It has no rice to feed them, no money to pay them. This, too, is like building a castle in the air.[xiv]

The two plans are ill-suited to the times. We could wait several hundred years, and they would still be unsuitable. If we want to unite *shizoku* and persuade them to take the same path, we must present firmly fixed goals and show the way to progress and reform, find jobs for those outside of government so that they can fulfill these goals, and thereby indirectly change the function of conservatives. If we treat conservative *shizoku* as enemies and aim at destroying them head on, they may seem to be reduced to nothing, but they will still possess something distinctive that can be transformed and be of practical use to the country.[xv]

There are people who claim that *shizoku* are completely useless. Many are admittedly useless and it is hardly worth the effort to change them, but we should not generalize from extreme examples. Also, when I say *shizoku*, I do not refer exclusively to those who wore a pair of swords and received hereditary stipends. I include doctors, Confucian scholars, some merchants and farmers, in other words, people who read books, practiced the military arts, and thought seriously about the world. I call them *shizoku* because many, in fact eight or nine out of ten, are descended from samurai families. We should not dismiss *shizoku* as a whole as useless, in particular, those outside of government who have already changed their function and embraced the cause of progress and reform. They are capable and eminently qualified to serve the country.

Before discussing how men outside of government can secure a proper station in life and have their function changed indirectly, I shall first explain the different kinds of government power. One is political power (*seiken*); in English, it is called **government**. The other is administrative power (*chiken*); in English it is called **administration**.[7]

The government (*seiken*) has the power to determine general laws; conscript soldiers and control the army and navy; levy taxes to support the central government; conduct foreign relations and make decisions on matters of war or peace; mint coins and determine their value. In short, the central government's authority extends to the entire country and creates a uniform whole. The administration (*chiken*) takes local factors into consideration to maintain order in each region and ensure the happiness of the people. Which is to say, local administration draws up police laws, constructs or repairs roads, bridges, and river banks; builds schools, temples, shrines, and parks; sets up regulations concerning public health; collects taxes to cover local expenses.

The government's power extends uniformly throughout the country, whereas the power of local government is limited. Regions differ in wealth and customs, and it would be impossible to treat them in the same way. For example, the law forbids people in cities from appearing naked in public or urinating in the streets; this could never be enforced in the countryside. Again, in cities, big bridges are built over rivers to facilitate travel and adorn surrounding areas; in rural areas, simple embankments suffice to prevent floods and save money.

Differences are found not only between cities and rural areas but also between towns and villages. To mention a few, a big and imposing school is built in a poverty stricken village and funds are exhausted, with nothing left to educate the students or repair the building. Only a primary school is built in a former castle town, leaving the talented children of *shizoku* unable to pursue higher studies, such as Western learning. The image of a tutelary god enshrined for hundreds of years is removed, or the statue of Buddha long revered by villagers is sent to another temple, as if the gods and Buddha have been demoted or promoted. As a result, local residents lose their object of worship and tradesmen who cater to pilgrims lose their livelihood. A town congested with shops requires proper drainage to guard against pestilential illness, but instead of attending to this, a brothel, something hitherto unknown in the area, is built, and syphilis, a far more pernicious disease, infects the residents.

None of the examples gives any consideration to local conditions. Customs also differ greatly between north and south, mountainous and coastal areas. Names of objects differ, as do shapes in tools, styles in houses and clothes, pastimes and entertainments, and, most notably, tastes in food and drink. A cursory glance makes one wonder whether country folk are capable of judging the quality or utility of things, but this is hardly the case. Customs and habits change according to the workings of human nature, and those judged worthless or inconvenient by outsiders have their own distinctive uses to residents in the countryside, the differences too subtle and minute for outsiders to grasp. Local government must take these differences into account if it hopes to give people their proper due. That is why local government varies from region to region and is never the same. Only long-time residents know the customs in their area in detail. Thus, the purpose of central and local government is entirely different.[xvi]

When scholars discuss government power and the respective advantages and disadvantages of centralized versus decentralized power, they should first distinguish between the types of power in each category. Do advocates of local government want political power to be divided? If they think each region should have its own laws, its own military, its own system of taxation, and its own right to determine war or peace, Japan would be like a collection of many independent nations. The Tokugawa bakufu was known for its subtle refinement of autocracy, but it eventually collapsed because successive heads failed to centralize political power sufficiently. A nation cannot be a nation if it does not centralize political power. Whatever the circumstances, the government must never hand out this power.

Again, some advocates of local government are unable to differentiate between central and local government and want to take power from the center and give it to local officials. If they have their way, what would be the consequences? Giving a portion of central power to local officials would increase the number of head ministers, with the government appointing thirty, or as many as fifty. This would lead to an imbalance in the government, and regional officials would wield power such that people will think that they are being ruled by a second generation of feudal lords and be even more discouraged. Misinterpreting the purpose of local government will only concentrate even greater power in the central government.

Others contend that a popular elective assembly will decentralize political power. But establishing an assembly in the nation's capital and giving power to local areas are two separate things, with no relation to each other. With or without a popular assembly, power must be given to local government and power must also be centralized. In short, the utility of an elective popular assembly lies in preventing the misuse of centralized power, and as such, plays an important role in the government. Those who want to give power to local government should first distinguish the two kinds of power before making their demands.

Proponents of greater centralized power misunderstand the statement that a nation cannot be a nation without a strong central government. They want to invest all political power in the central government, place all and sundry aspects of local government under its control, have it govern the entire country in the same way, and in complete disregard of differences in regional customs, put everything on the same level. If their ideas were carried out, in appearance, the conduct of government may be admirable, but how will this arrangement affect the people's spirit? They should think carefully about this. As it happens, my friend and colleague Obata [Tokujirō] has translated portions of a book by the Frenchman [Alexis] de Tocqueville, so I shall quote a pertinent passage:[8]

> It is evident that a central government acquires immense power when united to administrative centralization. Thus combined, it accustoms men to set their own will habitually and completely aside; to submit, not only for once or upon one point, but in every respect, and at all times. Not only, therefore, does this union of power subdue them by force, but it affects them in the ordinary habits of life, and influences each individual, first separately and then collectively.
>
> The partisans of centralization in Europe maintain that the government directs the affairs of each locality better than the citizens can do it for themselves: this may be true when the central power is enlightened, and when the local authorities are ignorant; when it is as alert as they are slow; when it is accustomed to act, and they to obey. Indeed, it is evident that this double tendency must augment with the increase of centralization, and that the readiness of the one, and the incapacity of the others, must become more and more prominent.

I have urged my friend to go over his translation and publish it in the *Katei sōdan* series.

The same proponents of greater centralized power go a step further and think that the government should not only control local government but also put commerce and industry under its authority and so control all private enterprise. But the people in commerce and trade in Japan have not been asleep, or in a stupor for hundreds of years, so benumbed that they merely followed orders. They sought work eagerly and with enthusiasm staked much on their endeavors. Left on their own, there is no limit to what they can accomplish. If commerce and trade had remained unchanged for the last ten or hundred years, of course, a strategy to arouse them from slumber and awaken their senses is necessary.

Regardless of rank or past career, in terms of intellectual capacity alone, men in government are the most advanced and foresighted of all Japanese. The advanced must guide those who lag, the foresighted, teach those who have yet to look ahead; this is the only way to rouse the people and awaken their senses. On this score, the Japanese government differs slightly from those of Western countries in having unofficial as well as official duties. Thus, to listen to abstract Western theories, without thinking about conditions in Japan, or to criticize the government for taking on too much work and insist that everything should be left to run its course, is nothing but a futile academic exercise, which ignores the reality.

Even so, the government should give careful thought to the way it guides and teaches the people and not undertake things lightly. The leaders are prescient and have many ideas about what to do, but have yet to formulate practical strategies. The people, on the other hand, are knowledgeable about certain things because of long-standing customs, and while their practical strategies may lack a theoretical foundation, in some instances, they will know far better than the government what to do.[xvii] Someone who draws a ship does not necessarily know how to build or navigate one; someone who has studied books on pathology is not necessarily skilled in diagnosing or healing a sickness. Therefore, in guiding the people, the government is right to tell them its ideas about what they should do, but wrong to carry out strategies it has not fully thought through.

Before making something, one must first draw a chart and make a small-scale model. This applies to establishing banks, reclaiming land, [or] constructing machines, buildings, schools, and hospitals. Making a small-scale model reduces expenses, but a model alone does not serve one's final purpose; eventually, a school or hospital has to be built and a machine has to be used. Also, the model should not be crude or excessively large but as small and finely detailed as possible. It is as if the central government is holding up the objects of civilization for all the people to see and leading them to a level of enlightenment where they will attain that state. The government does not like to control the private lives of the people, nor does it have the right to do so. The government also understands the futility of trying to control or force the people into specified activities. Thus, the government's only choice is to make it appear as if the people are being told that it is up to them to decide whether to go forward or not. This is what I mean when I say the government must tell the people its ideas about what they should do.

If the government misses this essential point, and confuses its stated ideas with the strategies for putting them into practice, it will run into endless trouble when carrying them out. The leaders are of samurai background and completely ignorant of the practical aspects of commerce and industry, yet the government has more capital at its disposal than any other entity in Japan. When people with no practical experience handle large sums of money, it is a foregone conclusion that the funds will be squandered and misused. This was amply borne out during the closing years of Tokugawa rule and the years since the Restoration. No doubt some critics will say that the evils of wasteful spending are unavoidable and should be taken into account from the start. Or that people should not think of short-term profits and losses but of profits and losses over the long term. What they say may seem highly persuasive, but even then, they should be more circumspect in making such claims, and consider a wide range of ideas and examine each one thoroughly before determining their respective merits and demerits.

Let us say the government decides to start an industry that requires 100,000 yen in capital. In the entire country, there is no such thing as monies that cannot be used. Funds are duly raised, an old industry is discontinued, a new one started; the results will have to be compared. Ten years later, the old industry, which was deprived of money, has declined and incurred a loss of 1 million yen; meantime, the new one has made a profit of 500,000 yen, leaving the government with a deficit of 500,000 yen. If the new and old industries had been treated equally, there would be no profit and no loss. Also, in assessing the results, the government would have to take into account not only the costs of salaries and extraneous office expenses, but the government's relationship with the people and the effect on their spirit and morale.

Now, let us say the government did not start the new industry. Would someone from among the ignorant and powerless commoners have started one within ten or twenty years whether or not funds were available? Are the government's efforts all in vain when it alone tries to increase the country's prosperity and the people remain benighted? Or could it be that commoners are unexpectedly intelligent, aware of the country's future direction, capable of raising private funds, and many times more competent than inexperienced officials? All these factors must be taken into consideration. And this is precisely what I mean when I say the critics should think about a wide range of ideas before making a judgment.

The government could use its authority to interfere with people's private lives by needlessly protecting them or putting up prohibitions, but in fact, such efforts will be futile and even hurtful. Western writers on political economy have keenly argued that there are ways to protect and limits to what can be prohibited.

People with an interest in public affairs are aware of this, but those in charge of these affairs see things differently. Claiming that conditions in Japan should not be judged by Western theories, they say their own policies on protection and prohibition will prove highly effective, and appear to be undeterred by the work entailed. To refute their views, rather than quoting Western books on political economy, I shall quote from a Japanese work that is factual and easier to understand. Entitled *Thoughts on Raising Domain Productivity* (*Kōeki kokusan-kō*), the book was written in Tenpō 15 [1844] by Ōkura Nagatsune, a samurai in the service of the Hamamatsu domain. The gist of the book is that the interests of subordinates should take precedence over those of the daimyo house. Couched in the language of the feudal past, the book contains ideas that often differ from those of our own age, but its overall argument about the harmful effects of government interference in private affairs is consonant with Western economic theory. The quote is from page 8 in volume 1:

> There was once a ruling daimyo who hoped to increase the wealth of his house by taking over a business hitherto entrusted to merchants in the castle town. He established an agency to handle commercial transactions and forbade peasants from selling their products directly to merchants. Profits accumulated, the financial conditions of the daimyo house immediately improved, and in due course, a clever retainer suggested to the officers in charge that if they did such and such, profits would rise even more. The officers followed his suggestion and profits increased. Then, another retainer came with a suggestion, which was taken, and in time, many claiming to be knowledgeable about profit making came to the agency. The merchants secretly resented this, since their rightful profits were being taken over by the daimyo, but intimidated by his power and authority, no one dared to speak out. They could only hope that an incident of some kind would restore things to their former state, and eventually, many resisted openly. The daimyo had established the agency to improve the finances of his house, so one hesitates to say it was a bad plan, but when a plan goes against Heaven's reason and ignores the well-being of the common people, it will often end in failure. Daimyo would be well advised to think carefully about taking business away from those under their rule. The retainers entrusted with the domain's prosperity should have known that people would be loath to comply. Instead, they followed first one, and then another of the suggestions from those claiming to be knowledgeable, and in all likelihood, would have extended their reach to other things as well. A scheme like this must be given serious thought and on no account should be taken lightly.

When a government undertakes an enterprise, money is inevitably squandered. This is unavoidable and not necessarily the fault of those in charge but the result of spending money without calculating revenues. Nevertheless, the whole point of finance is to make sure that money is available to cover expenses. We spend capital to build ships and obtain profits from freight. We spend capital to buy goods and obtain profits from sales. People are the same the world over: they act according to their own interests, compare cost and profit, and spend as they see fit, all this in keeping with the laws of competition in the market place. If some spend more than what comes in or spend heedlessly in total disregard of income, over and above the losses incurred, the laws of competition in business that ought to prevail in society are violated and the repercussions, disastrous and far ranging. Thus, if wasteful spending by government is indeed unavoidable, the 100,000 or 200,000 yen it spends will indirectly inflict on others a loss of 1,000,000 or 2,000,000 yen.[xviii]

The losses can be twofold: first, the money lost because of insufficient profits, as in the case of the hypothetical industry I described earlier; second, the damage done by obstructing competition in society. In a word, two losses in one stroke. In fact, some of the negative consequences are already apparent. For example, the government has built hospitals, hired foreign and Japanese doctors, paid salaries, and purchased ample equipment and medicine to take care of patients. Meanwhile, those who want to open a private hospital and practice medicine are unable to compete and have given up all hope. In the West, patients in government hospitals are mostly from the upper class [the Japanese editor suggests Fukuzawa means lower class], whereas in Japan, patients in government hospitals are from the middle class and above, thus depriving private practitioners of patients with social influence. To give another example, scholars of Western studies who completed their studies in Japan or abroad are unable to make a living, and after searching far and wide, reluctantly take jobs in government, and as humdrum civil servants, they make little use of their talents. Even if they founded private academies, the schools would be unable to compete with those funded by the government. Again, in recent years, only a handful of scholars devote themselves to translating books and no one bothers to study the art of translation because they know that the sales from their work cannot compete with cheaper government editions.

To choose a somewhat different example, according to one merchant, since the last years of the Tokugawa period, government officials have dealt directly with foreigners and handled most of the purchases from abroad, leaving Japanese merchants to look on with their hands clasped, so to speak. When a Japanese merchant handles a purchase, by the time it goes through two or three middlemen, the original price of 100 yen rises to 105 yen, but when a foreign agent handles it, the price is 103 yen. The difference is 2 yen, but since Japan as a country is making the purchase, as long as the original price of 100 yen remains the same, the 2 yen difference is negligible. The government gains 2 yen and Japan as a country loses 3 yen. For Japanese merchants, conducting business with foreigners is like going to school; thus, it is particularly important that they are given the chance to build up the spirit of enterprise.

I have digressed from the point and been rather long-winded, so I shall sum up my views. A clear distinction must be made between political power and administrative power. Political power must be concentrated in the central government, and administrative power must be given to every region throughout the country; the two powers must not be merged, or merged and then dispersed. The government's political power is like the gravitational force of the earth's center. Nothing on the earth's surface is exempt from the law of gravity, and yet we go about our daily lives unaware of its force. Things move up and down freely, to the left and to the right; in some cases, instead of falling to the ground, something rises upwards, as if to defy gravity. Objects on earth relate to one another and move unimpeded by gravity; even amidst confusion and disorder, the force of gravity never disturbs reason; it is truly a marvel of nature. If administrative power is allocated to local government and used freely, confusion and disorder may ensue and people may be bewildered for a while, but as long as the central government—the country's gravitational center—retains political power, there is no need to worry. What is perceived as confusion and disorder is really a sign of the country's health and vigor—a matter for rejoicing, in truth, a marvel of the political process.

Assuming that my views are correct, I shall return to my initial argument, namely, that the reason for the country's troubles is the conflict between progressive and conservative *shizoku*. I hope to prove this with facts from the recent past. Also, even if the power of conservatives is destroyed in the near future, we should not dismiss all the others who are concerned for the country yet unable to take part in its affairs. Whether their function is transformed or not, they have a measure of power but are troubled because they have no place to use it.[xix] They are like a horseman without a horse, or an archer without a bow. Today, the only place where they can find a horse or a bow is local government, which, duly empowered, will give them jobs. And giving them a proper station in life will indirectly change their function. As I stated at the beginning of the essay, in the entire universe, power can never emerge from nothing, nor can it be reduced to nothing. The function of *shizoku* is their power. That power must not be reduced to nothing. It must be transformed and put to good use. In this connection, I shall quote several passages from de Tocqueville's book that Obata Tokujirō has translated and published in issue 23 of *Katei sōdan*.

> There is one sort of patriotic attachment which principally arises from that instinctive, disinterested, and undefinable feeling which connects the affections of man with his birthplace. This natural fondness is united to a taste for ancient customs, and to a reverence for ancestral traditions of the past; those who cherish it love their country as they love the mansions of their fathers. They enjoy the tranquility which it affords them; they cling to the peaceful habits which they have contracted within its bosom; they are attached to the reminiscences which it awakens, and they are even pleased by the state of obedience in which they are placed. This patriotism is sometimes stimulated by religious enthusiasm, and then it is capable of making the most prodigious efforts. It is in itself a kind of religion: it does not reason, but it acts from the impulse of faith and of sentiment. By some nations the monarch has been regarded as a personification of the country; and, the fervor of patriotism being converted into the fervor of loyalty, they took a sympathetic pride in his conquests, and gloried in his power. At one time, under the ancient monarchy, the French felt a sort of satisfaction in the sense of their dependence upon the arbitrary pleasure of their king, and they were wont to say with pride: "We are the subjects of the most powerful king in the world."
>
> Like all instinctive passions, however, this kind of patriotism is more apt to prompt transient exertion than to supply the motives of continuous endeavor. It may save the state in critical circumstances, but it will not infrequently allow the nation to decline in the midst of peace. While the manners of a people are simple, and its faith unshaken; while society is steadily based upon traditional institutions, whose legitimacy has never been contested, this instinctive patriotism is wont to endure.
>
> But there is another species of attachment to country, which is more rational than the one we have been describing. It is perhaps less generous and less ardent, but it is more fruitful and more lasting; it is coeval with the spread of knowledge, it is nurtured by the laws; it grows by the exercise of civil rights; and, in the end, it is confounded with the personal interest of the citizen. A man comprehends the influence which the prosperity of his country has upon his own welfare; he is aware that the laws authorize him to contribute his assistance to that prosperity, and he labors to promote it as a portion of his interest in the first place, and as a portion of his right in the second.
>
> But epochs sometimes occur, in the course of the existence of a nation, at which the ancient customs of a people are changed, public morality destroyed, religious belief disturbed, and the spell of tradition broken, while the diffusion of knowledge is yet imperfect, and the civil rights of the community are ill

secured, or confined within very narrow limits. The country then assumes a dim and dubious shape in the eyes of the citizens; they no longer behold it in the soil which they inhabit, for that soil is to them a dull inanimate clod; nor in the usages of their forefathers, which they have been taught to look upon as a debasing yoke; nor in religion, for of that they doubt; nor in the laws, which do not originate in their own authority; nor in the legislator, whom they fear and despise. The country is lost to their senses; they can neither discover it under its own, nor under borrowed features, and they intrench themselves within the dull precincts of a narrow egotism. They are emancipated from prejudice, without having acknowledged the empire of reason; they are animated neither by the instinctive patriotism of monarchical subjects nor by the thinking patriotism of republican citizens; but they have stopped half-way between the two, in the midst of confusion and of distress.

In this predicament, to retreat is impossible; for a people cannot restore the vivacity of its earlier times any more than a man can return to the innocence and the bloom of childhood; such things may be regretted, but they cannot be renewed. The only thing, then, which remains to be done, is to proceed, and to accelerate the union of private with public interests, since the period of disinterested patriotism is gone by forever.

I am certainly very far from averring, that, in order to obtain this result, the exercise of political rights should be immediately granted to all the members of the community. But I maintain that the most powerful, and perhaps the only means of interesting men in the welfare of their country, which we still possess, is to make them partakers in the government. At the present time civic zeal seems to me to be inseparable from the exercise of political rights; and I hold that the number of citizens will be found to augment or decrease in Europe in proportion as those rights are extended.[9]

In quoting these passages, I am not saying that the ideas are suited in their entirety to present-day Japan. When the author, a French scholar, wrote about old customs and practices, France was on the verge of a sweeping reform, and he may have been referring implicitly to the past when the country was without a monarch, and anarchy reigned for a while. But Japan is not the same as France. We have an emperor; we have a government. There is simply no comparison between the two countries. Still, I am in complete agreement with the author's statement that the only way to change the attitude of the nation's citizens and direct their hearts and minds to the public good is to let them participate in government. It is only when the nation's citizens have the proper attitude, the central government is in full possession of political authority, the people in the countryside are allowed to participate in local government, and the two sides support each other and jointly resolve to maintain the peace of the country that everyone will know for the first time what Japan as a nation should do, and understand that public and private interests converge and are one and the same.

I also agree with the French scholar's statement that the government should not grant political rights to the people immediately. My one wish is that it grants administrative power to local government. Administrative power and political power are closely linked and frequently difficult to distinguish. Thus, in granting administrative power, the government will have to think of a multitude of orderly procedures, but even then, it should waste no time in indicating its future direction. Consider someone who decides to take a trip: he should set off as soon as he makes up his mind where to go; even if he is only halfway to his destination, he need not worry as long as he knows which road to take. At present, administrative government on the local level is generally underway, with only an occasional blunder. Those already in charge will have to meet with men in the central government and discuss the benefits and drawbacks of political power, as well as the relationship between central and local government. They will also have to make sure that neither side is too strong or too weak and that a balance of power is maintained. In other words, a popular elective assembly will have to be established. This is the first step.[xx]

A certain critic has stated that while he wholeheartedly approves of granting administrative power to local government he sees no need for further action. District heads have already been selected in each region, given a certain amount of power, and elevated to a status higher than that of ordinary commoners. Isn't this the purpose of local government?

I fear the critic has only looked at the surface of things and knows nothing about the actual situation. To begin with, what is the nature of the power given to a district head? In my opinion, his power is but a miniscule portion of the power held by the central government, a tiny particle of power dispensed to local inhabitants. Whenever a district head is selected, people say this and that about the government or the public being involved in the procedure, but such talk is really quite pointless. Whether selected by the government or public, the power held by the official is only the minutest portion of central power and the same in nature. The district head is really a lowly bureaucrat, a functionary at the bottom rung of the central government. And what are his duties? He must dance attendance on his superior, the regional official, and meekly submit to his orders; put on his straw sandals and rush to the village outskirts to greet a prefectural official on an inspection tour; clear the streets of noisy children as he guides the official—important duties indeed! When the critic gave his opinion on local government, did he have this in mind? Then, once the district head is back at his office, he is the proverbial bat in a village without birds. He affects the airs of a government official and insults the poor farmers; he tells his underlings the words and style of *kanji* to use in a petition; he scolds them for not using strong Mino paper; he orders them to write three or four copies of a single document; he sends them running four, five times to deliver a report. Is this what is meant by local government? In my opinion, this is not local government but a miniature version of the central government. As proof, rather than being paid with commoner funds, the majority of district heads prefer to receive their pay in the form of salaries from the regional government office. Why? Because they want to gain entry into the inner precincts of political power. Not that one can blame them. And because a district head has no hope of escaping from the bottom rung of officialdom, it is small wonder that no competent person wants the position.

As the situation stands, if someone capable became a district head, the social consequences could well be painful. Let us say a capable and learned man of high repute sets aside his ambitions to become district head. He is like the proverbial dragon lying in wait while submerged in a rice paddy. Officials will be partly pleased and partly apprehensive, even suspicious of his motives. It is as if a highly paid leading actor in a troupe has suddenly decided to join the audience, or play the part of a horse's legs. His fellow actors will be greatly displeased; even if he does not actually perform with them, just having his name listed at the top of the program is reassuring. Why would he go out of his way to play the part of a horse's legs? The actor playing the role of the warrior Kumagai Naozane may say he is reluctant to mount the horse. Another, more impetuous, actor may say if the leading actor wants to play the part of a horse's legs, go ahead and let him, and do not hesitate to strike him. Again, unless he has no talent, an actor assigned the part of a horse's legs may secretly scoff at the actor playing Kumagai. The situation can become intolerably unpleasant. And this is the reason I say that giving power to a district official hardly serves the purpose of local government. In rare instances, someone capable may accept the position, but the consequences, I predict, will not necessarily be good.

In rebuttal, another critic has said that while he generally understands the purpose of granting administrative power to local government, he is against it. Look at the masses, he says. As far as public works is concerned, they do not even know how to treat sewage or dispose of garbage. Or look at former samurai who stubbornly cling to outmoded customs. Unduly attached to their pair of rusted swords, reluctant to follow government orders to cut off their topknots, incapable of taking adequate care of their families, how could they possibly think about public affairs? Discussing local government with men of their ilk would be like consulting a stone statue of Buddha about arrangements for a lecture meeting. Does the government actually intend to appoint the more ambitious among them? They will either be irresponsible young scholars who stumble about in the dark, or polemicists with a hodgepodge of Eastern and Western learning, outwardly up-to-date but old-fashioned in spirit. Commoner or *shizoku*, ambitious scholar or educated gentleman, they will all be inexperienced in public affairs and completely useless and harmful. The critic's rebuttal is lively and seemingly reflects the wisdom of experience, but his conclusion can be summed up in two words: useless and harmful. He fails to give sufficient thought to the nature of what is useful or harmful. Since I cannot bring myself to admire him, I shall take the liberty of giving my own views on the matter.

First, let us posit a base of "point zero" that is neither harmful nor useful, and say that anything above it is harmless and useful, and anything below it is harmful and useless. If we speak of the human body in these terms, we can say that an absence of illness is point zero. If a person grows stronger and rises above zero, he becomes useful, but if he becomes sick, he will sink below zero and be harmful. But in human health it is often difficult to give point zero a permanent position since it tends to fluctuate. If a person becomes sick, then sickness is the base. If he recovers, he rises above the base and is useful. But if he dies, he does harm for there is no possibility of his regaining strength. Alternatively, if we made his condition when he is not sick the base, he may be too busy trying to avoid harm and have no time to plan for what is useful.

Let us apply the same logic to the division of administrative power. The original plan was, first, to eliminate the harmful elements in society, and then, to promote what is useful. As I said earlier, capable *shizoku* excluded from power are like a horseman without a horse or an archer without a bow. They could direct their skills in horsemanship or archery to other ends, but this might disturb the country's peace and stability.[xxi] Then again, if they are suppressed, society will be that much weaker, the dying embers of their power will turn into deceit and cunning, and the prosperity of the country will be damaged forever. In which case, the government will be too busy getting rid of the harmful elements to promote what is useful; the country will be at point zero. The only place where the horseman can find a horse, or the archer a bow, is local government. Giving *shizoku* a share in local government and a position from which to develop their strengths will put their minds at rest, leave the authority of the central government intact, and even if the advantages are not immediately apparent, eliminate the harmful elements. When the aforementioned critic stated that giving power to local government would be harmful and useless, he was doubtless thinking of a world in which the Japanese would literally exercise their rights from the very next day and participate in an orderly fashion like the citizens of England and the United States. His expectations are set too high and for the near future, whereas mine are set low and for the distant future. We are poles apart in our thinking; I fail to be impressed with him.

Will the same critic object to my statement that the government should give the horseman and archer a position in which they can develop their strengths and attain peace of mind? Will he say this would be pandering to the people? If so, this would be an egregious misunderstanding. A sycophant is someone who yields his rights to agree with another. In contrast, someone who satisfies another without yielding his rights is respected and admired. Outwardly, the two may appear the same, but the reality is completely different. At present, the right to govern resides in the central government. But if there is a way to win popular favor without damaging that right, the government should do its utmost to follow it. In brief, the wisest way to win the hearts and minds of the people is to grant administrative power to local government, and if at all practicable, even adopt the ideas of a bullheaded farmer.

Many a country farmer goes to Tokyo, looks with envy at the soaring buildings, and bemoans the sorry state of his home village. As long as the government is not affected unfavorably, it has no need to build tall buildings. Again, plain-living country folk are often incensed by the extravagant and dissolute ways of city people. As long as the government is not affected unfavorably, it should encourage frugal and simple living. Many *shizoku* in the countryside complain of the arrogant behavior of low-ranking local bureaucrats. As long as the government is not affected unfavorably, it should restrain excessive behavior of this kind. More urgent yet, the government should try to win the allegiance of influential popular rightists and journalists and awaken feelings of mutual sympathy as a way of expediting its own work. The government must gain the people's respect. At the same time, it must never forget the importance of making a clear distinction between the spheres where it can assert its right to govern and where it cannot; on this point, it must be absolutely firm.[xxii]

The critic I mentioned has also asserted that *shizoku* and commoners who are concerned for the country lack the habit of dealing with public affairs. His statement is completely unfounded. By habit, does he mean something that has to do with personal character, or with social position? He should be more exact. If he means personal character, no human being is endowed with an inborn ability to handle public affairs. A person acquires the habit after months and years of trial and error; without a suitable position, he cannot possibly acquire such skills.

To prove my point, I shall give an example close at hand. All the officials in the present government are *shizoku* concerned with national affairs. But were they all born predestined to become officials and endowed by nature with the ability to handle public duties? They most certainly were not. They acquired their skills by obtaining suitable positions and going through a succession of trials and errors. Is there any reason to expect people, who only yesterday were ordinary commoners and *shizoku*, to be free from error the moment they become government officials? Habit is not a matter of personal character but of social position. Or is the critic saying that, apart from those presently in office, there is not a single person in Japan with sufficient talent? If so, why are so many in the country eager to be government officials? They seek office because they want to take part in public affairs. Let us say the government decides to establish a ministry in addition to the present nine and hires men who have passed the required examinations. Within a month, the ministry will have all the able men it needs. If it needs a thousand, a thousand men will come; if it needs ten thousand, ten thousand will come immediately. I rather imagine the ministry will be inundated by zealous applicants. So let me be clear: the critic should not say that those excluded from government are incapable of acquiring the habit of handling public affairs, or that in all of Japan, there is no one who is up to the task.

Thus far, I have limited myself to admonishing the critic for his hasty judgment, but I shall add a few words of caution. To say people do not have the habit of dealing with public affairs is merely another way of saying they do not have the position to do this. And to say they do not have the position is no different from saying they have no power. Therefore, in the event the government decides to grant administrative power to local government, people will be able to take part in public affairs and obtain positions commensurate with their mental and physical abilities. Let us say a position is available and a competent person is duly appointed. As much as I would like to say that he goes about his tasks with the "unstoppable force of splitting bamboo and rushing water," I fear I cannot do so. A person acquires the habit of dealing with public affairs by obtaining a suitable position, and many in Japan are competent. But regrettably enough, no matter how competent, the aforementioned person has been given such a position for the first time in our history; we can hardly expect him to work effectively from the day of his appointment.

The central government has models passed down over hundreds of years, whereas commoners have none and must create a model anew. They will have to proceed by trial and error, learn from their mistakes, be misled at times by temporary success, and encounter all manner of unfamiliar incidents. We will have to wait for ten or as many as twenty years before local government is put in good order. Indeed, I rather imagine that not even in my lifetime will we see whether local government has succeeded. And this is why I previously said that my expectations are set low and for the distant future.

Now that I have finished my rebuttal to the critic's objections, I shall address the question of whether the government should retain full control of administrative power or apportion it out to the people. I shall put aside the permanent advantages and disadvantages in order to discuss the more immediate effects. The government can easily act with speed and vigor. Goals are set by the select few and once determined, are rarely changed and often admirably achieved. To cite several examples, within the last decade, the government has built roads and bridges throughout Japan to facilitate travel; constructed brick houses in cities to protect against fire; established schools, large and small, in almost every town and village. The achievements are unprecedented; it takes no special intelligence to understand that, in the hands of the people, the same work would have taken much longer. Speed and vigor is one great advantage of government.

In human society, no law in existence decrees that something very difficult is easy to accomplish. On the surface, something may look easy, but difficulties of one kind or another will always stand in the way. For example, someone wants to eat a tangerine in midsummer, or a watermelon in midwinter. While not impossible, realistically speaking, he will have difficulty finding the fruit. And what difficulty will he face? He will have to spend money. If we saw the watermelon, without knowing he has spent money, we would assume that he had no trouble getting it in midwinter, when in fact he has spent money to deal with the difficulty.

A government dealing with public affairs is not like a small household making its own bean paste to save money. Spending money recklessly is an abuse common to all nations; Japan alone is not to be reproved, since the country's wealth or poverty must be taken into consideration along with the pressing needs of the times. But just because a certain abuse is common, there is no reason to condone it along with other abuses. An abuse is truly an abuse when its harmful effects cannot be eliminated even after all possible means have been employed. Again, just because an abuse is common in this restless and ever changing world, there is no reason to feel complacent.

If we look into the money the government spends on buildings and schools and compare the costs with the product, we will find that it is no different from someone buying a tangerine in midsummer or a watermelon in midwinter. A school is like an article of commerce used for educating students. Or, put more crassly, students are articles of commerce, and entrance fee, the price. How much will it cost per *tsubo* to open a school, totaling all expenses, including those for the building, equipment, schoolyard, and surroundings? How much will it cost per student? If the building costs 300,000 yen and three hundred students attend, the cost per student will be 1,000 yen; at an interest rate of 10 percent, each student will need an additional 100 yen aside from the expenses for food, clothing, and tuition. The building is finished, but there are still so-called fixed expenses: hiring teachers; appointing government officials; making repairs; replacing books and equipment; purchasing brushes, paper, ink, firewood, charcoal, cleaning cloths. When we divide the fixed expenses by the number of students, add the interest on the principal, and calculate the average for one or three years, we find that students at government schools are by no means cheap commercial articles. Expenses for starting a school are but one example of profligate government spending. If we looked more carefully, we are certain to find many other similar examples. The government is swift and vigorous in taking action, but in many cases, the returns are not worth the outlay of money. This is one disadvantage of central government.

It is human nature to be deeply attached to one's place of birth, to think fondly of home, village, and childhood friends, to rejoice or lament the rise or fall of others. Also, needless to say, people look after their own property and are careful about its proper management. Thus, when people work for the public good, it is as if each person is suppressing his self-interest and self-love, and putting these private feelings up as security so that when they manage public money, there is little danger of confusion or trouble. Furthermore, people make allowances for old customs and practices that are distinctive to each region and difficult for outsiders to understand, and when suitable to their purpose, they make minute and subtle adjustments to prevent future difficulties.

For example, in the past, farmers in the countryside formed groups akin to public associations. In the spring, after preparing the ground for barley and rice, they would put money into a mutual savings association (*kō*) so that some of the members could go on a pilgrimage to Ise Shrine; in the summer, after planting the seedlings, they would repair the roads; in the autumn, after the harvest, they would prepare for the winter festival of the local shrine. All these activities were carried out smoothly, in orderly sequence. In fact, when villagers decided to build a bridge, road, or school, the less coerced by the government, the more they planned for the long term.

Expenses for maintaining a government school are incomparably higher than those for a private school; the same money could easily support two or three private schools. Also, when a private school teacher is hired by a government school, he becomes an official and is more difficult to control. This is not because of any defect in his personal character, but because of his new status. When commoners handle finances on their own, they follow a certain order and act consistently. This is one advantage of local government. When they have to decide on a goal, however, they tend to waver, and even after they reach an agreement, someone invariably raises objections, rejects what has already been decided, slows down work, and needlessly wastes time. Another example, albeit trivial, is the disarray in attire at funerals and confusion at meetings of mutual aid associations. In a word, the government tends to waste money and people tend to waste time.

When people in fear of authority and accustomed to following orders find that the government has been stripped of its power, they feel that the order of things has also collapsed, and bend this way and that like boneless limbs. At such a time, they will turn to someone of exceptional character in their midst, and if he succeeds in winning their support with his talents and virtue, the situation may be set aright. But such a person is invariably cautious and prudent, and if the government suddenly decides to grant administrative power to the people, no one may be willing to act and things will be as inert as before. Worse, some of the more thoughtless *shizoku* who have been given this power may well clap their hands with glee, put on airs like privileged rulers, and give free rein to their erstwhile despotic ways. Or, in the absence of a clear distinction between political and administrative power, they may set up countless miniature governments situated somewhere between the central government and lowly commoners; next they will forbid this, order that, take bribes on a wide scale, and as a result, people will complain bitterly. This, then, is another disadvantage of giving power to local government.

As we see, the practical advantages and disadvantages of local government are about the same, and it is difficult to determine the right course. Things would be more peaceful and settled if old customs were retained and power withheld from local government. But if we want the people to have a sense of Japan as a nation and nurture a thoughtful and reasoned patriotism for the ages in order to bequeath to posterity the blessings of national independence, we have no choice but to determine our course of action now. Granting political power to the people is like giving a sharp knife to a child. The child does not know the knife is dangerous, and he may even injure himself. In his ignorance, he may also wound someone. We cannot afford to stand idly by, but alas, what can we do? If the child is to learn how to use it, our only choice is to hand him the knife without further ado and wait for the day when, after much pain and frustration, he learns how to handle it on his own.

How much more so does this hold true in our country at present, when, besides planning for the distant future, we must deal immediately with the issue of *shizoku* who aspire to a place in society! The only way to satisfy them is to let them participate in local government. Again, as I mentioned in a previous passage, even if the justification for local government is nominally established, there is always the danger of despotism if the distinction between political and administrative power is not made clear. The base of administrative power differs from the base of political power, and if local government tries to use its power to rule despotically, it will have to contend with the very base from which it derives power. The relationship will be like that of a hired hand who tries to put pressure on his master, or a guest who tries to control his host. Why would a host, well established in his home, tolerate the guest's behavior? If the guest is not to the host's liking, the host has only to chase him out. In this world, the conduct of human affairs is more often based on imaginings rather than on realistic reasoning. Let us say a representative who is elected to administer local government acts like a despot. The people have the right to demote him, but since they rely more on their imagined ideas about his capacities rather than on what he actually does, they do not demote him; instead they may assign him temporary work in which he can give full play to his abilities. It is precisely in this regard that we say the human mind is free and independent. Is this the time to proceed with local government? If so, let us not worry needlessly and miss the opportunity to act.

Until the Kaei year period [1848–53] Japan was secluded from the rest of the world. The country was organized like a family, with the government acting as parent, teacher, and main financial support. All matters were left to officials, while commoners followed orders, looked on passively in times of war or peace, prosperity or decline, and never interfered with the flesh and blood life of society. To quote a Chinese proverb, they were like the subjects of an ancient Chinese kingdom "who lived in an era of peace and patted their stomachs in perfect contentment." Since the opening of foreign relations, however, Japan has been forced to compete with foreign nations in commerce and industry, learning and technical arts; the two sides are like enemies. Not only is the government pitted against foreign governments, the people have been thrust into contact with foreigners, the confrontation such that retreating even one step gives these outsiders that much more room to attack us.

As parent, teacher, and financial support, the government tries to protect the people, but the present reality makes this impossible. It is like the head of a family who takes care of his children as long as the house is empty of guests, but once he opens the gate, he finds himself too busy in the ensuing confusion to convey instructions to his children. To avoid future inconvenience, he must choose to have the children and servants learn how to handle guests and to think of ways to do this on their own. For a nation's people, this means instilling them with the habit of self-reliance so that they can themselves deal with foreigners. But how can they acquire this habit? The only way is, first, to serve in a position in the country that calls for self-reliance, and then, have them deal with foreigners. And the only practical way to obtain such a position is to work for local government and participate in public affairs. Indeed, one could say that local government serves as the training ground for handling foreign relations. This, in brief, is why I stress the urgent need to give power to local government and maintain that now is the time.

There are two ways to found a nation. One is to plant a cluster of small roots and wait for the roots to entwine into a thick trunk and grow into a big tree that supports the entire nation and enables the leaves and branches of civilization to flourish. The other is to plant the trunk of a tree in a shallow hole, and through some kind of force, have it absorb the moisture in the soil until it sends forth an abundance of leaves and branches. In appearance, the trees look exactly the same; only when they are exposed to a typhoon or torrential rain will we know which is stronger. A tree that grows from a cluster of small roots is better than a tree that was originally a single large trunk. A **table** with four legs is stable; an open umbrella on the ground is not. Scholars who give this matter their careful consideration will perhaps discover something new.

In closing this essay, I would like to add one more remark: I developed my argument with members of the *shizoku* class uppermost in my mind, but as I mentioned earlier, I do not necessarily confine my remarks to those of that status. The world has changed, the four classes are now equal, and we no longer talk about status distinctions decreed by man. Our concern is limited to a person's mental and physical functions. Thus, if we lump together the four classes to assess their distinctive functions in the nation's politics, we will be pouring sand, ashes, and dust into a jar of water and stirring everything together. The sand will sink to the bottom, a layer of ash will cover it, and the dust will float to the surface.

Mixed in this manner, more than a few *shizoku* will float to the top and many in the lower three classes will sink to the bottom, but for the most part, *shizoku* will be heavier and commoners lighter. Among the heavier *shizoku* will be those who have changed their function and those who have not. The main point of my argument is that those who have changed should be the first to be given a suitable position, and then have them influence those who remain unchanged. In other words, the function of the latter group should be changed indirectly. Some in that group may have a function peculiarly their own and cling to old habits, even when they have a chance to change. But we have no time to worry about them since they are fated to shrivel, disgruntled to the last. As to those who float to the top, if they have no function worth changing, we will have to wait until they acquire one on their own. In this respect, schools are like factories in that they create functions and increase them. I hope to go into this subject at a later date.

From beginning to end, this essay has dealt solely with the nation's politics. Scholars will undoubtedly find my argument superficial and dry; I can only hope that my descendants will live at a time when this kind of superficial argument is no longer necessary. Be that as it may, at present, the people do not know what Japan, as a nation, should do. They are like a person without a house. Without a roof over his head, he cannot possibly study or pursue a trade. Let us say you ask a young scholar why he is studying and he answers he wants to be a government official or a teacher. You say, with many already in government, there's little chance of finding an opening, so you will probably become a teacher. What will you teach and will your students be useful? Will they also become teachers and teach others? Some of your students will be from merchant and farming families, so what use will their education be? If they use their knowledge to set up regulations in trade and industry, start businesses and accumulate money, what will they do with that money? Will they leave it to their children and descendants, and what will they do with the money? Will they live in ease and comfort with their inheritance? If they are idle and think only of their physical health, they will be no different from birds and beasts. Or will they use the capital to start large industries, build schools, improve roads for transportation, and in other ways, contribute to the public good and enable the country to compete in wealth and power with foreign countries? What is Japan's place in the world? The people certainly do not know. Your students will study by day and by night, but to what end? What is their goal? By the time you finish asking these questions, the young scholar will be completely befuddled and at a loss for words. I set about writing this essay, without hesitation, because I wish to clarify Japan's task as a nation.

A scholar of broad vision will often wander beyond the perimeters of national affairs, dismiss patriotism as a species of fevered passion, and project the progress of human society into hundreds or thousands of years in the future. His arguments will be high-minded and carefully thought out; he will show other scholars a place where they can attain spiritual peace and certitude, but sad to say, how many wise and intelligent men are there in this world? The scholar's arguments will be lofty, but how many will really understand him? I, for one, know for a fact that there are extremely few. Now is the time to come to the aid of the times. The rest we leave for another day.

Commentary

Fukuzawa began "The Division of Power" with a disquisition on the conservation of energy. This was not unusual; he often invoked the authority of science to bolster his arguments. He wrote that the energy stored in plants comes from the sun, and plants, under the right geological conditions, turn into coal. Coal when burned generates heat, which boils water and propels steam engines. The form of energy changes but the energy itself does not disappear. Assuming that his readers would accept the application of the first law of thermodynamics to society, Fukuzawa contends that the energy of the samurai class, as manifested in the rebellions, cannot be extinguished; instead, it can and must be transformed.

In the essay, Fukuzawa refers to former samurai as *shizoku*, but he extends the post-Restoration term to include educated and politically minded non-samurai—journalists, lawyers, doctors, and teachers, "people who read books, practiced the military arts, and thought seriously about the world." The *shizoku* class, Fukuzawa states, is "completely different from the other three classes, almost a race apart." It is highly political. A samurai without a role in government is like a knight without a sword, or an archer without a bow. Fukuzawa had read de Tocqueville's *Democracy in America*, which describes Americans as an exceptionally political people. Japanese samurai, Fukuzawa avers, are even more so. For hundreds of years their entire lives had centered on political matters, they had ruled the country and conducted military affairs. They knew nothing of agriculture or commerce, nor had they any ability in such occupations.

Of the four hundred thousand samurai families in Japan, Fukuzawa distinguishes three categories: progressives with jobs, progressives without jobs, and conservatives. Progressives with jobs work for "civilization, progress, and reform," whereas many in the second and third categories join uprisings;

Fukuzawa then gives a long list of what he calls the proximate and remote causes of samurai revolts. The most important proximate cause was the samurai loss of their traditional role in society. Not only had samurai lost their stipends and rank, "their special privileges had been utterly swept away," with nothing to replace them.

The second cause of the rebellions was the changed nature of government. Before the Restoration, government had been shrouded in secrecy and office had depended on rank; an "iron gate" had barred from office all but the upper stratum of samurai. But now, with government offices open to all men of ability, the iron gate was replaced by a "glass door." The new transparency increased the visibility of government and intensified the resentments of those who had failed to obtain official preferment. Fukuzawa laments: "compared with the past, sentiments like envy and jealously, sycophancy and deceit, have increased many times over, with truly deplorable consequences."

Another factor, too obvious to be mentioned by Fukuzawa, was the difficulty in mounting effective rebellions. The four hundred thousand samurai families were distributed among three hundred or so domains. Of these, only twenty or so were big enough to carry out a meaningful rebellion. A few "masterless samurai" from smaller domains were drawn to larger uprisings, more during the Satsuma Rebellion, but most samurai were enclosed tightly in the web of their own domain, despite sharing class similarities.

Fukuzawa envisioned participation in local government as a mechanism that would redirect samurai energy. Local assemblies would give a new political role to the most able of unemployed samurai and assuage their discontent. The energy that had fueled revolts would thus be contained and put to constructive purposes.

What authority, what powers, would the proposed elective local assemblies possess? In his essay Fukuzawa draws on de Tocqueville's distinction between two kinds of government power—political and administrative (or local). He translates the former as *seiken*, and the latter as *chiken*.[10] Local assemblies would be entrusted with *chiken*. Fukuzawa's distinction between *seiken* and *chiken* is admittedly confusing. Political decisions are made, after all, at both the central and local levels. Why should the powers of local assemblies be called administrative (*chiken*), and not governmental (*seiken*)?

Later in the essay it becomes clear that, as Fukuzawa uses the term, *seiken* means central government affairs, both foreign and domestic, and also those local government functions that are uniform throughout Japan. *Seiken* includes both decision-making and administration. The compass of *seiken* is thus overwhelmingly large. In contrast, *chiken* refers to local authority over lesser matters that vary from prefecture to prefecture, matters that are better left to more knowledgeable local officials and of little concern to the central government. The use of local monies to build bridges, dikes, schools, and so on would come under local authority. Local bodies would both determine and administer such matters. Thus, the actual power of Fukuzawa's proposed elective bodies, of the *chiken*, while not without substance, was limited.

Despite the limited nature of his proposals, Fukuzawa counsels his readers to keep their expectations low. "We will have to wait for ten or as many as twenty years before local government is put in good order. Indeed, I rather imagine that not even in my lifetime will we see whether local government has succeeded." He writes that giving ex-samurai even local legislative authority is like giving a child a sharp knife. The knife is dangerous, but how else will the child learn to respect its sharpness? His outlook is less than optimistic, but he maintains that there is no going back to the institutions of an earlier age. For Fukuzawa, elective local assemblies were the sole means available to absorb and transform samurai energies.

Fukuzawa further states that prefectural assemblies will nurture politically minded men in every area of Japan, and that in the long run it will contribute to national strength and stability. Local assemblies will prepare them for larger roles in a future national assembly. Comparing Japan to a tree, he suggests that a tree with many rootlets will withstand the force of a typhoon, whereas a tree with a single big root might easily be toppled. Also, "a **table** with four legs is stable; an open umbrella on the ground is not." In other words, a despotic Japan, a Japan without local assemblies, would lack a solid foundation.

Does this essay indicate that Fukuzawa was almost ready for a national assembly? Not in the least. Local assemblies were a very specific remedy for a very specific problem. However, like training wheels, they would give experience to local figures and prepare them for future roles in a national assembly. But the establishment of such an assembly was not just around the corner. "Perhaps not in my lifetime," he predicts.

4

On a National Assembly (*Kokkairon*), 1879

Introduction

"On a National Assembly" was published from July 29 to August 1879 in the *Yūbin hōchi shinbun*, a prominent popular rights newspaper founded in 1872. Fujita Mokichi and Minoura Katsundo are listed as the authors of the newspaper editorials and the book that followed.[1] Both were former Keiō students who had become editors at the newspaper. Despite the listings, Fukuzawa was assuredly the author. Not only is the essay included in the three editions of his collected works, in his autobiography he proclaims his authorship:

> I said to them [Fujita and Minoura], "If you can use this piece as an editorial, do so. I am sure the readers will be interested. But, as it stands, it is too obviously my writing. So change some wording to hide my style. It will be fun to see how the public will take it."[2]

The word translated as "fun" is *omoshiroi*, which can also mean "interesting." The public no doubt found the essay *omoshiroi*, but that is not a sufficient explanation for listing Fujita and Minoura as the authors. Perhaps Fukuzawa felt sheepish at having so suddenly changed his mind: slightly less than two years earlier, in "The Division of Power," he had predicted that even local assemblies would probably not succeed in his lifetime. Now he was supporting an elective national assembly. Was this abrupt turnaround the real reason he chose not to publish it in his own name? Or, as he wrote later, was it because of the "circumstances of the times?" We are left in the dark.

The essay is presented as a dialogue between two opposing views: is it still too early for a national assembly or is Japan ready for one? Fukuzawa gives compelling arguments for both sides of the question; but while the argument against an assembly is presented with considerable force, in the end he comes out decisively in favor of an assembly. (This mode of presentation contrasts sharply with "The Division of Power," in which his argument is cut and dry: analyzing a specific ill, samurai uprisings, and proposing a specific cure, local assemblies. In the earlier essay, he felt it unnecessary to offer contrary arguments.)

There are several explanations for Fukuzawa's abrupt shift. One is the changed political situation in Japan. By the summer of 1879, Japan was far more stable than it had been two years earlier. In January 1877, after many local uprisings, the land tax had been lowered substantially and Japan's villages had become fairly quiet. In June of the same year, the Risshisha, a popular rights party, had petitioned for a national assembly. In September, after the suppression of the Satsuma Rebellion, many disaffected samurai had turned to the party movement. In July 1878, the Three New Laws were enacted, and prefectural and local assemblies were gradually established. Another popular rights party, the Aikokusha (Patriotic Party) held its first national convocation in November 1878, and its second, in July 1879. The people's rights movement burgeoned, as wealthy farmers who wanted lower taxes joined its ranks.

The top tier of the Meiji government also changed. Kido Takayoshi succumbed to disease in May 1877; Saigō Takamori died by his own hand in September 1877 at the end of the Satsuma Rebellion; Ōkubo Toshimichi, the author of the Three New Laws, was assassinated in May 1878. The deaths of the three leading figures of the Meiji Restoration led to a jockeying for power, which continued into 1881. The day after Ōkubo's death, Itō Hirobumi became interior minister. The same month, Sasaki Takayuki, a Confucian-minded advisor to the emperor, argued for direct imperial rule. Five months later, Itō abolished Sasaki's office and took over control of the emperor. Other changes also indicated the "new face" of Japanese society. In April 1877, Tokyo Imperial University was founded. In June 1878, the Tokyo Stock Exchange was established. Both within the government and without, the idea of a national assembly was vigorously discussed. It was amid this continuing swirl of opinion and smaller institutional changes that Fukuzawa set down his thoughts on a national assembly.

A more personal explanation for the leap in Fukuzawa's thinking may have been his desire to maintain his position as a leading figure in Japanese thought. *Conditions in the West*, as noted earlier, was unmatched as a source for Western history; *An Outline of Theories of Civilization* situated Japan along the path of European development and warned of the threat of European imperialism. No other Japanese thinker was capable of writing such works. "The Division of Power" was also ahead of most thinkers in Japan at the time. For good reason, Fukuzawa felt he understood history better than others. But given the momentum for a national assembly that had gained force within the government after the Satsuma Rebellion, and given the radical proposals of the new political parties, by 1879, he may have felt he was losing influence. This may have led him to advocate a national assembly, despite lingering doubts. This could also explain why he initially names the newspaper editors as the authors.

Fukuzawa's reading of more seminal Western works also prompted him to reexamine the basic tenets of his thought. During the late 1870s he had read John Stuart Mill, Herbert Spencer, Alexis de Tocqueville, Walter Bagehot, and other luminaries of the contemporary West who wrote works of far greater originality than the textbooks he had read earlier. Americans who taught at Keiō may have assigned books by these authors in their courses.

In "On People's Rights" (*Tsūzoku minkenron*, 1878), he presented a broader definition of rights than that upheld by the popular right's movement; he contended that individual independence and the ability to support oneself must be added to the definition of rights. In *National Rights* (*Tsūzoku kokkenron*), a companion essay published the same year, he stressed the importance of upholding central government authority and safeguarding national independence vis-à-vis foreign powers. Of all of his writings at the time, *Renewal of Popular Sentiments* (*Minjō isshin*), published in July 1879, just one month before "On a National Assembly," was especially important. In it he proposed a new theory of history and discussed at length British Parliament, which he admired and held up as a model for Japan.

Four years earlier, in *An Outline of Theories of Civilization*, Fukuzawa had stressed the spiritual dimension of civilization. What counted was not "iron bridges" but the advance of the "human spirit," an animating force that is intangible yet informs an entire population and defines its character, a force that develops slowly over centuries. But in *Renewal of Popular Sentiments*, he introduced a new set of causal factors, together with a revised timetable by which great historical changes could take place in decades, not centuries. He had not completely abandoned his stage theory but had repackaged it as an accelerated model. The West itself, he wrote, had only recently attained "civilization and enlightenment." To be sure, Western civilization had its roots in the Magna Carta and other distant events, but it was only after 1800 that Europe had been able to attain its present strength and refinement.

Rather than the slow evolution of the human spirit described in *Conditions in the West*, his new model stressed accelerated advance propelled by four recent inventions or innovations: the steam engine, the telegraph, printing, and the postal system. These led to revolutions in transportation and communication, which in turn transformed entire societies and gave rise to new ideas and feelings.

This new stress on technology and its consequences was Fukuzawa's second major interpretation of history, one that substantially altered his basic outlook. Without this new theory, he would not have proposed a national assembly in 1879, or if he had, he would have handled it differently.[3]

Japan had imported this modern technology. As Fukuzawa observes, "In the past twenty years, Japan has accomplished 200 years of progress." Because of these changes, the "caterpillar" of the Tokugawa past had turned into the "butterfly" of the present. The next year, in *Brief Comments on the Times* (*Jiji shōgen*), he would change the image of a butterfly to that of a "winged tiger."

Fukuzawa felt that his new theory was universally applicable. He applies the theory to China, for example, and argues that the country faced a choice: It could adopt the new technologies and undergo the same revolutions as Europe and Japan. If it did, a more progressive government would inevitably replace the existing Qing dynasty. But if it shunned the new technologies, it would inevitably become a Western colony. The choice was either/or.

Translation

It has recently come to our notice that not a few scholars and critics have turned their attention to the nation's affairs. Professing dismay with the way these affairs are handled, they say that they wish to promote the happiness and well-being of the Japanese people. Yet, when we listen to what they say, or read what they write, we find that most of their arguments are like casual conversations, phrases strung together, with no clear conclusion. They spend months and years on one particular issue, do not ever change their views, and rarely miss a chance to discuss them.[4]

Our argument for establishing a national assembly is based on views we have firmly held for several years and never changed. Indeed, we are confident that we were among the first to support the idea when it was initially proposed in Japan. The argument for a popular elective assembly was first made five years ago, early in 1874. When we expressed our support at the time, we were certain the public would oppose the idea and regard us as madmen. Much to our surprise, however, we found that people were favorably disposed to establishing a national assembly and united in voicing their approval. To be sure, a few opposed it, not because they were against a national assembly as such but because they felt it was too soon to establish one in Japan. It should be known, then, that when the proposal for an elective assembly was made five years ago, the people in Japan had already accepted the idea in their hearts.

The Japanese have thus desired a national assembly from early on, and today, anyone who opposes it is universally dismissed as a madman. When we first made the proposal, we feared we would be seen as madmen; now it is quite the other way: the opponents are the madmen. The times have changed indeed! We should add, however, that in the meantime, perhaps due to personal circumstances, the ideas of the principal advocates have gradually changed. They have not retracted their previous arguments; instead, they cling to them tenaciously. But they have been unable to realize their goals at every turn, so some of the advocates have begun to espouse wild and extreme views. Consequently, their arguments for a national assembly have been largely ignored by the public.

Meanwhile, our own arguments have also failed to attract people's attention. Nevertheless, we have seized every opportunity to put the matter to the people; in truth, the past five years have passed quickly like a single day. What is more, because we find ourselves well situated to gather opinions, and hold positions eminently conducive to predicting future trends, we have been able during these years to build a solid base for disseminating our views. Whenever we had energy to act and time to think, we have gone over our arguments with scrupulous care and weighed their merits and demerits; the words we have published number in the hundreds of thousands. We have therefore decided to lay bare our heartfelt thoughts, to our full satisfaction, and argue at length the pros and cons of establishing a national assembly. We beg our readers not to treat these essays as just another series of editorials. We have labored over them for years; they represent nothing less than the distillation of our thoughts. We feel most fortunate to be able to present them to the public, and if there is anyone who takes pity on our foolish ways and differs from us, we urge him to express his views unreservedly so that, together, we can analyze the rights and wrongs of our respective positions. Also, if anyone shares our hopes and wholeheartedly agrees with us, we urge him to join us in persuading the public.

With this purpose in mind, my colleague Minoura Katsundo and I have collected our thoughts, formed our arguments, and written the essays. To reach a wider audience, we eventually plan to publish these as a book. We ask our readers to bear in mind that we have devoted months and years to the essays, and not to dismiss them lightly. I should add that Mr. Minoura and I have written the essays jointly, each contributing an equal share, and that they do not solely represent my personal views. With this brief preface, we now present them to the public.

July 27, 1879
Fujita Mokichi

I.

Both the government and the people recognize the need to establish a national assembly and to give the people the right to participate in politics. An imperial edict issued several years ago [in April 1875] has clearly stated that Japan will adopt a constitutional system of government, and thus far, not a single commoner has been known to raise an objection. We can therefore state with utmost certitude that all the people in Japan look forward to the establishment of a national assembly and have given the matter their full attention. Despite this, however, we see no signs of progress now or in the past year. We have written these essays for public consideration to examine why we have no national assembly.

Needless to say, no one finds fault with a national assembly as such; nevertheless, there are people who argue that it is too soon and that the country should prepare gradually for such an institution. We have thought about this, too, and can see why some people think it is premature. To begin with, when we look at the general state of knowledge and virtue in this country, we find that people have yet to attain a high level of self-respect and dignity, and that they are still wanting in the spirit of autonomy and independence. Dependent on others and under their control for thousands of years, the people are devoid of so-called **political ideas** (*seiji no shisō*), ignorant of what it means to participate in government, and do not seem particularly eager to do so. To force on them something they do not want, to urge them to do something they know nothing about, is like teaching a song to a mute person, or teaching a lame person how to ride a horse. Not only will the person feel no pleasure, he will most likely feel pain. A national assembly composed of people as insensate as wood or stone will be nothing but a gathering of fools.

But not all Japanese are like wood or stone. Quite a few, such as former samurai who served their domains, are energetic and self-reliant, but while they may not be entirely deficient in political ideas, they have regrettably been brought up to think just as their ancestors did under the feudal system: they know how to rule but not how to be ruled; they advocate people's rights on behalf of others but do not know how to assert their own rights, and when they do assert their rights, they are really trying to fulfill their long-held **ambition** (*kōmyōshin*) to wrest political power from the men in government and soar to the heights of worldly success. Then, when they feel thwarted, their desire for fame turns into discontent, and resenting those in office, they fervently hope for social turmoil and in extreme cases resort to reckless and violent action. We shall call men of their ilk the **anti-government party** (*hiseifutō*).

We could cite even more egregious cases: men who were once proud to serve in government but because of some disappointment changed their allegiance overnight and now advocate so-called popular rights; others who have become professional speechmakers or newspapermen and curry favor with the masses by recklessly railing against those in or outside of government. They are not arguing to set aright the evils of the world but to give vent to their personal dissatisfaction with reversals in fortune; their arguments are nothing more than a litany of grievances. Yet, if we hope to find people with a modicum of political ideas in Japan, we have no choice but to turn to these people. Nevertheless, it would be unwise to have such men form a national assembly, for even if an assembly were established, it would only destroy society. Incapable of conducting its affairs, arrogant and extreme, they would disrupt the necessary spirit of moderation and deference, and eventually the assembly would turn into a body of rude and unruly men.

If the situation is in fact as we have depicted, it is much too soon to establish a national assembly, and we shall have to wait and proceed with caution until the people reach a sufficiently high level of knowledge and virtue. Look at the French Revolution: in their haste to form a national assembly, the radicals murdered the king. Little good came of this violent act and their bad name lingers to this day. A national assembly is not a mirage that fortuitously appears out of nowhere. Or look at the history of politics in Britain: after the signing of the Magna Carta, in 1215, during the reign of King John, the power of the government and people waxed and waned by turns, each threatening or tolerating the other. Two hundred years passed as one hundred; then, three hundred, four hundred, and finally, some six hundred and fifty years later, the British system of constitutional government finally took its present shape. Disaster will result if we did not keep this in mind, and, in hopes of emulating Britain, immediately established a national assembly in Tokyo, the capital of our great country of Japan. We may not make the same mistake as the French, but we will most certainly be criticized for "building a castle in the air."

There is also the fact that, by its very nature, a **national assembly** (*shūsho kaigi*) is slow in reaching decisions and prone to miscalculate the timing appropriate to the implementation of these decisions; we have only to look at world events past and present. Even if an assembly is opened in Tokyo, somehow obtains wondrous results, and in external form succeeds, it will still be dilatory. Decisions that hitherto took the government two or three days will take three or four months; an ordinance that required one sheet of paper will require several hundred sheets of drafts and many discussions. The end result will hardly be worth the effort. As for important undertakings such as reforming the military and tax system, laying railroads and telegraphs, building harbors and developing mines, two or three government officials would of course be more expeditious than a popular assembly. Speed and efficiency always benefits the country as a whole. A case in point is the cholera epidemic this year: had the government not acted promptly, such effective control would not have been possible. The containment of epidemics requires the strong hand of government. If the central government loses a small portion of its present power, the conduct of state affairs suffers by the same amount. Only those mature and experienced can fully appreciate this.

In forming a country's government, there must be a body of fixed and immutable laws. Governance of the country would be impossible if the government deferred to the feelings of every person, high and low, rich and poor. Efforts to mollify everyone by considering one thing and disregarding another or needlessly worrying about what others think is not only shameful but actually harmful. Rather than depending on a dilatory and inefficient assembly and missing the opportunity to act, delegation of all political power to the government is preferable. There is nothing wrong with a national assembly in itself; political expediency simply requires that the issue be set aside for a while until the time is ripe.

Up to this point we have described thoughts that occurred to us but refrained from expressing openly; we have also summed up the general drift of arguments presented from time to time in newspaper editorials and speeches. The arguments admittedly reflect only one segment of public opinion, but when we look at recent social developments in the light of past events and ponder what the future may bring, we have reason to think that the critics should not be rejected outright. Then again, this may simply be a case of myopia: unaware of the momentum of progress and civilization, these critics may have forgotten the past, as though it were an evanescent springtime dream, and peer at the future, as through a bank of clouds and mist, their eyes unable to gauge the distant view. With hopes of disabusing the critics of their delusions, we offer our own argument in the following essays.

II.

Let us go over the gist of the arguments put forth by critics who claim it is too soon to establish a national assembly. First, they argue that we should wait because the people lack the spirit of self-reliance. And when they say wait, they presumably mean we should wait until the people are sufficiently imbued with that spirit. But how can this be brought about? Schools are for imparting learning, but it would be foolish to think that classroom education alone will suffice, especially since the skills acquired at school differ distinctly from those required for politics. If we want to instill people with political ideas, the best course is to get them acquainted with these ideas.

In Britain and the United States, everyone, not just scholars, is knowledgeable about politics. A pertinent comparison would be the merchants and farmers of feudal Japan. Though they were not scholars of Chinese learning or retainers obligated to die for their masters, many understood what it meant to live in a society based on nationwide customs and the moral principle binding lord and retainer. More recently, all manner of theories have been propounded about popular assemblies, yet many uneducated commoners know about them and have no trouble understanding their underlying principles. This has been borne out by the prefectural assemblies, which opened earlier this year: the assemblies have yet to operate smoothly, but neither have they run into any serious difficulty. Thus, when critics say that a national assembly should be established only after the people have attained a sufficient level of knowledge and virtue, they are like a person who says he will postpone a trip until he is certain it will not rain for an entire year. He will never set off. Their excuse is lame and simply not worth considering.

Second, the critics argue that those with a modicum of political ideas are all disgruntled advocates of popular rights who belong to what we called the "anti-government party" and unceasingly criticize and resent officials. A national assembly composed of these arrogant extremists would be harmful and destroy the necessary spirit of moderation and deference. This may well be true. And when the critics say we should wait because some people are disgruntled, they presumably mean we should wait until these feelings disappear. If that is true, we should immediately look for a way to mollify these people and put an end to their resentment.

The critics, however, have not once offered a solution. They tell us to prepare and wait until the time is right, but when will that be? Will we have to wait forever? In our opinion, the popular rightists will become even more disgruntled, not less, if we wait for what critics say is the right time. As the critics say, these inveterate complainers are no doubt disgruntled because they were unable to attain high office or were excluded from government, and perhaps they are justifiably called the anti-government party. But whether disgruntled or anti-government, these people are all Japanese. There is no reason to kill them until no one of their persuasion is left in Japan. Nor is there any point in trying to persuade them to set aside their grudges, since past experience has shown that not one such attempt has proved effective. We should neither kill nor rebuke them. In fact, if their dissatisfaction is focused on the single issue of the right to political participation, they will never be satisfied until they are given that right. To forbid them from participating in national affairs for the simple reason that they are disgruntled, and to abandon them without presenting a timely solution, or even thinking of one, will only make them more disgruntled. If we discover a fire but stay away because of the flames and do nothing, the fire will only continue to spread.

Again, the source of dissatisfaction may not turn on the single issue of being excluded from politics; personal poverty or a desire for honor and fame may be the reason. But whatever the truth, we should not reproach them, for they openly advocate a fair and sound argument for the people's right to participate in politics. Even if some advocates are sincere and others are duplicitous, should all be rejected because we are unable to distinguish between the two? Saying so-and-so is sincere, or so-and-so is duplicitous, is pure speculation and will lead us nowhere. We would do well to wait and give their arguments a try. For once the national assembly is clearly seen as beneficial and necessary. Would anyone still say that it is impossible to tell one group from another? We have yet to think of a basis for saying this.

Discontent in this world is like the grass in spring that thrives on warmth and moisture. Leave the grass alone and it will keep growing; one day's growth will lead to another day's growth, the grass will never cease growing. Or to use another analogy: advocates of popular rights are unhappy because they are excluded from government and behave like a stepchild forbidden to enter the front gate of the house. Scold the child for crying and he will cry louder. He may even take up a weapon and threaten to kill his stepparents; no one can stop him. Even if he does not kill them right away, what is to prevent him, if he is at all clever, from committing a heinous deed in the future? Thus, for critics to say that we should wait until the disaffected calm down, and this, without offering a plan or solution, will aggravate them all the more. A day's delay only adds another day of discontent.

III.

When critics call popular rightists the anti-government party, they would seem to be rejecting them out of hand. The "anti" (*hi*) in the phrase is a translation of the English prefix that means "opposition." It is not particularly offensive and merely denotes an opposing viewpoint or position. For example, readers who disagree with our views on a national assembly would be anti-national assembly. Yet they would not dream of inflicting harm on our newspaper company or defaming our journalists, nor would we waste our time worrying. People who oppose our views do so in public and in private are often good friends. Just because they challenge our views, we see no need to be indignant and confront them as sworn enemies. If we did, we would be left without a friend in the world of scholars and critics. The prefix "anti" is by no means offensive.

The present government has succeeded in bringing the country together—the highborn and lowly, the rich and poor—and with a fixed body of laws, controls the nation as a single society. Of course, the laws do not suit each individual person: what suits A does not necessarily suit B, what suits C does not suit A. Someone is bound to be inconvenienced and complain loudly. Or even if a person does not personally suffer, he will be irritated because his views differ from those of the government and feel frustrated, like someone "trying to scratch his itchy foot through his shoe."

People who disagree with government policy are, by definition, anti-government, but this does not mean that they will try to harm the government or insult officials. Given the nature of government, a degree of dissatisfaction is unavoidable, but this, too, is no cause for worry. The primary purpose of government is to take the measure of public sentiment, mollify the many who are dissatisfied, win over intelligent and influential commoners and have them lead society. In Britain, there are two political parties: the Conservative and the Liberal. They confront each other constantly, now advancing, now retreating, now ascendant, now dormant. When one party gains power and takes over the government, the other party becomes the anti-government party, but soon enough, that party takes over and the ruling party becomes the anti-government party. The kind of person who hates the anti-government party and rejects everything about it either misunderstands the prefix "anti," or is small-minded, intolerant, dishonest, and invariably likes to win.

The same critics also seem deeply worried that popular rightists will become even more arrogant, extreme, and disruptive of the spirit of moderation and deference if they are elected to the national assembly and put in a position to lead society. But this, too, is simply not worth worrying about. We do not have to point this out, for the critics must surely know that, in the general scheme of things, something beneficial can also be harmful. They must also know that one should consider both the harmful and beneficial and find a middle ground, instead of just looking at the most extreme of harmful cases. Arrogance and extremism are at the far end of bad, moderation and deference are at the far end of good; the two are not to be compared. Two phrases in the *Analects* come to mind: one is "firmness and simplicity of character," the other, "flattery and ingratiating manner." It is obvious which phrase corresponds to which extreme, namely, that arrogance is firmness of character carried to an extreme, and flattery is moderation and deference carried to an extreme.[5] If we look at only the negative side of things and cite extreme cases, we will find fault with the conduct of virtually everyone in positions of leadership.

Barely ten years have passed since the Restoration, and extravagance and dissipation are becoming more pronounced by the day. Besotted by women and wine, men carouse in the pleasure quarters; no party is complete without the plangent strum of instruments; no customer is happy unless attended by slender-waisted beauties. Worse still are those upper-class gentlemen who have taken up gambling to enliven social gatherings. This is what passes for social intercourse today. Relations between a married couple and between siblings have also become more intimate, and while this might reflect the spirit of moderation and deference, when carried to extreme, this, too, can border on "flattery and ingratiating behavior."[6]

Consider, too, the people who only ten years earlier criticized bakufu retainers for their extravagant and effete ways, and accused them of behavior typical of long-time residents in Edo. They eyed the retainers as though they were vipers, but now, they themselves indulge in the same manner of life. Those in important positions may exercise political control over Edo, but in their fondness for luxury and ease, the city controls them. Needless to say, our remarks apply to the more conspicuous examples of this deplorable tendency and are not meant to criticize upper-class society as a whole. Thus, when critics accuse the popular rights activists of arrogance and extremism, they, too, are no doubt singling out one segment and not generalizing about the entire group. Popular rights advocates are not necessarily arrogant and extreme; it is their "firmness and simplicity of character" that makes them seem that way, their only fault, a certain rustic crudeness. Some advocates are probably cunning and deceitful, and in their eagerness to ride the wave of popular rights, try to trick the public into thinking that they support the cause, but they, too, represent only one segment and should not be taken as the majority. In general, Japanese today are not sophisticated or knowledgeable about the ways of the world and many still live by old-fashioned moral values. Given the present state of people's minds and behavior in this moral universe, what is more conducive to the advancement of civilization—firmness and simplicity of character, which can lead to arrogance and extremism, or moderation and deference, which borders on flattery and ingratiating behavior? One would be hard put to answer.

IV.

From what we have said thus far, there would seem to be no obstacle to establishing an elective national assembly. So why do critics say it is too soon, insist that we wait until some unspecified time, and procrastinate? It is because they are intellectually weak, incapable of seeing ahead, and even when they have a glimmer of insight, lack the courage to act. To be sure, we, too, lack intelligence and courage and tend to dither and waver. But by great good fortune, we were born during the Kaei and Ansei years [1840s and 1850s], a time of epochal change in Japan. As children, we heard about developments in our country from our fathers, older brothers, and teachers, some of us even witnessing events first hand and forming our own judgments. We also read books on Western history and learned about the role of the French National Assembly during the upheaval in France, as well as the development of the parliamentary system in Britain.

But East and West differ, and the present is not like the past. We cannot always draw on British and French precedents to judge affairs of the state in Japan, not least because these countries have recently made great strides in their civilization and Japan has only begun to take in its modern elements. Too many precedents in Britain and France do not apply to our present situation. Relying on historical arguments is not enough. We thus propose to look to our own past for evidence to support our view that we should establish a national assembly. We leave the final judgment to our readers.

If people today say it is too soon to establish a national assembly, they would also have to say the Restoration of 1868 took place too early. Consider for a moment that until the Restoration, the Tokugawa bakufu in Edo presided over the country in full dignity and exercised complete control over the country's three hundred odd daimyo, the prescribed relationship between lord and vassal unchanged since early Edo times (the Kan'ei period, 1624–43). But then, in 1854, the bakufu suddenly abandoned its long-standing policy of excluding foreigners and opened the country. The decision stirred up heated debate, and samurai who opposed it—so-called men of high purpose—left their domains to act on their own. Some sought shelter at domain residences in Edo, while others established ties with court nobles in Kyoto, or worked to convince daimyo (today's nobles) and important retainers of the justice of their cause. They eventually formed a loose alliance and espoused three principles: reverence for the Imperial House, expulsion of foreigners, and overthrow of the bakufu.

The bakufu, however, knew that expulsion of the foreigners was impossible: it had already signed a series of treaties with foreign powers and opened several ports for trade. Confronting the advanced state of civilization in the outside world, the bakufu also realized that Japan would have to master Western learning and technology: it forthwith founded a school for Western learning in Edo and a school for naval science in Nagasaki; invited teachers in the military and literary arts from abroad; and sent the brightest young men to study in Europe and the United States. The subsequent progress was not inconsiderable.

The bakufu was also aware that internal peace had to be maintained, and took great pains to achieve this, but it was too slow to act and failed to rally the people. In order to maintain its own governing position, the bakufu often resorted to physical force to suppress samurai activists and tried to compel the more intractable domains to control them, which further inflamed the activists and added to the crisis. The activists on their part accused the bakufu of abusing its traditional claim to unchallenged power and glory, and without weighing the rights or wrongs of bakufu policies, they single-mindedly pursued their goal to restore the honor of the Imperial House, expel barbarians, and overthrow the old regime.

Meanwhile, some of the more thoughtful and farsighted samurai had come to realize that expelling foreigners was impracticable and opening the country was to their own advantage. They set about making plans for the future but did this without telling the younger, hotheaded members of their group, who still fervently believed in the cause. This younger group was determined to take over the country and willing to upset the social order as long as this embarrassed the bakufu. They murdered, set houses on fire at random, fought in broad daylight and thieved at night, thinking nothing of committing crimes against the state or openly interfering with the affairs of commoners.

What was the reaction of the bakufu leaders, who were entrusted with maintaining public peace? They labeled all the activists *rōnin*—footloose samurai allegiant to no lord or domain—and regarded them, with some justification, as out-and-out enemies no better than vipers and scorpions. Nor were the bakufu leaders alone in their thinking. Prominent members of society, or those known for their discernment and experience, also looked askance at the movement to restore imperial rule and expel the foreigners. Or even if some believed in the cause, they argued that it was too soon to act.

But no human power can stay the momentum of forces at large in the country. The bakufu eventually fell, the reins of government were returned to the emperor, and after a battle at Fushimi and the defeat of armed resistance by domains in the northeast, the new Restoration government was established. The bakufu officials' undue reliance on bakufu power and prestige was wrongheaded; their desperate efforts to maintain internal peace were wrongheaded; their attempts to stamp out "viperous" *rōnin* were wrongheaded. Furthermore, the *rōnin* activists, who were condemned for their reckless and lawless behavior, were not rough and violent as supposed, but upstanding samurai, with a strong sense of loyalty. Put in positions of leadership, they acted with moderation such that even former supporters of the bakufu, who had previously vilified them, had to concede that the new government's policies were admirable and beyond cavil. In short, the Restoration, which had been viewed by some as premature in 1868, had in fact taken place at just the right time. Now, supposing the great work of the Restoration had not been carried out and the bakufu were still in power today, the same people would still be saying that it was too early for a change, which only illustrates the feebleness and utter unreliability of human intelligence!

The Meiji Restoration—the downfall of the old regime and establishment of a new government—was a change of the greatest magnitude, the result of action carried out with iron resolve. By contrast, we want only one thing: an elective national assembly, an institution that will neither affect the fate of government nor harm the officials in power. All we seek is the people's right to participate in politics. Even if we look at this from the viewpoint of our opponents, we would be unable to find fault with this quest. Let us make this clear: in today's world, anyone who says the Restoration was not too early twelve years ago should not dare say it is too soon to open a national assembly today!

V.

According to the Chinese chronicle *Shiji*, when Pei Gong[7] became governor of Guanzhong, he, together with village elders, revised the harsh laws laid down by the previous Qin rulers and declared that henceforth, the laws would cover only three crimes: [murder, physical harm to others, and robbery]. The villagers were overjoyed. Now, it would appear that Pei Gong revised the laws because he was magnanimous by nature. But his act was not motivated by any personal consideration. Rather, he had looked into the hearts and minds of the people in Guanzhong, and, having ascertained their hatred for the harsh laws, decided to take their feelings into account. Which is to say, what prompted Pei Gong to revise the laws was not his sense of compassion so much as the sentiments of the people in Guanzhong. And what had made the people suffer was none other than the laws imposed by the Qin. Things in this world do not happen by accident; they always have a remote cause.

One of the first acts of the Restoration government was to issue the Charter Oath [in the name of the emperor]. The first of five articles read: "Deliberative assemblies shall be established widely and all matters decided by public discussion." When we consider this document with due reverence, we do not doubt for a moment that it derives from the special grace and favor of our most virtuous emperor, and yet, when we ask where this most benevolent gesture came from, we find that it is the emperor's profound understanding of the minds of his subjects and his wise decision to rule accordingly. Clearly, the Charter Oath was at once an expression of imperial grace and favor, and the hopes and aspirations of the people.

In other words, at the time of the Restoration, the people were already acquainted with recent developments in Western civilization, hated and despised the traditional system of hereditary rule, and longed for political renewal. In truth, the Charter Oath was like rain after a long drought. (The people's eagerness to learn about Western civilization is proven by the popularity of *Conditions in the West*, the book by Fukuzawa-sensei.) The fifth [*sic*, fourth] article in the Charter Oath called for the "destruction of evil customs of the past and the need to base all matters on the just laws of nature." Here, too, the intent of the emperor is abundantly clear. Not only are we deeply moved by this most gracious gesture, we also rejoice that the people are well on their way to progress and reform. Some of the more radical elements in society tend to cite the Oath to support their arguments and rely on it at every turn. We beg to differ; we predict the future state of the people's hearts and minds will be in accord with the sentiments behind the issuance of the Oath, and rejoice that progress has been made in the name of civilization.

The Japanese are thus on their way to progress and reform; the principle of hereditary rule by men of high lineage has been all but abolished. Those who seek evidence for these developments have only to look at the Restoration in its entirety. The first and immediate requirement for carrying out the revolution in one stroke was military power. At the time only three domains—Satsuma, Chōshū, and Tosa—filled that need. The three domains quickly mobilized their soldiers, overthrew the bakufu, and founded a new government. In the normal course of events, these domains would have assumed full political power, and if the system of hereditary rule had been kept, one of three daimyo—Shimazu, Mōri, or Yamauchi—would have been designated shogun by the emperor and replaced the Tokugawa. Or conceivably, the three domains would have stood in opposition and pitched the country into armed conflict. When we look at the past seven hundred years in Japan, we would expect this to happen. The Restoration of 1868 proved the exception. The government did not fall into the hands of the lords of the three domains; instead, wonder of wonders, it was taken over by their samurai retainers! Not only that, but once the country settled down, the samurai who commanded the troops in the name of their domains abolished the domain system, stripped all daimyo of their power, excluded them from government, and no one in the country thought this strange. Had someone from Japan's feudal past witnessed these events, he would have been struck dumb and wondered whether the world had been turned upside down. If the people had not so hated the evil customs of old and so yearned for progress and reform, they would never have tolerated an upheaval of this magnitude! Let it be known, then, that within twenty years of opening the country, imperial Japan has created nothing less than a new social order.

As noted, the reins of government were not taken over by people of privileged lineage, and former daimyo were rendered completely powerless. Leaders of the Restoration gathered the ablest men in civil and military fields, established deliberative assemblies widely, decided all matters by public discussions, and looked up to the emperor to rule the country. The men accordingly took part in these public discussions and governed in conformance with the decisions. It little mattered that they had once been retainers in service to their domain lords and had no distinguished forebears to speak of, for in these deliberative assemblies and public discussions, there was no need for people of high birth and lineage.

It is quite possible that the same leaders will stay in office for years to come and accomplish great deeds, but these are no longer the times to revive the custom of hereditary office. If, by any chance, high lineage determines who should serve in an office, former daimyo are always at hand. But will they ever let their former retainers corner the market, as it were, and take possession of all the gains? Even a three-year-old knows the answer. Present leaders serve in government wholly because they are competent and authorized to act in compliance with the imperial injunction to establish assemblies and publicly deliberate all matters. Their participation in open discussions is proof enough that the spirit underlying an elective national assembly is already at work. The spirit is there, only its tangible form is lacking. All we ask is that it be given tangible form. We do not ask for an illusory mirage but for a tangible body that conjoins the will of the people and the spirit that presently informs the government.

There is a saying in the *Yi jing* [*Book of Changes*] that the first appearance of frost presages the season of ice. Japan has already trodden the frost-covered ground of public assemblies and discussions; the people have seen that abandoning hereditary rule has had no adverse effects. Like the ice that follows frost, is not a national assembly also a force of nature? The force is as unstoppable as a bullet fired from a gun, its trajectory predetermined. Who but a fool would wish it to stop midair!

VI.

The critics we spoke of claim that assemblies are dilatory by nature and prone to miss the opportune moment for action, and that a national assembly will inevitably have the same defect. Rather than criticizing the institution as such, they seem more concerned with the possible consequences. But this, too, is no cause for worry. To begin with, civilization in the modern age advances by leaps and bounds and occasionally takes people by surprise. As it happens, we recently read a book by Fukuzawa-sensei entitled *Renewal of Popular Sentiments* (*Minjō isshin*). We found it highly stimulating, so we shall quote a passage:[8]

> The four basic elements of recent civilization are steam power, telegraphs, printing, and the postal system. All four were invented during the 1800s, and once these conveniences were adopted, their influence increased a hundredfold. Work that required seventy years took but three; projects that required one hundred people took but one. Before the 1800s, people were caterpillars; now they are butterflies. We should not address butterflies as if they were caterpillars, nor judge them as caterpillars.

Sensei's words truly hit the mark.

For the past twenty years, Japan has adopted the learning of recent Western civilization, and the resulting increased energy of the people has been nothing short of amazing. Indeed, it is as though Japan has achieved in twenty years what took other countries two hundred. In this, the government did not always act alone; the people initiated much of the work in commerce, industry, learning, and technology. For example, the Education Act expedited the work of the Ministry of Education, but people had already made changes without waiting for official directives. Or consider books, newspapers, and magazines presently in circulation; eight or nine out of ten writers are graduates of private academies and not government schools. Clearly, learning had flourished among the people even before the establishment of the Ministry of Education. To give yet another example, consider public lectures, debates, and the like: until 1874, no one in Japan had ever delivered a speech in public, but in the early summer of that year, when we ourselves were at Keiō Gijuku Academy, some of the students formed a debating society called the Mita Enzetsukai, the first of its kind in Japan, the first to lead the way.

Today, public speeches and debates are a common occurrence in official and private circles and show no signs of abating. In fact, such is the persuasive power of speech in society that even government officials have been observers at these events. When we consider how these talks became popular barely five years ago, we can only marvel at the speed with which learning and scholarship have advanced.

As with the world of learning, so with the development of commerce: the government took the initiative and enacted regulations for national banks [in 1872], but within several years, nearly two hundred banks were established, with many more applying for permission. Under this and that company name, rice and money exchanges also opened business. Men drawn to these businesses are often speculators, some owners and customers no better than gamblers. But putting aside the personal character of these tradesmen, there is no question that business is a hundred times more prosperous than in the past, a sign, surely, of even more vigorous commercial activity in the future. People today are easily bored when nothing excites their interest, but give them work, and there is no need to worry that they will be slow and dilatory; a look at the actual results will confirm this. Only a person who remains unaware of people's transformation into butterflies and fancies them still caterpillars would fret about the future and hesitate.

At this point, it may be worthwhile to take a step back and put ourselves in the position of critics who say people are slow in getting things done. If this were indeed the case, we would have to admit that it is a blessing to society. As noted earlier, our country adopted the recent learning of the West and used it to good effect. In so doing, the government took the lead: within a space of ten years, the country discarded obsolete customs and practices, instituted new laws, left nothing, large or small, untouched. To accomplish this, the human capacity to look ahead to the future was, of course, absolutely essential. But it must also be said that the government was at times too bold and precipitate in replacing the old with the new. We might cite the adoption of the Western calendar and abolition of the five major festivals; the expenditure of huge sums of local money to enact the land tax reform; the destruction of Buddhist temples and consequent damage to historic and scenic sites; the renaming of towns and villages, to the confusion of the residents; and the razing of castles and roadside trees.

Of course, we are not saying that each of these measures was misguided; no doubt there were benefits, both direct and indirect. Yet, in life, something beneficial can also be harmful. Something good and true may be right for a particular time but not for a particular place. In other words, during the past ten years, the government acted admirably in innumerable ways but also made mistakes, not because of indecision but because of excessive boldness and forcefulness. The fault, in short, lay with its unchallenged power to appropriate the fruits of recent civilization for its own purposes. Thus, if the critics are correct in saying that a national assembly will be dilatory in deciding matters of state, this will prevent the government from acting with undue haste.

For example, if the recent decision to destroy temples to end the commingling of Buddhist and Shinto elements had been left to local residents, they may have held back on the grounds that certain customs ought to be preserved, and the country would have been spared the subsequent ruin and desolation. The characters for "hold back" are not necessarily objectionable; depending on the circumstances, the word differs not a hair's breadth from scrupulous attention.[9] In this turbulent and ever changing world, getting carried away must be restrained all the more, and so it is with deep appreciation of the critics' concern that we conclude this essay.

VII.

We have now devoted six editorials to present our case for establishing a national assembly. (The preceding editorials have been serialized in our newspaper for ten days or so.) We have yet to hear a word of objection from our readers, which would seem to confirm our opening statement in the first essay that people throughout Japan are favorably disposed to a national assembly and have given it their thorough consideration. But we also know that, in general, something that exists at the midpoint of a continuum can be useful on the one hand and useless on the other. After a long drought, hundreds of thousands of people desperately hope for rain, but not those who live in areas that abound in rivers, marshes, and ponds. Most people welcome the cool of autumn, but not those who suffer from consumption. If this is the case with natural phenomena, how much more so is it true of human affairs! If A gains, B incurs a loss; what is beneficial for B is hurtful to C. Hardly anything is completely flawless and benefits millions and millions of people.

At present the country's people are favorably disposed to a national assembly and the benefits will accrue to everyone. Nevertheless, when we examine the institution closely, we will find that at the same time it brings benefits, it will bring losses. The purpose of an elective assembly is to give the people the right to participate in government, that is to say, to give them a share of governmental power. But what they gain, the government loses. In short, the people will get a share of the power hitherto held by seven or eight government leaders, and what they acquire, the leaders will have to relinquish. For the people, a national assembly will be like rain after a long drought, its establishment as welcome as the cool of autumn. But the country is large, with areas abounding in rivers, marshes, and ponds, and among the many inhabitants are some afflicted with consumption. The government corresponds to the area with many rivers and ponds, and like consumptives, the present leaders will gain nothing from the change. It is as though gains and losses cannot exist together in a single entity. And this, we see as the one and only temporary obstacle to establishing a national assembly.

Human beings live in the society of men and are innately fond of power; no one disputes this. They are allowed to be fond of power and they are allowed to acquire it. And having once acquired power, would anyone want to give it up? The people's ardent desire for a national assembly is no different; it arises from an innate fondness for power. Government leaders are no less fond of power. They only differ in status and can hardly be expected to relinquish their power willingly, nor should we reproach them for this. The leaders want to hold on to power, the people want what they have yet to possess; both express the truth of human nature. Government leaders may resort to every sort of stratagem to aggrandize their own power, or worse, feel no compunction about being accused of tyrannical and arbitrary behavior and even boast in public that they are upholding the principle of autocratic government. We shall refrain from making meddlesome remarks about this, and merely say that in their mutual desire for power, the government and people are being true to themselves as members of the human race. They should be allowed to seek power and they should be allowed to covet it; this is what is meant by the competitive instinct in humans. And if competition is the driving force of civilization and enlightenment, should we not rejoice for the country because government and people compete with each other?

Critics with radical views are wont to complain loudly about government policy. Pointing to this as despotic or to that as repressive, they seem to think the government should be compassionate and magnanimous in all things. Their complaints, however, are ultimately futile. In a civilized world, a government may want to carry out a policy that is generous to everyone, but this is impracticable. If a government actually did this, both the policy and the government would come to naught. Therefore, the government must do its utmost to maintain power, and the leaders, too, have little choice but to strengthen their position. As for the people, should they look on passively like craven villagers grumbling about the festive activities in a neighboring village? It is far better to stand up and ask than to just sit and watch; the people have only to seek the way. Society today is like an immense stage for competition. The government cannot be compelled to be compassionate and large-hearted, nor can the government force the people into submission. The two sides have no choice but to go forward in their respective quest for power and let unremitting competition be the normal condition of life.

The line of reasoning in the foregoing argument seemingly leads to the conclusion that we should not establish a national assembly even if the people are favorably disposed, since establishing such a body would conflict with the principle to maintain and support the present government. Have the country's scholars given thought to this matter? And if so, have they reached a conclusion? We would be delighted to know. In the meantime, we will offer our own humble opinion in the next essay.

VIII.

People who call for a national assembly are of the opinion that government officials should not be allowed to stand for election and that the government should be composed of officials and the national assembly of commoners, with the two sides in opposition and each staying within the designated limits of political power. At one time we, too, believed that an elective assembly should be established along these lines. A case in point is the exclusion of government officials from this year's elections for prefectural assemblies. But as we gave the matter further thought, we had a sudden insight: if we wanted a Western model for electing members, we should choose the British system. In this regard, British Parliament and the US Congress offer a good comparison. In form and power they are much the same, but in the United States, government officials are not allowed to run for Congress, whereas in Britain, officials in high office are usually Members of Parliament. In government, they are administrators (*gyōseikan*), and in Parliament, they are legislators (*giseikan*). And because they fulfill both administrative and legislative functions, the government is able to win over the majority in Parliament and act as it sees fit.

We decided to write an essay on the subject, but in the midst of rewriting the draft, we came across a section in Fukuzawa-sensei's *Renewal of Popular Sentiments*, in which he praised the virtues of the British government and with great enthusiasm, explained the structure and powers of British Parliament as they relate to contemporary events. (We have already quoted a passage from the book in the sixth essay.) We found it highly instructive, and though Sensei's arguments do not bear directly on the establishment of a national assembly in Japan, we felt they were pertinent to the point we have just raised (the election of assembly members). So rather than presenting our arguments, we have obtained his permission to quote the following passages:[10]

> What I particularly admire about the British government is not the past achievements so much as its resourcefulness in adapting to a given situation without going against the present and future progress of human culture. There are two political parties in Britain—the Conservatives and the Liberals. The parties are in constant opposition and seemingly unwilling to compromise, but this does not mean that Conservatives are necessarily stubborn and inflexible, or that Liberals are necessarily rough and unruly. It simply means that, in keeping with age-old traditions, people with different views have separated themselves into two factions. Men from these factions are chosen by popular vote to discuss matters of state; the place where they convene is called Parliament. Those elected by the people serve in the House of Commons. Those not elected serve in the House of Lords, which is virtually powerless. Thus, one may say that the political power of Parliament resides exclusively in the House of Commons. Parliament, then, is the place where men from the two parties meet to discuss and debate issues.
>
> Members of Parliament disagree on almost every issue, but final decisions are made by majority vote. Cabinet ministers belong to one of the two parties, and the head of the party always serves as prime minister. In this position, he exercises full control over the government, appoints party members to important posts, and with the support of his majority in Parliament, determines and enacts policies without any interference. Members of Parliament appointed to government office retain their seats in Parliament; in government, they are officials, in Parliament, they are debating members. Because they serve concurrently in both capacities, they are naturally very powerful and carry out their work with great efficiency. With the passage of time, however, public opinion eventually turns against the ruling party, support for its policies declines,

and, as the opposition gains power and most of its bills win the majority vote, the government acknowledges the change in the public mood and holds a **vote of credit** (*seifu kaikaku no tōhyō*).[11] If the government fails to win the vote, the prime minister and his subordinates resign, hand over the reins of government to the opposition, and become ordinary Members of Parliament again.

But just because they are ousted from office, they do not have to remain silent. As head of his party, the former prime minister weighs matters of policy and speaks out as he did while in office; he merely lacks the necessary authority to enact them. The handing over of power is smooth and conducted with consummate skill.

The names of the two parties—Conservative and Liberal—might imply that they are as inimical as fire and water, and that the frequent alternation in government would immediately affect government offices throughout the country, but this is not the case. As mentioned earlier, the Conservatives are not necessarily stubborn and inflexible, nor are the Liberals rough and unruly. They are all civilized Englishmen with the same general outlook, their points of contention differing only minutely. To use a clothing simile, Conservatives and Liberals wear the same long-sleeved or short-sleeved clothes, the only difference is in the tailoring. They are not like the monarchy and Nihilists in Russia, who eye each other as archenemies, or like those in our own country, who, in years past, were either for or against opening Japan, each implacably opposed to the other's point of view. On this score scholars should not be misled.

Nevertheless, when the two parties in Britain compete for political power and the time comes for one to replace the other, the government in power is ousted and a new one is installed; by any definition, the government is overturned. Indeed, one could say the British government topples every few years. But this is never achieved by military force. And this illustrates precisely what I mean by the resourcefulness of the government in adjusting to political change.

IX.

[Continuation of quote]

As mentioned, the change in government and cabinet ministers wholly depends on the decision of Parliament. The ministers of the losing party become ordinary Members of Parliament, and inasmuch as Parliament is recognized as the public meeting place for expressing the will of the people, there is no shame in leaving the government in compliance with a parliamentary resolution. Even if some of the men are disgruntled, they have no grounds for protesting. At the same time, the new government cannot complacently bask in glory, for it knows only too well that its continuance does not depend solely on its own power but on the will of others.

One party advances, the other party retreats; only very rarely does a party stay in power for more than five years, the average being closer to three or four at most. Dissatisfaction lasts three or four years, so too, satisfaction; feelings of shame or pride are weak and fleeting, the human heart accommodates both. For the same reason, an argument, however novel or immoderate, is never rejected outright. The party out of power is free to declare, discuss, and disseminate its views, and if the people in the country are sufficiently persuaded, the party in power gracefully withdraws. The government in Britain holds a fixed position for a fixed period of time and is not immutable for the ages. A party taking office upholds its views during its tenure and is unlikely to change them. This is what is meant by a fixed position. But when the government resigns in deference to public opinion and the changing times, its earlier fixed position is no longer tenable. In brief, policy positions are not immutable.

In the countryside, there are simple waterwheels. The shaft of the wheel, like the letter T, has two arms, and at the end of each, a bucket is attached. Each bucket is filled with water from a bamboo pipe. As the shaft turns, one bucket catches water and empties, then the other bucket takes its place. Each bucket fills and empties in turn; the mechanism is extremely clever. But if the shaft is prevented from turning, all the water would fill only one bucket, and unable to bear the pressure, the supporting arm would eventually break.

The British government is just like the waterwheel. During the 1800s, the government encountered the onward march of civilization but endured its pressures without any harm to its political structure. The two parties advanced and retreated. One must say that the mechanism is wondrous.

Switzerland and the Netherlands are presently peaceful and stable, with their civilization making great progress. This is because their government is like the British system. In Russia, however, the government, the arm, has only one enormous bucket. The waterwheel tries mightily to counter the force of gushing water, but is unable to stop it at its source. The leaders in government must realize that their policies are ineffective, but what can they do? When they survey the vast expanse of the Russian Empire, they see no leeway for a liberal policy wherever they look; they have no choice but to be harsh and repressive, a policy that is surely the last resort of a temporizing government. We can only imagine their anguish and pain.

China is at the center of the Asian continent and seemingly untroubled, with its society in good order, but this is only because the people are uninformed and still ignorant of civilization. But let us suppose the government lays down railroads and telegraphs, installs printing machines, and establishes a national postal system. It takes no special intelligence or knowledge to predict that the people will not remain silent and that society will be thrown into great turmoil. Whether the officials in the Qing government are aware of this and so refuse to adopt [Western] civilization, or whether they happen to dislike it out of their own ignorance, we do not know. All we can say is they cannot hope to take in nineteenth-century civilization and maintain the present mode of government.

In Japan, the Tokugawa bakufu fell because of such an attempt. Is there any reason to think that the Qing government would be able to withstand the consequences? If the government does not adopt civilization, the country is certain to be invaded by foreign powers and perish. If, on the other hand, the government decides to adopt it, the people will assert their rights and overturn what they perceive as an outdated government. One or the other is unavoidable. Future generations, I predict, will witness what is fated to take place.

In Britain, the power to change the government and appoint or depose cabinet ministers wholly resides in the people. It is as though the country has and does not have a monarch. Yet, if you ask whether the monarch is disdained and ignored, the response will be "No." Reverence for the royal family is a custom peculiar to the British; not even the most radical member of the Liberal Party would openly challenge the venerable authority of the royal house. Not only would the Liberal Party member refrain from doing so publicly, he probably respects the royal family in his innermost thoughts. One might even say that the British are old-fashioned in character and highly progressive in action, or that, as a people, they are broad-minded and singularly tolerant. They are not to be compared with the French and other peoples, who immediately attack the king in the name of freedom and reform, or say that restoring the monarchy will obstruct the people's freedom.

Habit and custom basically determine whether one is lenient or strict in dealing with others. Look at the lower stratum of society: the children are obstreperous and do not take easily to obeying their elders. In associating with one another, too, they use rough language, and in extreme cases, use physical force to intimidate others; even the parents are not above striking the children. Compare this with families of the upper class: the children are sensitive to the changing moods of their parents and happy or sad as the case may be. What accounts for this difference? None other than family custom. The parents and children of the upper class are tolerant and forbearing; affectionate with one another, they would not dream of harming someone in the family. Relations between the British royal family and the people are like those in upper-class families; they would never inflict harm on each other, nor would it occur to them to do so. A monarch who does no harm to his subjects receives greater reverence; subjects who do no harm to the monarch are treated with greater warmth. The maintenance of social order in this manner is, beyond all doubt, mankind's most admirable achievement.

Civilization is like a vast ocean. The ocean takes in rivers large and small, clean and unclean, and yet remains unchanged. Civilization embraces the ruler, the aristocracy, the rich and poor, the peaceable and headstrong. It encompasses all things, pure and impure, hard and pliant, and yet never disturbs the order of things. Civilization alone takes us closer to the highest realm of spiritual enlightenment. Because of this, the timid and fainthearted are undeserving of our attention. When opinion shifts to reverence for the emperor, they look at proponents of popular rights as though they were vipers and despise the very term. When opinion shifts to the cause of political freedom, they regard the monarchy and aristocracy as a heavy burden they must bear. When one group calls for abolishing rule by lineage, another group, to everyone's bewilderment, calls for suppressing popular rights. The spectacle of these people running from one extreme to the other, without the slightest tolerance or forbearance, suggests a hypochondriac who fears dirt and washes everything in sight. His behavior is ridiculous, his state of mind pitiful. Beware of people of this ilk for they are the first to disrupt the social order.

X.

The passages we quoted are from chapter 5 in *Renewal of Popular Sentiments*. Our readers should be aware that the book was most helpful in formulating our thoughts. The book also points out that, although political power in Britain resides entirely in Parliament, the ruling party is firmly in place because many of its members serve concurrently in the government. In order to stay in power, however, leaders must work tirelessly to keep the party united; to this end, they publish the government's views in newspapers, hold meetings, give public speeches, and in some extreme cases, travel far and wide and form secret plots to win popular support. Their sole objective is to crush the opposition and defend the government's position. Outwardly, their behavior would seem to be base and dishonorable, but, as we stated, society today is like an immense stage for competition, and if civilization and enlightenment are the result of competition, there is no need to censure these political leaders. Unlike a mean-spirited and unscrupulous person, who tries to bolster his own position by furtively relying on one or two people to get rid of his rivals, political parties try to win over all the people and control their future course of action. The competition for the reins of government takes place everywhere, on every street and corner; the rivalry is between vigorous men in their prime and amounts to nothing less than a contest between gentlemen. The winning party controls the government and the country; the defeated party yields and waits for another day.

During the struggle all manner of schemes and stratagems are deployed. It is a battle of wits and ability, a fight to seize the moment, a competition to persuade the majority of the people and win over public opinion, a rivalry that takes place in full view of the world. Win or lose, each side survives. And all this is played out in the open! In truth, a spirit as refreshing as cool water animates such activities.

For the people of Japan, a national assembly will be as welcome as rain after a long drought. Men in government, however, will find little benefit. That one side should benefit to the exclusion of the other may seem worrisome, but let us say we follow the British model, and instead of barring government officials, we let them stand for election and have the people decide. (We have our own opinions on the subject of voting.) What would the outcome be? Would government officials be elected? In our view, the government is a place where men of talent naturally congregate, as fish to water and birds to trees. To be sure, there are competent men outside of government, but we are convinced that the greater part of intelligent and upright men in Japan work for the government. We hardly need to point this out since the officials must themselves be well aware of it. Thus, when we call for a national assembly, we are not saying that leaders in government are stupid and should be replaced by men of intelligence. The argument of our essays rests on the single issue of sharing political power. We are saying that the power held by two or three people in government should by shared by twenty or thirty, that the concerns of five or six people should be evenly apportioned among five or six hundred. For this reason we believe that government officials will have a fair chance of winning when elections are held.

If, as we think, present leaders in government are elected to the national assembly, they will play an important role in both the government and the assembly. Isn't this what is meant by killing two birds with one stone? Rather than diminishing the power of government leaders, a national assembly will enhance that power. In other words, a national assembly will work to the advantage of government leaders, the conduct of state affairs, the common people, and the interests of the entire country. The establishment of such an institution will pose no hindrance whatsoever.

Needless to say, a national assembly is a forum for political debate, a battleground for opposing theories and arguments. Party members will doubtless disagree among themselves, split into two or even three factions as they oppose the party in power. But this is the very purpose of an assembly and certainly no reason for apprehension. The ruling party will spare no effort to defend its power, arguing strenuously to check the opposition and conferring secretly to draw up plans. It will scheme and manipulate, make use of books, newspapers, public meetings and speeches. (Government officials will be obliged to give public speeches.) Physically and mentally, the ruling party will do everything possible to defend its political principles. But in course of time, the party's professed principles will no longer prevail, and submitting to the public will, it will forthrightly give up its seats, think of ways to prevail once again, and wait for another day.

What is politics but a competition between men at the peak of their power? Present leaders in government were never gentle or peaceable. They weathered the treacherous storms of the Restoration, encountered untold mishaps and disturbances, and suffered a multitude of reversals, yet not once did they give in. People know full well that our leaders are men of extraordinary vigor and determination. Why would they be content in a period of calm to fret and dither like a child or old woman? Why would they fight for the mere satisfaction of winning the battle? Readers, we urge you to keep your eyes open in order to see what the future brings.

Commentary

This essay opens with a careful presentation of the arguments against a national assembly. While the arguments are not new, Fukuzawa's presentation is compelling. The Japanese people have a low level of "knowledge and virtue," they lack independence, political ideas, and moral autonomy: "A national assembly composed of people as insensate as wood or stone will be nothing but a gathering of fools." Former samurai know how to rule but not how to be ruled. Some political party leaders are ambitious or even hope for social turmoil; given free rein, they may well use a national assembly to wreak havoc on Japanese society. Some who had left the government want to regain their former positions, or even to replace the present leaders. They are malcontents and a national assembly made up of their likes would be disastrous. Fukuzawa sternly cautions his readers: "Look at the French Revolution: in their haste to form a national assembly, the radicals murdered the king."

The previous year, in his 1878 essay "On People's Rights," Fukuzawa had written:

> Confronted by a swordsman wielding a three-foot blade, a man, however good-natured or composed, would not think of asking the swordsman his intentions but would immediately get out of the way. In our present day society, there are those who advocate people's rights ... I am not familiar with the details

of their proposals, but in general they seem to want a large assembly hall in the capital, where men of public spirit can come together to discuss affairs of state. But today, to suddenly open an assembly of such men and have them discuss national matters would be no different from establishing governments at two places in the capital. Such an assembly would divide the authority of the present government and weaken its power. The advocates of people's rights seek to confront the government, as it were, with a sword poised to strike. The government has no choice but to get out of the way.[12]

In the present essay, Fukuzawa further asserts that an assembly is "not a mirage that fortuitously appears out of nowhere." Beginning with the Magna Carta, it took the English people six hundred and fifty years to establish their present-day parliamentary system. He asks, if such an assembly were immediately established in Tokyo, even if it did not lead to the murder of the sovereign, would it not be a "castle in the air?"

These and other negative arguments carry considerable force. But despite his apprehensions, Fukuzawa goes on to present an even greater array of arguments in support of a national assembly. Among these, perhaps two historical arguments provide the key to his thinking. The first and most important, already discussed, was the transformative power of new technologies.

The second argument is that history, which is moved by the totality of existing forces (*tenka no taisei*), has a direction that is understood by human reason only after it unfolds. Prior to the Meiji Restoration "the Tokugawa bakufu in Edo presided over the country in full dignity and exercised complete control over the country's three hundred odd daimyo." It was too early for a change in rule, yet young hotheads, enraged by the bakufu's weakness toward foreign powers, used the figure of the emperor to attack it, committed criminal acts, and eventually succeeded in its overthrow. With such men in charge, the future looked dire and many thought that the Restoration had come too soon. But sober men of good judgment existed among the hotheads. They adapted to the existing reality, upheld the treaties, and formed a new government along Western lines. The Restoration, in fact, had not come too soon. But if the "great work of the Restoration had not been carried out and the bakufu were still in power today, people would still be saying that it was too early for a change." Fukuzawa is suggesting that in 1879 Japan's situation is not unlike that in 1868: it faces a formidable challenge. But if the challenge is met and a national assembly is formed, good men will come forth and all will go well.

Most of Fukuzawa's arguments in favor of a national assembly are clear and require no further comment. But his political stance is ambiguous. He hedges and tries to play this down, but he does not quite succeed. He has nothing but praise for the accomplishments of the Meiji leaders. He suggests that even after a national assembly is created, they will continue to rule and may possibly gain greater power. Furthermore, since they are men of proven ability, they will be elected to the national assembly and thus gain a new legislative authority on top of the executive authority they already wield. To ensure such a development, he recommends the British practice, which permits government officials to be elected to Parliament, and not the American practice, which bars officials from Congress.

Fukuzawa also points out that establishing a national assembly "will be [welcomed] like rain after a long drought," but it will not be a fundamental change like the Meiji Restoration, which created a wholly new system of government; it will merely add one more institution to those already in place. His argument suggests that other parts of the government would remain under the control of leaders already in the government.

Quoting arguments that he himself had made earlier in *Renewal of Popular Sentiments*, Fukuzawa praises the British parliamentary system and recommends it as a model for Japan. As he saw it, the resilience of the British institution was a product of the regular alternation in power of the two major parties. In an election, one party, either the Liberal or the Conservative, is voted into power, and the other party becomes the anti-government party. In time, popular discontent gradually collects around the party out of power, until it has sufficient support to win an election and return to power. Each party takes its turn; the shift in power is accomplished peacefully. This regular alternation, he maintains, is the mechanism that ensures domestic harmony and peace, which in turn makes Britain strong in the world.

Needless to say, when Fukuzawa wrote the present essay, no such mechanism existed in Japan. What Fukuzawa does not acknowledge, or mentions only in passing, is that if the British system were adopted by Japan, the government leaders would not win an election. Anti-government parties were in the ascendant; the votes of the enfranchised portion of the population would almost certainly go to those parties. Thus, to the extent that a national assembly possessed real powers, the likely outcome of an election would be the diminution of the power of the Meiji leaders.

So after praising the Meiji leaders effusively, Fukuzawa adds somewhat sanctimoniously that if, by chance, they are not returned to office, "their vigor and determination" would not desert them during a period out of office; nor would they "fret and dither like a child or old woman." Of course, the Meiji leaders had not the slightest intention of being put out of office. We can only imagine what the oligarch Itō Hirobumi thought when he read Fukuzawa's essay.

5

The Trend of the Times
(*Jiji taiseiron*), 1882

Introduction

"The Trend of the Times" provides no new historical model but is a vital link in the progression of Fukuzawa's thought. It was published in April 1882.[1] The essay is relatively short and differs from earlier works in that it is based not on European history but on events within Japan, particularly those following "the political crisis of 1881" that reshaped the top level of Meiji government. The crisis, while complicated in its ramifications, developed out of a power struggle between Ōkuma Shigenobu and Itō Hirobumi. Ōkuma, originally a Saga samurai, had become a powerful government leader. Itō, his rival, was originally a very low-ranking samurai from Chōshū, who had also risen to power. As a result of the struggle, Ōkuma was ousted, and Itō, who would go on to become the "father of the Meiji Constitution," gained new authority. Many officials sympathetic to Ōkuma also resigned and subsequently joined the party movement.

One byproduct of the shake-up was the government's promise to establish a national assembly within ten years. This was announced on October 11, the day of Ōkuma's ouster. The imperial edict containing the promise was traditional in form. It spoke of "ancestors in heaven who watch our acts," and warned of imperial displeasure against those who "advocate sudden and violent change." But despite traditional trappings, the heart of the edict was the promise of a national assembly, the long-held goal of the party movement.

Meanwhile, the settling down that had started in 1877 with the termination of the Satsuma Rebellion continued. Large reforms of the earlier 1868–76 period were followed by smaller reforms of the police system, laws, taxes, ministries, and other government offices. Officials, political parties, and the Kōjunsha, a political association of which Fukuzawa was a prominent member, wrote draft constitutions. Comparable changes also occurred in the economy and the scholarly world.

Fukuzawa wrote "The Trend of the Times" six months after the crisis of 1881. Since the promise of a national assembly had been made, he does not dwell on it. Instead, he focuses on a growing phenomenon within Japanese politics: the conflict between the government and political parties. He asks, why were the political parties still belligerent toward the government? The government had promised them what they wanted. Why were they not satisfied? Why did they not quietly prepare for their role in the forthcoming assembly?

The essay can be divided into three parts. The first treats the concept of "human rights" in Japan up until 1878. The second, the main argument of the essay, analyzes three government reforms, which turned out very differently from what the government expected. The third offers a solution to the political strife, to the "trend of the times" that was weakening Japan.

Translation

The six essays in this book, which were drafted by Fukuzawa-sensei and written down by Nakamigawa-sensei, first appeared as editorials in our newspaper *Jiji shinpō*. Owing to a lack of space, we were unable to publish all six editorials in one issue or in daily installments, and so we spread them out over ten or so days. Since then, perhaps because our readers found the editorials useful, we have received many requests for copies of the newspapers. For the readers' convenience, we have decided to publish the six editorials as a book.[2]

April 1882
Editorial Staff

I.

The full attainment of property, life, and honor are human rights. Without good reason, such rights are not to be violated even by one iota. We call such rights human rights, and by this we mean the rights due every human being. Nevertheless, in a world where the good and bad in human nature and behavior commingle, individuals lack the power to protect their human rights. Governments were presumably formed to protect the rights of a country's people. The workings of government are called politics (*seiji*). Politics is the means by which people are able to attain their human rights. In a monarchical country, the monarch makes all the decisions in governing. In a country under a constitutional government, the citizens (*kokumin*) are allowed to take part in the political process; this is called the right to participate in politics, that is to say, political rights (*sansei no kenri*). Citizens under a constitutional government are divided into two, as it were: from the viewpoint of human rights, they receive protection of their rights; from the viewpoint of political rights, they exercise their rights to assure their own protection. Therein lies the distinction between human and political rights.

By tradition, Japan was ruled by a monarchical government. During the feudal period of hereditary rule, commoners had no political rights, and in many cases, their human rights were violated. Throughout the country, people very rarely possessed equal rights. Only after Japan opened relations with foreign countries, and people read Western books and learned about Western civilization did they discover that commoners were also entitled to certain rights. Japanese wrote about these matters for the first time and coined the term "popular rights." This took place about seventeen or eighteen years ago, during the mid-1860s.

The people's minds were further renewed at the time of the Meiji Restoration. As discussions about popular rights filled the air, the government duly took notice and zealously set about eliminating outmoded customs and usages: it put an end to the system of hereditary rule. In one bold move, it abolished daimyo domains and established a centralized prefectural system; it made taxation more equitable, revised laws to stress fairness, and instituted a host of other measures each of which, compared with the feudal past, improved the human rights of citizens.

On the single issue of political rights, however, the government showed no signs of making any concessions, and the people, too, seemed disinclined to demand any; both sides seemed to have forgotten about the issue. Commoners had suffered hundreds of years of hereditary rule, and perhaps were too preoccupied with gaining human rights to think about political rights.

Then, in 1874, the former senior councilors Gotō Shinpei, Itagaki Taisuke, Soejima Taneomi, and Yuri Kimimasa submitted a memorial to the government for an elective popular assembly. They stated that they were gravely concerned about the ineffectiveness of government ordinances and had come to the conclusion that the only way to rectify the situation was to establish an elective assembly that would curtail the powers of government officials; they apparently thought that such an institution would serve as a corrective to the government.

Needless to say, the memorial contained words to the effect that the obligation to pay taxes entitled the people to have a voice in affairs of the state, though I rather doubt the petitioners had the people's political rights uppermost in their minds. As former government officials whose chief concern was the conduct of government, they were hardly likely, even in their hearts, to be putting pressure on the government on behalf of the people. As it was, very few commoners at the time were interested in discussing the right to participate in politics.

By 1875 or 1876, however, the work of abolishing old customs had been completed, and both the government and people were showing signs of boredom. (One sign of the change in the public mood was the reappearance in the marketplace of art, antiques, utensils for the tea ceremony, and other objects considered obsolete since the Restoration.) The people had also become more informed. But then, in 1877, just as they were beginning to question several aspects of government, the Satsuma Rebellion broke out, and since all were deeply disturbed, arguments about popular rights were set aside. The rebellion was soon suppressed, and in 1878, the government issued the Regulations for Prefectural Assemblies. Early the next year, elective assemblies were simultaneously opened throughout the country. This marked a turning point in popular sentiment.

The establishment of prefectural assemblies was by no means spurred by popular demand. Nor was the government under any illusion that this was the case. Apparently, the government intended to use the local assemblies for its own political purposes. The results were not as expected, however. Once the assemblies opened, the people listened and observed, and for the first time realized what it meant to have political rights. What they expected had turned out to be the unexpected; the outcome was indeed fortuitous. Farmers and merchants, who hitherto had not dared to look even lowly officials in the eye, now sit in lofty assembly halls, discuss local taxes, and question the budget. When their decisions become prefectural laws, even prefectural governors cannot change them. Previously, the daimyo levied taxes on the cultivators, the amount decreed as if from heaven. Who would have imagined that today, the farmers themselves would legislate their own taxes! (For the elderly acquainted with the past, the new local taxes were no different from the old yearly taxes in kind.) Truly, high and low had become topsy-turvy. As a popular expression put it, "the farmers act in place of the lord." Is it any wonder that the people's feelings have changed?

Prefectural assemblies are just like schools for teaching the idea of political rights. Also, since all the assemblies had opened for business at the same time, with the same set of laws, they could communicate with one another by newspaper or mail, and widely distribute their reports. Thirty-four million pairs of eyes and ears see and hear these simultaneously. Given the human proclivity to move forward, it is only natural that the people now wish to take one more step and demand a national assembly. If the prefectural assembly served as the side gate for everyday use, a national assembly would serve as the main gate. With the side gate already open, one could hardly blame them for wanting the main gate to open as well.

In hindsight, it might have been better to keep the side gate closed, go forward full speed to build the main gate, and have the two open at the same time, after all the groundwork was completed. But human intelligence has its limitations; one cannot foresee everything. The government most certainly did not, nor did I, a mere spectator, and there is no point in going over what is over and done with. Still, the first proximate cause of the present clamorous debate on participatory government and popular unrest is none other than the opening of prefectural assemblies. I shall list this as the first cause and proceed to the next.

II.

There is a saying that people can only act properly after being adequately fed and clothed. In other words, if people hope to think about matters beyond their physical needs, they must first be physically comfortable. And since discussing politics goes beyond physical needs, we cannot expect people to voice their concerns while they are too busy securing their daily necessities. To be sure, some commoners are rich, but two or three rich men can hardly argue about politics when they are beset on all sides by poverty and loud complaints about hunger; this would be as dispiriting as viewing flowers in the wind and rain. When people are suffering from cold and hunger, it is futile to expect them to be interested in political ideas.

Until the last years of bakufu rule and the first years of the Meiji era, farmers were always farmers, ill fed and ill clothed, their circumstances unchanged for three hundred years. Their burden was slightly lightened when the prefectural system was established in 1871, and daimyo, who had become more attuned to the times, reduced local taxes before relinquishing their domains. The farmers' pride and self-respect was further bolstered with the sweeping land tax reform [in 1875]. This, together with the devaluation of paper currency in the last two or three years, the steep increase in rice prices, and the consequent rise in the value of land, enabled farmers to set aside much of their yearly harvest and accumulate a sizable amount of wealth. Also, having seen the value of their land go steadily up, they knew that even if they did not sell it right away, they could always get hundreds and thousands of yen and be quite well off. Rich in name and in fact, farmers no longer had to suffer from cold and hunger.

As it happened, political speechmakers were then roaming the countryside calling for the destruction of age-old customs. Newspapers, too, were publishing articles intended to incite political fervor and change dull and apathetic farmers into fervid and hotheaded politicians. Yet, no matter how eloquent the speechmakers or ingenious the articles, the farmers would have paid no attention if they were still shivering from cold and hunger. But now, they were willing to listen and discuss politics, the remote cause of this change in attitude was none other than the abolition of feudal domains, establishment of the centralized prefectural system, land tax reform, devaluation of paper currency, and rise in rice prices. I count this as the second cause of the present political unrest.

In 1873, the Ministry of Education issued the Regulations for Universal Education. Standards were raised in primary and secondary schools throughout Japan and the number of entering students increased by the year. As of today, there are no fewer than thirty thousand primary schools and more than two million students. Students who were seven or eight years old when the regulations were issued are now seventeen or eighteen; those who were ten are almost adults. But if I were asked what the general run of these young people think about politics, I would be at a complete loss, my mind "as blank as a sheet of white paper, my tongue as mute as an untouched instrument."

To begin with, most of the primary schools are public and lack the guidance of an individual headmaster. One person might be in charge, but he is merely discharging his official duties as chief administrator; he bears no comparison with the headmaster of a private school, who has founded the school and assumes complete responsibility for matters both tangible and intangible. More different still is a teacher at a public primary school: his period of employment is indeterminate, and since he can be dismissed at any time, he has no reason to regard the school as his home. The students, too, attend classes because it is the proper thing to do; they naturally have little interest in regarding the administrator or teachers as suitable models of behavior. Without such models, they are deprived of the benefits of moral guidance and merely study the subjects taught in the classroom.

But school education should not be limited to the instruction of tangible subjects; of far greater importance is the inculcation of a certain intangible spirit. When we look at traditional Confucian education in the past, we find that many of Ogyū Sorai's disciples take after Sorai, and Itō Jinsai's disciples take after Jinsai. This was true not only of their direct disciples but also of succeeding generations, who made distinctions among themselves according to the founder of their particular school. What mattered was a certain intangible spirit, the effect of which was greater than the tangible instruction given in the classroom. The times have changed, however, and with it, the relationship between teacher and student. Nevertheless, it would certainly not be amiss to keep the old tradition alive.

The thirty thousand primary schools in the country are thus devoid of moral guidance. Students learn only reading, writing, and arithmetic, and are told next to nothing about the moral principles they should uphold. Nor, for that matter, do they believe in Buddhism like the elderly, or honor the tenets of Confucianism like previous generations of students. The government for its part encourages moral education and tries to instill the proper virtues in students. The textbooks they issue are admirable, but no one is qualified to teach them. A sufficient number of teachers may be on the staff, but rarely is there someone mature and experienced. This is to say nothing of their former students, who finished school during the last decade and wander aimlessly around the country. Those of peasant background have forgotten how to till the soil; those of merchant background are too proud to mind the shop. These youths, whose very literacy causes them grief, can be found throughout Japan. If a lively and forceful political speaker were to tell them to go west, they would promptly go west; if they were told to go east, they would go east. Persuading them is as easy as coloring a blank piece of paper red or black. They are silent now, but this is not because they are unable to speak, but because they have never had the chance to express themselves, or met someone who will teach them how to do this. Given the chance, there is no telling what they will say. The youths, in short, are like untouched instruments.

One hears that many of the political activists in the countryside today are primary school teachers. Of course, they will maintain a calm demeanor at work, but one cannot judge the inner person from his outward appearance. One also hears that the majority of youths who have been politically active since last summer and autumn are graduates of primary school. This may well be true, and in the coming years, the number will undoubtedly increase, rather than decrease. No matter what kind of law is established, it is already too late. Graduates, I predict, will year by year become more contentious. This, then, is the third cause.

III.

As I mentioned in the preceding sections, the proximate and remote causes of the recent clamor for popular rights and the criticism that has been leveled against the government are: one, the establishment of prefectural assemblies; two, the creation of the prefectural system and reform in the land tax; three, the increase in youths who have completed a primary school education. The three developments brought about completely unexpected consequences; no one, not a single person in the country, anticipated what would happen. Consider the prefectural assemblies: they were originally intended to put popular discussions to some use, but they led to a plethora of public disputes. Consider the centralized prefectural system and land tax reform: they were intended to simplify government ordinances and ease people's lives, but they became fodder for endless public criticism. Consider universal school education: it was intended to broaden people's knowledge and secure the blessings of civilization, but the schools produced a multitude of petty political critics.

Although this is a matter of opinion, the proliferation of popular discussions, ceaseless arguing, and increase in political critics do not signal a regression in national power but rather, when seen over the long term of a hundred years, are matters for rejoicing. Intellectuals, however, are troubled by the present situation. But they should not condemn plans that were made in the past just because they are troubled at present.

Putting aside which view is correct, there are certain tendencies that emerge unforeseen in the world; these I call the spirit of the times (*kiun*). When a certain spirit has already set in, one should not be angry and try to reverse it. Floods occur because riverbanks are destroyed by continuous rain. Rushing water cannot be held back, and nature must be left to run its course. Floods are extremely difficult to control; so, too, are people difficult to govern. How, then, has the spirit of the times influenced present society? And what does this mean for the future?

I shall begin my discussion by referring to the Imperial Edict of October 1881, which promised the establishment of a national assembly. The edict satisfied all the people; even those who long desired such an institution have no cause to argue or protest. The people have only to wait with due reverence until 1890; one can reasonably expect public arguments to quieten down and government regulations to be more lenient.

The reality, however, is altogether different. For some inexplicable reason, the people complain about the lack of freedom, the government constantly worries that its laws are being ignored, and the number of unscrupulous speakers and newspapermen grows by the year. I do not know whether this is the fault of the government or the people; all I can say is that when I look across the entire nation, I find that, compared with the past, the people are neither more orderly nor more peaceful. If, by any chance, the opening of a national assembly in 1890 is cancelled or delayed, they will have ample reason to be disturbed. Nevertheless, when one considers how they were suddenly promised an assembly within ten years, and this, after being denied earlier on and resigned to wait another several hundred years, I find it exceedingly strange that they are disgruntled. Could there be a reason unrelated to the opening of the assembly? If so, one would have to ascribe it to the spirit of the times. And speaking of the spirit of the times, I am particularly dismayed to think that the growing rift between the government and people may lead to the cancellation of the mutually anticipated assembly, or if the assembly does actually open, may give rise to yet another round of grievances.

The present government is unwilling to give detailed explanations of their various policies. If the government refuses to talk, the people have no way of knowing its guiding principles. They would like to speak out, but afraid of breaking the law, they resort to circumlocution and only hint at their resentment. Newspapers and public speakers are no less devious and speak with a "honeyed tongue and hidden sword." As a result, the government knows nothing about the people's true wishes or the principles they hold. Ignorant of what the other thinks, the two sides cannot help but be resentful and suspicious.

Mutually resentful, mutually suspicious, it is as though they view each other through eyeglasses of different colors. The government's glasses are tinted green so all the people look green. The people's glasses are tinted yellow so all the officials look yellow. Since it is human nature to hate anyone who is different, admonishing the two sides is useless. But if they took off their glasses and looked at each other with their naked eyes, they would be able to see the good points as well as the bad in each other. Once they discover this, they would be more realistic, perhaps more tolerant, and in the course of friendly conversation, even be able to reach an accord despite disagreement on the particulars. This has not happened, however. Without querying the other's position, the government and the people hate and despise each other; like religionists, who disagree and form sects, they have split into what I shall call the "government sect" (*seifushū*) and the "people's sect" (*jinminshū*). The government sect, furthermore, is not only silent as to its principles and loath to make any concessions, but in extreme cases, ousts officials who disagree with its policies. Generous and large-hearted it is not.

I have just stated flatly that the government ousts anyone who disagrees with its general policies. I shall qualify my statement: though the facts are not easy to ascertain, the government will occasionally dismiss an official who has merely come under suspicion. There is an old saying that one should be lenient when commission of a crime is in doubt. A government should be even more lenient in punishing a criminal if there is room for doubt, not to speak of a person merely suspected for his beliefs! To go to the extreme of ousting an official, without sufficient cause, runs counter to the fundamental principles of governance. In dismissing officials who happen to hold different principles, the government presumably intends to increase the number of officials who share the same principles. But behavior of this kind can only lead to fear and suspicion, and, more often than not, produces the opposite effect.

Ever since the Restoration, officials ousted from government have tended to turn into the government's political enemies overnight. Apart from whether the person sees the government as an enemy, or is seen by the government as such, the plain facts make clear that the government has not been magnanimous and forgiving. When people notice this, they do not know how to act and despair of being heeded by the government; instead of being docile and obliging, they give vent to their pent-up dissatisfaction with endless arguments. As they distance themselves from the government and refuse to have anything to do with it, the rift becomes ever wider. Indeed, to the great misfortune of the nation, the situation has reached the point that anyone who draws near the government is accused of being less than a full man.

IV.

Now, it is quite possible that a commoner will comply with the government's wishes and will secretly try to reconcile the two sides. But since he will not be acting openly, he is bound to anger the people. Excluded from society, he will not only suffer personally, but he will find that his efforts to reconcile the opposing sides have separated them even further. As for newspapers and magazines, not many will read the articles, unless they are written in a tendentious and provocative tone. At public lectures, too, the audience will not clap with approval, unless the speaker's heated arguments come close to breaking the law. Competition being a constant in human nature, if one speaker reaches a fever pitch of one hundred, another will aim for one hundred and ten, and so on without limit. One is reminded of the last years of the bakufu, when the argument for restoring imperial rule and expelling foreigners grew more impassioned by the day. Nothing would appease the activists, and they finally achieved their aims.

Public opinion today is completely different in import from the old call to expel foreigners, and the government, of course, is not like the bakufu. Nevertheless, the fervor for contentious argument is much the same. To sum up, the present public mood is the result of what I call the spirit of the times, a trend that has been gathering strength for several years, and to try to check it is now beyond human power.

Still more unfortunate, and granted that this, too, owes to the trend of the times, is the fact that some in government service are unhappy with their position. In general, a person takes a job or government position and stays with it because he is satisfied, and accordingly does his best to uphold the principles of his organization. The officials I have in mind, however, actually look down on their jobs. Without a hint of embarrassment, some even boast openly that they were never interested in working for the government but were willing to bend their principles because it was a novel way of making money. They joke about their behavior, as if they were above petty concerns. Their unseemly conduct can only strengthen the cause of what I called the people's sect. If this tendency becomes widespread, the sect will naturally take advantage of the situation and become more powerful and harder to restrain. Then, as it gains strength with the proverbial force of splintering bamboo, the work of government will inevitably slow down. As the two kanji for "slow down" indicate, the government will have difficulty governing the country and its work will be impeded.[3] "Slow down" is the opposite of "go smoothly." Each time the government issues an ordinance the people's sect will deliberately try to obstruct it, even when it does not directly concern the people at large. Whether in the form of an appeal or petition, the members will act so that what normally takes the government one day, takes ten, and ten days' paperwork will take a month and still be unfinished.

In this connection, I shall mention a case I happened to hear in passing. A certain prefectural assembly of forty members, each paid 1 yen a day, spent fifteen days discussing the draft of a proposal to raise or lower the regional tax by 300 yen. Needless to say, their pay came out of the local people's pockets. The assemblymen's expenses came to 40 yen a day, or a total of 600 yen for fifteen days. In other words, a total of 600 yen of public money was spent to discuss a sum of 300 yen, and this is not to mention the amount of time wasted. The end result of all the money and mental exertion was nothing but a delay in the work of government.

Obstructive and dilatory behavior of this kind is not limited to prefectural assemblies; it is found throughout the country and can be highly irksome. Will the government tolerate this? Whatever the circumstances, will it bend like the willow in the wind and sway this way and that? Will it continue to forebear and remain silent? Forbearance is important, true, but human nature can tolerate only so much, and in the end, the government will have no choice but to resort to military force. Controlling people with military force in order to realize long-term national goals is far easier than controlling people with words. The government could well be accused of cowardice if it chose not to fight "out of fear of damaging the treasure hidden in its bosom."[4] But if the situation is sufficiently urgent and the danger of a disturbance is imminent, the government will have no time to worry about the treasure. And if the government and people confront each other with physical force, the consequences will be calamitous. The government will lose face, the people will be cast into misery, and the great nation of Japan will be disgraced vis-à-vis foreign nations. Imagine for a moment such a misfortune befalling the country: the people would be the first to suffer. Advocates of popular rights have neither arms nor money; the only things they can count on are public opinion and the country's laws. But if the government covers its ears and refuses to listen to public opinion, decides to rely on force rather than the written law, or interpret the law to suit its own purpose, what can the people do? They would be in a terrible predicament.

In the recent past, when samurai activists called for the expulsion of foreigners, they were scattered far and wide and only a few had real power. But when they ran into debt or other difficulties, they could always turn to one of three hundred daimyo domains in the country and have their debts covered, without loss of face. Again, if they committed a crime or came under suspicion, they could seek refuge at any one of the daimyo residences in Edo, Osaka, and Kyoto; with the loosening of bakufu controls, the residences had become, so to say, extraterritorial, and safely hidden, the activists could plot their next move. In retaliation, the bakufu called the activists worthless drifters and outwardly despised them but secretly feared them.

Today's activists in the populist cause are altogether different. They may be effective in arguing, but as a physical force, they are weak because they are isolated from one another and must act as individuals. For money, they must rely on personal or family resources and have no domain treasury to back them. Even if they band together and vow to overcome every adversity, or succeed in getting the support of someone rich, they stand no comparison with the samurai activists of old. The present government, furthermore, is not militarily weak like the bakufu, nor its officials conservative and temporizing like bakufu senior councilors and their subordinate retainers. They are law-abiding officials now, but as recently as twenty years ago, they were doubtless killing people, setting houses on fire, calmly facing a rain of bullets in the thick of battle; they are by no means cowards. Once they make up their minds and show their true colors, they will act forcefully and crush the popular rights activists in one blow. Or even if they do not crush them completely, the country will be plunged into the depths of misery. As long as the conflict between the government and the people remains a matter of words, the situation will be tolerable enough, but if it reaches the point that the government uses force, the people will be the first to suffer. This would be a great misfortune for the advancement of civilization, a disaster for the health and vigor of the nation.

V.

Let us say we are fortunate enough to be spared witnessing the ominous scene that I have just described. Even so, there is something else that fills me with apprehension: the possibility that the government will see the people locked in argument and become even more suspicious of their motives. In fact, a few have already been irresponsible and unruly in some areas, though they should not be rebuked just because they behave suspiciously. Nor is the government alone in being angered by these incidents. Old-fashioned and honest people, who see only one aspect of things, are indignant. There are also cunning people who seek immediate gain; looking ahead to possible developments beneficial to themselves, they curry favor with the government by saying populists are nothing but a gang of violent extremists.

One is reminded of the last days of the bakufu when truly loyal retainers tried to shore up its fortunes, while others, fickle and duplicitous, took advantage of the turbulent times and proposed schemes that only added to the qualms of those already dubious of the bakufu's future and intensified the hatred of its long-time enemies. As a result, the bakufu became even more intransigent, denounced anti-bakufu samurai as worthless drifters, and "lumping together gems and stones," treated all of them with scorn. If popular rightists are regarded in the same manner, distrusted, rebuked, even ostracized or worse, rumored to hold suspicious views that violate the sanctity of the Imperial House, the nation will be mired in deeper trouble and the consequences will be even more far-reaching. At present, the people argue contentiously with the government, but their arguments are limited to politics: they declare that the political system should be like this, or that the government should not do such and such. At most, they criticize men in office and call for reforms in government laws. The political party in favor with the government and the parties out of favor also attack each other.[5] The government, meanwhile, barely listens to what the people have to say, but thus far, no one has discussed the importance of the Imperial House. From its position on high, the Imperial House looks down to the world far below where political arguments take place. Which side wins or loses has absolutely no effect on its sanctity; its majesty and sacredness has been unchanged from time immemorial and will remain so for ages eternal. That is what makes the Imperial House the Imperial House. But if, by any chance, the arguments allude to its sanctity, regardless of whether these are right or wrong, or even motivated by a sincere reverence for the Imperial House, the very occurrence of such statements will be seen as encroaching on sacred ground and open the way for a subject that should never be raised. People will be shocked and caught in a veritable storm of emotion. Indeed, one hears rumors that some people have begun to talk about the subject. I find this truly alarming for the nation's peace and security and deeply regret it.

The world is rife with tumult and disorder; nothing is as frightening as suspicion and distrust. To make a simple analogy, consider dogs and humans. If you walk by a dog calmly, it will also be calm, as if man and dog are unaware of the other's existence. But if you are a little suspicious, or having heard that the dog sometimes bites, you show signs of fear and hurry past, the dog will be on its guard. Or perhaps, you are filled with fear and suspicion, and hoping to chase the dog away, brandish a stick or stone. The dog will invariably bark and bite; even a fainthearted dog will bark as it runs away. Then, if you chase the dog in anger, it will continue to bark and make you angrier still. You could ignore it and retrace your steps, in which case, in a reversal of roles, the dog will chase after you. One dog barks and all the dogs in the neighborhood bark, as though they are holding a rancorous debate. I remember many instances like this from my childhood, and I am quite certain that readers will, too. All this happens because humans are suspicious of dogs and dogs suspicious of humans, going in different directions, as it were.

From the first, today's argument for popular rights has been a debate among the Japanese citizenry about the rights and wrongs of the political system. But let us say a certain political party judges the popular rightists suspect, casts its lot with the government, and, professing to honor and revere the Imperial House, invokes its name without any hesitation and publicly proclaims that anyone who opposes the party opposes the Imperial House.⁶ The other parties will naturally protest. They will say, "No, our party reveres the Imperial House, not yours," and instead of discussing politics, the parties will spend the time arguing about the Imperial House. They will be like children in the same family, who are squabbling about household matters but stray from the issue at hand and say, "The parents are the parents of the eldest child," or "No, they are the parents of the youngest," and so on. Nothing could be more ridiculous than children in the same family arguing about their parentage. Should such an unfortunate situation occur, there is little hope that a genuine political party will emerge in Japan. The root cause is none other than the mutual suspicion between the government and the people and their insistence on going in different directions. This will only end in the greatest misery for all.

Names and titles are extremely important in human affairs; to misuse them is to invite disaster. As one example, I shall mention an incident that took place in the last years of the Tokugawa bakufu, when the country was caught up in acrimonious disputes. At a certain place, in Kyoto, someone scribbled a few lines that mentioned the name of the shogun, Tokugawa Iemochi. I have forgotten whether the person did this intending to help the shogun, or to thwart him. In any event, a learned man, who heard about this at the time, privately lamented as follows:

> The unchallenged authority of the House of Tokugawa is no more. Throughout Japan, for two hundred fifty years, no one dared to utter or write the shogun's personal name. The shogun was the shogun precisely because he stood outside of politics. Because of this, people referred to the bakufu with vague terms like "Kantō" or "Official Place," and rarely mentioned the Tokugawa by their family name, much less the shogun by his personal name. The reluctance to refer to the shogun by name proves that he was not held personally responsible for the country's politics. But now, someone has written his name for all to see. I take this as a sign of stressful times ahead for the country and that the shogun will be held personally responsible for this.

If this was the case with the Tokugawa shogun, how much more so is it with the Imperial House! The name should never be used heedlessly, not even when it is invoked in the spirit of utmost reverence and loyalty. Anyone who wishes to serve the Imperial House with unswerving loyalty should maintain a respectful silence, and in this I mean both officials in government and ordinary people. A person may be loyal in his heart, but if he talks glibly about the Imperial House, he is disloyal in deed. Even raising the subject is the unfortunate consequence of the distrust between the government and the people. Fearful indeed are the evils of distrust.

VI.

As I mentioned, if, by any chance, the government decides to use military force, the people will be crushed immediately. But they will be vanquished only outwardly and not in spirit. You may seize a person by the arm but fail to control his mind. Not only will the government fail to control the people's minds, but the people will become even more wary and eager to redouble their opposition. Then, as they become increasingly intractable, the government will perforce become more repressive and destroy all hope for accord. During the last years of bakufu rule, when samurai activists agitated for the restoration of imperial rule and expulsion of foreigners, the bakufu acted decisively at first. It rounded up the activists and imprisoned them, even sentencing some to death, but unable to crush the collective will of the activists, it began to waver and temporize and finally collapsed. As I think this over now, the bakufu did not collapse because it failed to take decisive military action, but because it wavered and temporized knowing that brute force can never suppress people's minds.

The government and the people are at odds, political parties have sprung up everywhere, and the date for opening the national assembly is firmly fixed. If the assembly opens despite the present discord, who will take over the reins of government? For now, this is impossible to predict, since the decision rests with the majority, but will the party in favor with the government take power? If so, the other parties are certain to step up their criticism. Or will one of these parties take over the government? If so, the party will come under attack as soon as it takes office. The reason? Because the day such a party takes office, it will adopt the beliefs of what I called the "government sect." If the assembly opens before the government and people reach an understanding, and the two sides still refuse to listen to the particulars of each other's political principles, they will be looking at each other through different-colored eyeglasses and decide who is right and who is wrong according to the color they see. They will be like the two rival factions in the former Mito domain, which despised each other without discussing their respective principles. The factions finally resorted to violence, killed each other, and worse, slaughtered innocent women and children—as if women and children had any political beliefs! Clearly, they would not have committed these atrocities if they had asked what the other side believed.

A party under constitutional government and a party under military government are equally political parties; the only difference is whether a party is willing to question and discuss the other party's beliefs. A party under constitutional government relies on the written word and spars verbally. A party under military government relies on weapons, refuses to listen to the opposition, and eventually resorts to murder and butchery; accustomed to resolving arguments with murder, its political influence will be limited, its character, relentlessly harsh and cruel, even if it forms successive governments.

Today, Japan finds itself pitted against world powers and poised to compete on the world stage in military and civil matters. At this critical juncture, what is the most urgent task before us? Nothing less than to join together as one family and support the government unstintingly, thereby strengthening its rule and enabling it to further assert the nation's sovereign rights. But judging from prevailing trends, and what I imagine will be the situation a few years hence, I do not think the government will be that much stronger, or that it will assert Japan's sovereign rights more forcefully. At best, the country will be able to maintain internal peace and order, but even this is not certain. Putting aside minor differences in what the government or people say, is there any true Japanese who does not worry about the present situation? If there is, and he is proud of it, I pronounce him a fool, utterly incapable of feeling heat, cold, or pain.

In the final analysis, the present situation is the result of the spirit of the times. The spirit, however, is not a natural phenomenon but a human product and not totally beyond human power to retrieve. What matters is that we do not let it get out of hand, or try to check it in anger. The only difficulty lies in recognizing the force of its movement, ascertaining the true locus of its driving power, and taking appropriate measures to restrain it. Diagnosing social conditions is no different from diagnosing human sickness. The symptom does not necessarily appear where the sickness originates. A headache is located in the head but may originate in the stomach. A cluster of symptoms is particularly difficult to diagnose. The government is the nation's doctor and eminently capable of diagnosing its sickness. I happen to have several suggestions to make to the nation's doctor, but I will be unable to give an adequate explanation without laying out all the facts. And since I do not have enough space in this newspaper, I shall ask only who in Japan should take on the critical task of changing the spirit of the times, and clarify where that responsibility lies.

Men presently in government were samurai activists twenty years ago. Angered by the temporizing policies of the Tokugawa bakufu and alarmed that its indecision would foment unrest and cause untold misery to the people, they carried out a revolution (*kakumei*) at great personal sacrifice; what they accomplished was truly heroic. Throughout history, there have always been men willing to bear personal responsibility for the country in times of war or peace, even in a government that has lasted hundreds of years. This is to say nothing of men who replace a government to govern anew! I know for a fact that the leaders in our government have a firm sense of duty and a deep concern for society; their primary goal is social stability, and they will govern the country by peaceful means. Together with all the people in the country, I believe this beyond any doubt.

Nevertheless, when I cast my gaze across the entire nation, I do not find that people are calmer now than in the past, nor do I think that they will be any different in the near future. As I look on from the sidelines, I feel great sympathy for the men who labor so strenuously. Perhaps people have suddenly changed in the last three or four years and become more heedless, short-tempered, bold, and unruly. I have personally witnessed this on several occasions, but since these developments merely reflect the general trend in politics, I see no reason to admonish every person or lecture every family for their failings.

When we speak of social character, we mean something that is not distinctly attributable to individuals but to society as a whole. Thus, if people have in fact changed in the last three or four years and become more heedless, short-tempered, bold, and unruly, we must conclude that Japanese society has itself changed, and there is nothing one can do about it. Still, no matter how society in Japan changes, the Japanese will always be Japanese, and the Japanese government is responsible for governing them. Just because the Japanese have changed and become more difficult to govern, there is no reason to abandon them or to suppress them with force.

Changes that take place in people's minds and hearts are impossible to fathom. Leaders in government are judged by the skill with which they govern unruly people. In this, they are like horsemen and the people are like horses. There are many breeds of horses, each with a different temperament, some sluggish, others high-spirited. Handled improperly, the horse's temperament may change, but no matter how difficult to handle, a skilled horseman will never abandon a horse. No animal that bears the name of horse is untamable. Despite this, when a horse refuses to follow orders, the owner will sometimes accuse the animal of being stupid or wild and immediately abandon it. In extreme cases, when an improperly handled horse loses its temper, the owner will also lose his temper and whip it, in which case, he is no better than an unskilled laborer. A properly handled horse can always be trained; if it is untamable and abandoned, the fault lies with the owner and not with the horse. Similarly, there exist no people who cannot be governed if the government handles them skillfully. If they are abandoned as ungovernable, it is because the government lacks the skill. The peace or disorder of the country is the responsibility of the government;

the security of the people is the duty of the authorities in power. No excuse, no pretext, will absolve them of this obligation.

With this, I conclude "The Trends of the Times"—the six editorials that appeared in the *Jiji shinpō*. I shall watch with keen interest how the government acts three or five years hence.

Commentary

In the first part of this essay, Fukuzawa notes that the Western concept of "rights" did not exist in Tokugawa Japan and was introduced into Japan only during the 1860s. Once introduced, the idea quickly spread, and the reforms that followed the Restoration gave it body. Old customs and institutions were abolished, hereditary rule was ended, and taxes became more equitable. These measures, however, established "human rights," not "political rights"—the right to elect government representatives. The Japanese of that age, Fukuzawa states, did not understand the significance of participation in government.

The 1874 petition for a national assembly by Itagaki Taisuke and his followers had made "elective political rights" an issue, but the popular response had been weak. And just when elective rights might have gained popular support, the issue had been temporarily sidelined by the outbreak of the Satsuma Rebellion early in 1877.

In the second part, Fukuzawa discusses three government reforms that were undertaken to benefit Japan and to expedite the workings of the government. But the reforms had the unintended consequences of unleashing new forces within Japanese society, and gave new energy to the political parties. Fukuzawa examines in detail the consequences.

The first reform was the establishment of prefectural assemblies in 1878. The assemblies were intended to handle local matters that varied from prefecture to prefecture and distracted the central government from critical national concerns. But contrary to expectations, as party men were elected to fill the assembly seats, the assemblies became springboards for renewed agitation by the parties and the dissemination of popular rights doctrines. Fukuzawa writes:

> Once the assemblies opened, the people listened and observed, and for the first time realized what it meant to have political rights ... Farmers and merchants, who hitherto had not dared to look even lowly officials in the eye, now sit in lofty assembly halls, discuss local taxes, and question the budget. When their decisions become prefectural laws, even prefectural governors cannot change

them. Previously, the daimyo levied taxes on the cultivators ... as if from high heaven. Who would have imagined that today, the farmers themselves would legislate their own taxes! ... Truly, high and low had become topsy-turvy. As a popular expression put it, "the farmers act in place of the lord." Is it any wonder that the people's feelings have changed?

Fukuzawa makes clear in the essay that farmers and tradesmen, as well as samurai, were elected to the assemblies. He goes on to discuss the implications for the future.

Prefectural assemblies are just like schools for teaching the idea of political rights. Also, since all the assemblies had opened for business at the same time, with the same set of laws, they could communicate with one another by newspaper or mail, and widely distribute their reports. Thirty-four million pairs of eyes and ears see and hear these simultaneously. Given the human proclivity to move forward, it is only natural that the people now wish to take one more step and demand a national assembly.

Fukuzawa sums up his judgment of the reform: "The first proximate cause of the present clamorous debate on participatory government and popular unrest is none other than the opening of prefectural assemblies."

The second government reform was the land tax reform, completed in 1876. Until then, though taxes on land remained high, government revenues had fluctuated with the price of rice because a portion of the land tax was collected in kind. This made planning difficult. By reforming the tax, the government created an even stream of revenues. The unintended consequence of the reform was that farmers became prosperous. The inflation of the late 1870s had raised the price of rice, while the post-reform taxes that farmers paid remained fixed. Less of their income went to pay taxes and, as a result, farmers became affluent. Newly affluent, farmers for the first time had the leeway to think about politics, and the voices they heard were those of popular rights writers and speakers who promised to lower taxes even further. Fukuzawa describes the situation:

As it happened, political speechmakers were then roaming the countryside calling for the destruction of age-old customs. Newspapers, too, were publishing articles intended to incite political fervor and change dull and apathetic farmers into fervid and hotheaded politicians. Yet, no matter how eloquent the speechmakers or ingenious the articles, the farmers would have paid no attention if they were still shivering from cold and hunger. But now, they were willing to listen and discuss politics.

The third government reform was the Regulations for Universal Education, issued in 1873. The government's intention was to raise standards in primary and secondary schools to create a more able and responsible citizenry. In content the new education was Western and scientific; for instance, it taught that the earth revolved around the sun. But contrary to the government's intention, as Fukuzawa notes, the thirty thousand new primary schools, with over two million students, became centers for the spread of political rights thought. As was true of the other two causes, no one could have foreseen that universal education, which was intended "to broaden people's knowledge and secure the blessings of civilization," would give rise to a "multitude of petty political critics." The actual political consequences of the government's actions, Fukuzawa stated, were "completely unexpected."

> One hears that many of the political activists in the countryside today are primary school teachers ... One also hears that the majority of youths who have been politically active since last summer and autumn are graduates of primary school. This may well be true, and in the coming years, the number will undoubtedly increase, rather than decrease. No matter what kind of law is established, it is already too late. Graduates, I predict, will year by year become more contentious.

This, then, is the third cause.

In sum, the responsibility for the contentious political situation rested with the government. The three reforms, not simply the exertions of political activists, had fueled the fires of the popular rights movement during the early months of 1882. Fukuzawa calls these new forces a *kiun*, which can be translated as "trend" or "social dynamic," or "thrust," or "spirit of the times," or "moral momentum." This *kiun* was like "rushing water that cannot be held back but must be left to run its course." In another context he describes it as having "the force of splintering bamboo." The rising tide of these social forces explained the deepening rift between the government and political parties, even after the promise of an assembly.

Stepping back to view Japan as a whole, Fukuzawa stresses that, spurred on by this *kiun*, only an activist minority of the people had campaigned for a national assembly; the majority had remained unaffected by the party movement and resigned to wait for "another several hundred years." But then, unexpectedly, the government had made the promise of an assembly. Fukuzawa insists that this was not a caving in to the activist minority, but, rather, an internal decision made by the government on its own merits. Despite this, it had the consequence of splitting the country, as if into two religious sects—a government sect and a people's sect—and the two sects bitterly warred.

Mutually resentful, mutually suspicious, it is as though they view each other through eyeglasses of different colors. The government's glasses are tinted green so all the people look green. The people's glasses are tinted yellow so all the officials look yellow. Since it is human nature to hate anyone who is different, admonishing the two sides is useless.

More worrisome, the internal split endangered Japan's international position:

Today, Japan finds itself pitted against world powers and poised to compete on the world stage in military and civil matters. At this critical juncture, what is the most urgent task before us? Nothing less than to join together as one family and support the government unstintingly, thereby strengthening its rule and enabling it to further assert the nation's sovereign rights.

But will Japan unite as one family? Fukuzawa is fairly pessimistic.

Judging from prevailing trends, and what I imagine will be the situation a few years hence, I do not think the government will be that much stronger, or that it will assert Japan's sovereign rights more forcefully. At best, the country will be able to maintain internal peace and order, but even this is not certain.

Still, the situation is not hopeless. In Fukuzawa's eyes, the spirit of the times (*toki no kiun*) "is not a natural phenomenon but a human product and not totally beyond human power to retrieve." Like flood waters, the *kiun* cannot be dammed but it can be channeled.

At the end of the essay, Fukuzawa likens the relationship between a government and the people to that between a horseman and his horse:

A properly handled horse can always be trained; if it is untamable and abandoned, the fault lies with the owner and not with the horse. Similarly, there exist no people who cannot be governed if the government handles them skillfully. If they are abandoned as ungovernable, it is because the government lacks the skill. The peace or disorder of the country is the responsibility of the government; the security of the people is the duty of the authorities in power. No excuse, no pretext, will absolve them of this obligation.

What, then, can we gather from this essay? First, it was written in the aftermath of the political crisis of 1881 and raises the possibility that the government will use force to suppress the parties but then dismisses it. The essay assumes that the government will honor its promise of a general assembly in ten years and not resort to force; it encourages this course of action. Second, it points out that the majority of Japan's population is not involved in the political struggle, that they are apolitical and not concerned with an elective assembly. The struggle is solely between the government and the political parties. Third, the conflict is an unintended consequence of reforms taken by the government. Therefore, apart from its general responsibility of ruling Japan, the government is specifically responsible for having produced this situation. Fourth, the fact that the conflict is real does not mean that it is justified. Partially, at least, it owes to a misperception occasioned by each side wearing "eyeglasses of different colors," a misunderstanding that endangers Japan. The proper resolution is for each side to see the other with unbiased vision. Fifth, the ultimate responsibility for the resolution lies with the government; its basic function is to rule—to maintain peace and order. On this score, Fukuzawa is hopeful: "The government is the nation's doctor and eminently capable of diagnosing its sickness."

6

Revering the Emperor (*Sonnōron*), 1888

Introduction

Among Japanese thinkers, Fukuzawa might be categorized as a rationalist. He came to nineteenth-century Western thought with an intellect formed by a Confucian education and not from any Japanese religious belief. He grudgingly respected Buddhism as a religion that provided an ethic for those incapable of philosophy. He respected Christianity—which in his eyes resembled Buddhism—but only so long as it was practiced outside of Japan. He gave Shinto short shrift.

His low opinion of Shinto is clearly evident in the 1875 *An Outline of Theories of Civilization* in which he pooh-poohed Shinto and separated it from the Imperial House.

> Though one hears Shinto mentioned now and again in modern times, it has been nothing but an insignificant movement, one which barely managed at the Meiji Restoration to avail itself of the lingering glory of the Imperial House. Since it is something merely ephemeral and incidental, in my opinion we ought not to recognize it as an established religion.[1]

Putting aside the religion of Shinto, even the Imperial House possessed only a "lingering glory."

In *Brief Comments on the Times* (*Jiji shōgen*), published in 1881, Fukuzawa had commented more fully on the religions in Japan of his day.[2] He first made his position clear: just as Korea had taught the Japanese carpentry one thousand one hundred years before, the West was now teaching material subjects and this was wholly to the good. The single non-material Western import was Christianity. He wrote, "At the personal level, there is nothing reprehensible about giving up everything and embracing Christianity with one's whole heart and mind." Converts are "no more reprehensible than the ignorant masses who believe in Shinto gods and the Buddha." Nevertheless, he opposed the introduction of

Christianity; if it gained many converts, in a contest Christians would call on foreign powers for help, and Japan might become the possession of a foreign power. He professed neutrality: if it were the other way around, if Buddhism had not become Japan's native religion and if Christianity were, he would defend Christianity and seek to exclude Buddhism.

But Shinto, he insisted, was quite different. Properly speaking, it was not a real religion, for its concerns were this worldly. Fukuzawa admits that Shinto had gained a bit in recent times. Imitating Buddhism, it had initiated the practice of conducting burial rites. But this was not good; it should have stuck to its original identity.

But having said this, his thinking changed, or so it seems. The following year, in 1882, he wrote "The Imperial House" (*Teishitsuron*), and in 1888, he wrote the essay translated here, "Revering the Emperor" (*Sonnōron*).[3] Both essays presented the Imperial House as an institution possessed of far more than "a lingering glory." What did this change mean? Had Fukuzawa become less rational? Had he begun to see the Imperial House in a semi-religious light, perhaps even in a Shinto light? Many passages in the two essays suggest that possibility. But it is also possible that he was merely adding a shimmer of religious coloration to a philosophical view that had not undergone a fundamental change.

Politics certainly shaped the two essays. The 1882 essay was a direct response to the formation in the previous year of the Imperial Government Party (Teiseitō), which claimed to represent both the government and the emperor. The government had swiftly denied any connection to itself. Fukuzawa wrote in 1882 to deny that the party represented the emperor. Political parties, including the Teiseitō, he insisted, operated at an altogether lower and different level.

The first line of the 1882 essay made this point: "The Imperial House stands outside of the world of politics." (*Teishitsu wa seijisha gai no mono nari*.)[4] Fukuzawa went on to say that the emperor, who presides high above, "oversees" all government activity, but is not a part of it and does not "attend" to it. The emperor's appointed role is to firmly take hold of (*shūran*) the hearts and minds of the people and to promote order in society. In so doing, the emperor remains unsullied, an entity transcending the nitty-gritty of actual politics. Fukuzawa eloquently described the emperor's "impartial and non-partisan" position as follows:

> In a government with a parliament, two kinds of parties contend with each other like fire and water, like the full heat of summer and the bitter cold of winter, but the Imperial House alone is like eternal spring. The people look up to it and feel calm. The laws promulgated by a government with a national assembly will be

as cool as water and as unfeelingly thin as paper, but the benevolence and grace of the Imperial House will be as sweet as candy. Looking up to the emperor, the people's anger will dissolve.[5]

To illustrate the emperor's influence, Fukuzawa cited an event that took place soon after the 1877 Satsuma Rebellion. Thousands of government soldiers had assembled in front of the Imperial Palace to protest their poor treatment. Most were former samurai in the prime of life who had lost both status and income. But when an imperial edict expressing the emperor's gratitude was read aloud, the soldiers were reduced to tears and returned home.

Another point in the 1882 essay is that religion in the West differs from religion in Japan. In the West, it unites the members of society; in Japan, it needs help. He repeats the point in this second essay of 1888.

> In Western countries religion flourishes and is not just a matter of priests and temples. Within secular society, religious groups form and often carry out charitable works. In consequence, religion gathers people's hearts and minds and encourages morality. In our Japan, however, the effects of religion do not reach into secular society. Religion ends in sermons and temples. It is clear, therefore, that we cannot possibly rely on religion alone to uphold the virtue of the people but must rely on the Imperial House.[6]

Translation

"Revering the Emperor" was first published in daily installments in *Jiji shinpō* starting on September 26, 1888, and won high praise from our readers.[7] Because the essay appeared in installments, readers found it difficult to follow the argument as a whole, and even before the series were completed, they suggested that we gather the installments together in a book. We also received requests for past copies of the newspaper, but having printed only a limited number, we were unable to comply. Because of the overwhelming acclaim and our sincere wish that the argument in the essay be disseminated widely, we have decided to publish the installments as a small book.

October 1888
Ishikawa Hanjirō

The Imperial House of our great nation of Japan is majestic and sacrosanct (*songen shinsei*). As subjects, we know it is our duty to honor and revere it, and in rendering homage, we have no other purpose in mind. The sentiment would appear to be a distinctive characteristic that is found only in the Japanese; from ancient times to the present, no one has ever questioned this belief. Nevertheless, in view of the steady progress of human culture and the rise in society of numerous and diverse arguments since the opening of the country, I propose to go beyond the simple explanation that revering the emperor is inherent to the Japanese character. I also believe this great moral principle is necessary in the governance of the nation and should not be taken lightly, and useless though it may seem today, I have written this essay in the hope that my words will contribute to the peace and stability of our country's future and be of some use to future progeny. I raise three points in my argument:

One: Why is revering the Imperial House necessary in the governance of the nation?
Two: What is the basis for the majestic and sacrosanct character of the Imperial House?
Three: In what way can the majesty and sanctity of the Imperial House be maintained?

As to the first, for the most part, the Japanese respect and reverence for the Imperial House are spontaneous, natural feelings. If you ask ordinary men or women why they think the Imperial House is sacred, they will give a simple answer: the Imperial House is sacred because it is the Imperial House, as if there were no room for doubt. This is true not only of ordinary people but also of certain virtuous and learned gentlemen who habitually profess reverence for the Imperial House. Ask these worthy men why they feel this way, and they will say it is because the imperial line has continued unbroken since time immemorial. Few, if any, will give a detailed explanation.

As the situation now stands, I, for one, would hesitate to press them to elaborate further, and practically speaking, perhaps no explanation is necessary. Nevertheless, with the progress of civilization now unending and contentiousness in society on the rise, I can envisage the day when arguments appeal to reason rather than to human sentiment and when arguments regarding the Imperial House will also be based solely on reason and its usefulness in governance called into question. In anticipation of this, unlike the aforementioned common folk and so-called pro-emperor zealots who say the Imperial House is sacred because it is the Imperial House, I shall go one step further, and in answering the question, argue that reverence for the emperor is necessary for governing the nation. By appealing to both reason and emotion, I hope to give a satisfactory answer that will further strengthen the people's feelings for the emperor.

It is said that human nature is innately good. Yet, on observing human beings in this mundane world, we find that, in general, there is no one who does not like to win and gain a larger share in life. In other words, aspiring to fame and fortune is part of human nature, the starting point of all social activity. Again, there is no limit to the human capacity for contrivance: people will resort to any manner of means to obtain what they like or want, and on the whole, they will succeed. Some of these means are correct and some are wrong. In many cases, the person in question will think he is acting properly, whereas those around him think otherwise. Again, matters considered morally correct in the past may no longer be so in this day and age. There can be extremely complicated circumstances behind these actions, which are difficult to judge, and since the morally imperfect mortals in this ephemeral world will not give up their pursuit of fame and fortune, people are, quite naturally, wary and on edge. As long as these feelings are hidden, a semblance of peace and stability will prevail, but as soon as they are out in the open, on a small scale, individuals will disagree and argue, and on a larger scale, political parties will fight each other, and war may even erupt. Nothing more harmful to society can be imagined. And when we look for the root cause of all this, we will find that it is the human predilection for winning and getting the greater share, a trait that is extremely difficult to regulate.

Then, should we let everyone in the world win? Winning and losing are opposing terms; if no one loses, no one wins. Or, should we let everyone take the larger share? But large and small are also opposing terms; if no one has the smaller share, no one feels he has the larger share. Everyone in this mundane world covets fame and fortune, yet if a person wishes to attain satisfaction to his heart's desire, he would have to be given all the honor and riches in the world. But then, apart from that one person, everyone else will be dissatisfied. This will only worsen the situation and clearly should not be allowed.

The primary purpose of government is not to consign people to the depths of discontent and resentment, nor to raise them to the heights of pride and satisfaction. Rather, governments exist to give them a place in the middle so that they may be spared of extremes and be able to partake in an equal portion of pain and pleasure, joy and despair. This is what is called "each person receiving his due share" (*sono bun o etaru*). Laws, religion, and moral precepts are meant to clarify the rights and wrongs of human behavior and restrain or prohibit undue greed, but they have proven insufficient. This is especially true in Japan, where the customs and practices of the former samurai class persist and many are feverishly concerned with politics. Indeed, at times, the fervor for politics reaches such an extreme that laws and moral precepts are often rendered completely useless. History has shown this temperament to be peculiar to our country. In order to mitigate this unwarranted fervor in the world of politics, we must turn to a certain power that Japan alone possesses. By this, I mean none other than the majesty and sanctity of the Imperial House.

As I have said, human beings desire fame and fortune. But if I were asked which of the two is more important, I would have to say that human sentiment would put fame first and fortune second. When basic necessities are met, and physical health secured, a human being wholly aspires to fame and honor. Extravagance in mansions, money, fine clothes, and food has no limits, but one can physically consume only so much, the rest being all for show. In other words, people seek greater wealth to buy fame and honor. There are so-called slaves to money. They seem to think of nothing else; with no regard for pride or respectability, they accumulate money as if this were their sole purpose in life. Yet, when we examine their true motives, we find that they desire money because without it they would feel insecure and suffer untold misery and humiliation if they were thrust into abject poverty. Money is of primary importance in preventing such a situation, to say nothing of the fact that even in normal circumstances, money is the source of power and the measure of one's place in society. In short, they, too, pursue wealth for the sake of fame and honor.

When we consider the extent to which human beings are drawn to fame, and the fact that money is the most expedient way to achieve this, the abundant strife in the world of mortals is no surprise. Now, if winning or losing were as clear-cut as a sumo match, we would have nothing to worry about. But most human affairs are intangible, their complexities difficult to judge. To distinguish right from wrong, we could appeal to the country's laws, but laws are unsatisfactory in that they are effective only in external, concrete matters and are incapable of probing into matters of the heart. For this, we need an intermediary, and by intermediary, I do not mean an entity that merely handles conflicts, but one that also functions in the larger sphere of ordinary human affairs, mollifying and regulating heightened emotion. The entity acts much like an anodyne that eases sudden and acute pain.

Let us suppose that some hotheaded city youths come to blows at a festival or the scene of a fire, all because of a slight misunderstanding. The fight quickly escalates and each side stubbornly refuses to give in. Fearless of police intervention, the youths are determined to fight to the death, but just as the fight threatens to turn into an unforeseen calamity, a man widely known as the boss of the neighborhood gang elbows his way barehanded through the crowd of spectators and roars, "Leave this fight to me!" He separates the youths, and they immediately quiet down. They silently withdraw from the scene, and even make peace over cups of sake. Such incidents are not unusual in big cities.

Presumably, at one point, the impetuous youths had decided to give up their lives but changed their minds in an instant. And if we examine their true feelings, we will find that they are not particularly disposed to cruelty or bloodshed but were unwilling to withdraw out of manly pride. But once the neighborhood boss stepped in, both sides were able to withdraw without losing face. They may have been somewhat disgruntled, but honor bound as they were to the boss, they decided to let the matter pass, and precisely because they let him handle the fight, these high-spirited youths did not utter a word of complaint. They left everything to the boss because of his reputation, and, in fact, his intercession provided them a welcome opportunity to leave without loss of face. The reputation of one man had resolved the incident admirably and brought about a peaceful resolution for many young men.

Street fights of the kind I have described usually take place among youths from the lower reaches of society and are generally ignored by virtuous and learned gentlemen. But if we analyze actions taken in this mundane world to see their true character, will we find that these upper-class gentlemen are different from the youths of the streets? Merchants vie with one another for profit, scholars for fame, and politicians for power; on the surface they may seem calm and self-possessed, but as they compete with one another, the upper classes are no different from the lower classes and not particularly superior. If they were left to act as they pleased, there would be no end to controversy; not only would society be disturbed, but events would drive such individuals to refuse to give an inch and the situation would become even more troublesome.

Merchants who speculate and compete for profit confine their activities to moneymaking and usually stop short of buying honor, so matters among them are settled with a simple exchange of cash. Competition is more intense among those who have no interest in money or consider it secondary, putting fame and power first. Politicians who engage in extended disputes and sometimes stir up serious trouble are the worst: society, the country itself, becomes their plaything, vulnerable to unexpected disaster.

At such a time, the majestic and sacrosanct Imperial House, which in more normal times exerts its subtle and wondrous moral power to prevent disaster, is the only moderating force. It works in much the same way that a man of high purpose is persuaded to change his mind over a cup of sake, or a crafty villain plotting to take over the country is restrained with a gentle word of admonition;

nowhere else is such a power to be found. Needless to say, the Imperial House presides high above the world of politics and bears not the slightest responsibility for the merits or demerits of government. Indeed, the further removed from the frenzy of politics, the more exalted is its majesty and sanctity, and the greater its power to moderate and restrain. As attested abundantly by age-old customs and popular sentiment, the Imperial House is not only necessary for governing the nation, but any loss or infringement of its majesty and sanctity will immediately cast society into darkness.

In Western countries, human affairs have long been settled by the decisions of the majority; in Japan, following the orders of one great man has long been the custom. East and West thus differ in their approach, and judging the respective advantages and disadvantages is not a simple matter. The practice of the majority making decisions or one great man making them can be traced back thousands of years in history, and both have hitherto proven sufficient to set the people's minds at ease and maintain social stability. But then, thirty years ago, Japan suddenly abandoned its policy of national seclusion and started associating with Westerners. Because of this new influence, the Japanese carefully examined conditions in their own country and discovered that, in matters both tangible and intangible, the West possessed certain attributes that surpassed their own. They called these attributes the "civilization and enlightenment of the West." The Japanese zealously set about adopting these attributes, and in due course, learned that one of the principles of civilization was making decisions regarding human affairs by majority vote. They adopted this principle little by little, applying the rule of majority vote to settle affairs involving commoner affairs, or to issue endorsements of certain individuals, and extending it even to certain areas of politics. For example, the recent decision to establish a national assembly, an organization relying on majority vote to determine national affairs, heralds a change of unprecedented magnitude in Japan.

In today's world, Western civilization holds undisputed sway over human beings and is impossible to challenge. What is more, a close examination of its attributes will reveal that, on average, the virtues outweigh the failings, and that there is much to admire; the Japanese can only stand to gain by adopting its good points. Among these, the principle of majority vote is beyond criticism and certain to be adopted throughout the country in determining human affairs, public and private, large and small. I am wholeheartedly in favor of this; my only concern is that people accustomed for millennia to following the orders of one great man will not readily submit to a majority decision. Also, even when the Japanese have no choice but to comply, I doubt that, following the example of

Westerners, they will respect the opinion of the majority, ascribe to it a kind of mystical aura, and docilely submit without any hesitation.

Although this example is of a somewhat different nature, I will turn to a situation that has troubled top leaders of government since the early years of the Meiji: their inability to appear as if their decisions on promotions and enactment of ordinances reflect the will of one person. The present government appears to have been originally organized on the principle that one great man would be in charge. If this were indeed the case, there would be no need to look into his personal affairs or background. As the head of government, he would exercise full authority, determine policy single-handedly, push aside anyone who disagreed, and act just like the senior councilor, who stood at the head of the Tokugawa bakufu.

But from the start, the reality has been different: the top-ranking men in government are like brothers, with little difference in background. They are also said to make decisions as a group, and in some vague way settle matters according to the views of the majority. The arbitrary use of power by one great man is undesirable, but if the principle of majority vote is openly recognized and accepted as the basis for making decisions, the same principle could be used as the basis for giving full rein to despotic power. Such is not the case, however. The government may seem to be led by one great man, but this is not allowed; it may seem to rely on majority vote, but it is unclear what that majority is. In consequence, the government as a whole suffers. Nor is this sort of situation limited to government; it is found in private circles, and frequently causes dissension and disorder. This trend, which is common in Japan today, is a phenomenon that hinders the transition from rule by one great man to rule by the majority. Yet, as I mentioned, the forces of Western civilization know no bounds, and ultimately, in politics, as in other human affairs, rule by a single great man is certain to give way to majority rule. This, in short, is my prediction for the future.

What I have described above is the difficulty encountered in changing from one great leader to majority rule in political and human affairs; no one, I trust, will say the transition will be easy. Because of this, perhaps the principle of majority rule should be limited to tangible matters. In affairs relating to commoners or the government, there should be no objection to making decisions about issues and appointments by the number of votes. But the Japanese have yet to reach the stage where they look upon majority rule with something approaching religious awe; they may accept it in form but not emotionally. As a result, on the one hand, there are those who seek majority rule and fight for it, while on the other hand, there are those who are angered by the very idea and despise it. Also, there are those who fought for majority rule but, having failed, call for a single great man. Changes in human affairs give rise to turmoil, and inasmuch as venal mortals, who sink or swim with every current in this tumultuous world, have forsaken scientific reasoning and yielded to their troubled emotions, we cannot appeal to law or reason to mollify them. We must look elsewhere for an entity possessed of a strange and wondrous power that has a soothing and calming effect.

The situation may be likened to human sickness: if the sickness is physical, it can be healed by scientifically tested medicine. But if the sickness is mental, methods that go beyond the reach of scientific reasoning will often prove effective. From one viewpoint, the likes of those who sink or swim competing with each another are admirable, and a few are not without use to the country. From another viewpoint, however, many seem to suffer from a kind of mental illness that might be called a pathological desire for fame. To ease this condition and give such people occasional respite, we must look for a wondrous treatment that is nonrational and untested by science. This is why, in short, I put especial trust in the majesty and sanctity of the Imperial House.

Let us say two persons, A and B, are considered equal. If one is placed higher than the other, someone is bound to be dissatisfied. Give fruit to A and flowers to B, praise A in public and honor B in private, serve sake one day and tea the next. Try one thing and another, but the only thing that satisfies people in boundless ways and resonates with boundless significance is the effulgent glory of the Imperial House. Again, let us say politicians argue about the pros and cons of a policy and are as inimical as fire and water, or that a certain person is promoted and another demoted, resulting in a complete reversal of circumstances. Putting aside the legality of the matter, emotions are roused and mutual animosity reaches a fever pitch such that the parties are ready to resort to physical force or deadly weapons. At such a time, the mere mention of the profound concern of the Imperial House, which presides high above the world of politics, works a miracle: the fever immediately subsides and health is restored.

Patients who suffer from a pathological desire for fame are not innately cruel and cold-blooded, nor do they hatch malicious plots to let them rise at the expense of others. At times, they can be surprisingly calm and detached, and while inwardly reluctant, can persist in their errant ways for fear of losing their honor and reputation in society. By great good fortune, however, the mere mention of the emperor's concern is enough to make them swiftly abandon all thoughts of personal honor or shame, shed lingering resentments as if cleansed by water, and thereby keep their reputations intact. This not only redounds to their happiness but also secures the peace and stability of society and, in an important way, helps the conduct of government.

The historical antecedents of Western monarchs do not bear comparison with those of the Imperial House of Japan. Nevertheless, the majestic and sacrosanct (*songen shinsei*) authority of their office has in many instances helped to reconcile the conflicting emotions of subjects and subdue social unrest. Not a few Western monarchs have also indicated what people should do to benefit society, encouraged learning and the arts, and in many ways laid the foundation for the public and private weal. How much more so is it with our Imperial House, whose grace and benevolence have helped to govern the country to a far greater degree! The Imperial House is a jewel of inestimable value; I can only pray that nothing will tarnish it.

To proceed to the second part of my essay, everyone in the country knows the Imperial House is sacred, but no one has explained why this is so. Without an explanation, there can only be a weak basis for this belief. I thus hope my explanation will be of some use.

I base my argument on the fact that humans have always cherished the old and looked back to the past with fondness, and that the majesty and sanctity of the Imperial House appeals to these very feelings. Generally speaking, the value of a tangible object in human society is determined in two ways: by the amount of labor expended on its creation, or by the emotion attached to it. Cash is valued because of the enormous amount of labor expended in mining and refining gold and silver; clothes and luxurious household wares are valued because of the extensive labor required for weaving silk and wool and crafting metal and wood. In brief, the value of an object is rightly determined by the amount of labor invested; that is, its market value is determined in a highly rational way.

In practice, however, this is not always the case. For example, the value of a painting by a master artist or a rare object from a distant land is not determined in the way I have just described. A painting is valued not for its artistry but because the master artist is possessed of a lofty moral character and rarely takes up his brush; a foreign object is valued not for its usefulness but because it comes from afar and is not easily obtained. In human life, people appreciate what is rare. If someone says that an object is unique in Japan, with nothing comparable in the entire country, or that it is the very best in the world, with none other like it, then this object, whether a stone or piece of tile utterly useless to humans, will always be purchased for a huge sum of money. This is what is meant by the emotional value (**sentimental value**) of an object.

We tend to think that appreciation of old or rare objects is a dilettantish interest of the rich, but it is actually quite common among the people at large. Let us say there is a thousand-year-old pine tree in a remote village, a tree treasured by the people as something extraordinary and revered like a god. If the villagers chopped down the tree, the precious wood would not only fetch a handsome price, but the area hitherto shaded by it could be converted to a paddy of about three-fourths of an acre, with a yearly yield of so many bales of rice. The villagers hold a discussion to decide whether they should preserve the tree or cut it down. The majority, I daresay, would be in favor of preserving it. Why? Because the ancient pine tree is known throughout the neighboring provinces as something unique: it is at once an ornament of the village and the pride and joy of the villagers. A tree like this is found only in their village, and whenever it comes up in daily conversation, the villagers swell with pride, feeling that they alone possess such a tree. Out of respect for the tree, they would not dream of putting profit first. People will not only refuse to chop down a venerable tree but will often go to great lengths to put up a stone monument or bronze plaque to commemorate a place or person famous in history. Castle ruins, old battlegrounds, temples, shrines, and the like have no immediate use; from a cold and bleak economic point of view, they are completely useless. Yet, the public will not only oppose their destruction but will also gladly spend money for their preservation.

Assessing the value of objects in this world by the amount of labor invested is solely a matter of commerce and industry and does not necessarily apply to determining the price. Not only that, but an object considered rare and accorded the highest value invariably has little utility. Indeed, the more removed from practical use, the more valued an object is. A pleasure boat owned by a monarch may be considered a beautiful piece of craftsmanship but it will never inspire awe. But if the monarch owned a **diamond** of incomparable value, he can display it with great pride. If one were asked which is more practical, a jewel or a boat, one would of course pick the boat. But a boat is man-made; it can be purchased with money and is not particularly valuable. In contrast, it is not always possible to find a large diamond even after much labor. A **diamond** is an object bestowed by the gods, as it were, and beyond comparison with all the other objects in the world. In this respect, objects considered priceless treasures by humans have no practical value in an economic sense and are almost always useless. This may strike us as exceedingly strange, but such is the reality of human affairs. Even the most confirmed rationalist would have to accept this fact, assuming that he lives in the company of his fellow men. We look at the human race and say they are rational creatures, or survey the world and say we live in the age of reason, but such views apply to only a limited segment of human affairs. The masses of people in this world are like bits of flotsam tossed about in the restless sea of emotions; people who act according to reason are but one or two out of ten.

In the world of humans, a rare object is treasured, regardless of its practical use. The object acquires even greater value if it dates from antiquity, and especially if it is associated with a historical personage. The older the object or coin, the more highly it is prized. A mirror three thousand years old, or a copper coin two thousand years old, is extremely rare, but if the mirror was once owned by such and such an empress in the ancient past, or the coin handled by such and such an emperor, it will be accorded the highest value. With the passage of time, most objects are lost or forgotten; only the very rare object survives, and if it belonged to someone famous, it will acquire great sentimental value as the rarest of rare objects.

If the foregoing is true of inanimate things, it is undeniably true of living human beings. But how does one determine the value of a human being? None other than by his historical lineage. All human beings have ancestors, but given the complexities and vicissitudes of human fortunes, only a few are able to trace their ancestry back for several hundred or a thousand years. And even when they are able to do this, it is not because their ancestors were noted for great deeds but because the bloodline has somehow survived for generations without a serious setback. This in itself is nothing particularly admirable. But let us say there is a person whose lineage can be traced back in history for several hundred years: the founding ancestor has raised the family status by starting such and such an enterprise; an ancestor of another generation has revived the family fortune by such and such an achievement; their descendants have succeeded in preserving the family bloodline to this day. The present-day descendant may be ordinary in intelligence and virtue, but as long as he is not utterly stupid or immoral, vis-à-vis society, he can be justly proud of his lineage. This is to say nothing of a descendant who possesses more than ordinary intelligence and virtue! The respect he receives from society will exceed that of others many times over. And why? Not because society esteems the descendant himself, but because it esteems the ancient origins of his family and the accomplishments of his ancestors.

Assuming that what I have said about human emotions is correct, I shall turn to the Imperial House of Japan. The Imperial House is the oldest of countless families in Japan. It dates back to the very beginning of the country; before it, there existed no family (*kazoku*) in Japan. To this day, every Japanese citizen who lives and breathes in Japan has belonged to one of its branches. Other families, however ancient, cannot compare with its antiquity. All the families in the country distinguish among themselves by taking on surnames; the Imperial House alone has no need for one. Having no surname, subsumed under no kinship group, it is simply known as the Imperial House. The antiquity of its origins is truly extraordinary and unrivaled in the world. This is not to mention the fact that many emperors have been capable and wise, the renown of their learning, virtue, and military valor undiminished to this day. Apart from whether the results were beneficial or harmful, every important event in our history has been connected with the Imperial House. Needless to say, its presence is far removed, yet deeply felt in the minds and hearts of the people.

Is reverence for the old and attachment to the past a sentiment common among people today? Is there one citizen in Japan who does not esteem the antiquity of the Imperial House and appreciate its venerable history? Even an old piece of tile or stone is prized. A tree is spared when its past history is known. As for humans, who are on a much higher level, someone with an ancient bloodline is respected and honored by society, regardless of what his ancestors achieved. Furthermore, if he happens to be the descendant of a man of exceptional valor, he is respected, whether or not he is intelligent, because he represents that ancestor. The Imperial House is not only the oldest family in Japan, with a long unbroken lineage, it also lays claim to many ancestors whose good works are in evidence to this day. No mere coincidence it is then that all the people in the country look up to the Imperial House with awe and believe that it is majestic and sacrosanct.

Many educated men in society profess to revere the emperor and hold admirable views, but when they try to explain why the Imperial House is sacred, they merely say that it is sacred because it is sacred. In ancient times, when people were simple-hearted and lived in a simpler world, if anything, a simple explanation proved more persuasive. But the times have changed: with the gradual advancement of human culture and the increasing demands of worldly affairs, people's feelings have naturally become more complicated and their minds better informed. As they come into contact with a wide range of things, people want to know the whys and wherefores before resolving their doubts. I am certain that in matters regarding the Imperial House, too, some are unwilling to believe everything passively, and it is to these people and to future generations that I offer my humble opinion, which, as I mentioned, is based on the human respect for the old and strong attachment to the past. I count as my good friends gentlemen who profess reverence for the emperor. I deeply appreciate their good will, but these are no longer the times to encourage simple-hearted people to believe and accept something passively. I thus sincerely hope that even as they steadfastly hold on to their worthy sentiments, these gentlemen will go one step further and agree with the argument I present.

In stating my views, I have deliberately refrained from saying this or that about the emperor's virtues. I particularly dislike those critics who talk endlessly about the emperor's virtues and try to link these with politics. By nature, politics and law fall within the realm of reason, and in distinguishing their rights and wrongs, reason is the criterion. In a world where good and bad co-exist, at times it may seem to work to the government's advantage if the vast multitudes of commoners were made to believe that politics and imperial virtues have a direct influence on each other. But this can cause trouble to those very virtues. Politics is the politics of a temporary government; the Imperial House is the Imperial House of Japan for the ages. It transcends politics and presides from on high over the world of human emotions, and it is for this very reason that I have long hoped that its abiding virtues and benevolence will extend to the realm of reason and help ease tension in the country.

As to the third part of my essay, in what way can the majesty and sanctity of the Imperial House be maintained and preserved? I can think of two answers to this: the first is to trust in human nature; that is, the propensity to venerate the old and think fondly of the past—what I have said explains the people's reverence for the Imperial House. At a time when civilization advances by the day, my choice of words may seem inappropriate, suggesting as it does the views of an irresolute old man who clings to past customs and refuses to change. From a somewhat broader perspective, however, an old man's views may not necessarily be dated and may even lead to new and untried ways of looking at things. From the very beginning, I have upheld the sanctity of the Imperial House and looked to its never-ending continuance. This is because I regard it as the impartial and nonpartisan focal point at the center of Japanese society and the object of the people's devout affection. I thus hope that it will cast its sacred rays (*kōmyō o terashite*) from a place high above politics, ensuring an eternal spring, as it were, to enable all the people to live in peaceful accord, and thereby make for a stable and immovable national polity.

When we look at the everyday world of commoners, we see confusion and disorder everywhere. People feverishly seek fame or compete for monetary gain, scholars argue with one another, politicians hold forth endlessly. The ceaseless struggle to gain the upper hand in an infinite variety of pursuits often gives rise to bitterness and strife, but this is of their own devising and of no concern to the Imperial House. Competition is a constant in the progress of civilization, and it might seem the Imperial House takes no notice and disregards the myriad things in the secular world. In fact, the Imperial House encompasses all things, and by virtue of a certain limitless power, indirectly mollifies the people's hearts and prevents strife and competition from reaching extremes.

Nothing is more harmful to stability in the human world than extremism. When carried to an extreme, even a seemingly flawless opinion is dangerous. This is to say nothing of the opinion of those who accuse the human race of sullying the name of civilization but whose own conduct is childish and utterly irresponsible! Even more egregious are those Japanese whose lives are still bound by an age-old traditional education and who know only extreme views. Shallow-minded and timorous, with no idea of what self-respect and self-determination mean, they are like stupid and stubborn children. One can only imagine the dire consequences if they were allowed to have their way! As for the politicians mired in discord, they are like rocks grinding one against the other; caught up in mutual friction, both friend and foe are doomed to be crushed. Their behavior may look like the exercise of freedom, but it is really just the opposite. And this is why I look up to the majestic and sacrosanct Imperial House and humbly believe that its grace and beneficence will assuage and calm the hearts and minds of the people, prevent competition and strife from reaching extremes, and enable everyone to live free from harm. In this day of ever renewing civilization, respect for the old and attachment to the past is an essential element in maintaining and preserving the Imperial House.

Assuming, then, that respect for the old and attachment to the past are of the greatest importance in protecting the Imperial House, I shall discuss the ways in which one can make use of this sentiment. Nothing in this world is superior in and of itself. Something is superior only when it is compared with other things, and the larger the field of comparison the more evident its unchallenged superiority. Consider a certain figure from the past: a scholar of Chinese learning known as the "Great Master." He was called the Great Master because he was the most outstanding among many scholars at a time when Chinese learning was popular. Or consider a sumo wrestler who has earned the title of *ōzeki*. He was given the title because he proved to be the strongest among his fellow sumo wrestlers. If there were no one to compare them with, no matter how learned or strong, the scholar or wrestler would not have been called the Great Master or given the title of *ōzeki*. The Imperial House is venerable, its antiquity unmatched in our country. And since people will naturally appreciate its antiquity more fully when they compare it with other things from the past, we should preserve a wide range of old things to strengthen this sentiment and render even more distinctive the glorious antiquity of the Imperial House.

The [Usa] Hachiman Shrine [dedicated to the Emperor Ōjin] and the Tenman Shrine [dedicated to Sugawara no Michizane] are old and venerable. The Buddhist monastery at Mount Kōya also dates from the distant past, as does the Honganji Temple. These institutions are highly esteemed for their antiquity, but in comparison with the Imperial House, they are not particularly old. Ōnin [sic, Ōjin] was the fifteenth emperor [and reigned during the fifth century]; Sugawara no Michizane served at the court only a thousand years ago. The monastery at Mount Kōya was established under the patronage of a certain emperor, and the Honganji Temple, during the reign of another emperor.

When people hear of the ancient origins of these institutions and their historical ties to the Imperial House, human emotions being such, they are struck anew by its exalted position, their respect for the past is further strengthened, and the moral foundation of the Imperial House rendered ever firmer. I do not know the reasons for recent government efforts to preserve shrines and temples, but whatever the purpose, I am emphatically in favor of it. Why? Because most of the shrines and temples in our country date back to antiquity, and when people reflect on their great age, they naturally associate it with the Imperial House. In other words, these institutions provide a broad base of comparison with the Imperial House. The head priests of Izumo Shrine, Aso Shrine, and Honganji Temple have traditionally come from old families of noble lineage and are venerated by the people as though they were Shinto gods or Buddhas. One could dismiss this as undue credulity on the part of the benighted masses, but given the puerile and intellectually imperfect state of present society, perhaps the wiser course is to let them continue to believe in their gods and Buddhas, since this strengthens their fondness for the past and redounds to the glory of the Imperial House.

More recently, these gods and Buddhas have descended to the world of mortals and become members of the newly designated class of nobles (*kizoku*). These strange half-human, half-godly beings may have felt morally obligated to set up family registers in compliance with the Family Registration Law, but this is what I call an instance of intellectual fastidiousness. Human society is too complex to approach everything with the precision of a carpenter using a plumb line; such an approach is naive and childish. The world of civilization and enlightenment is immense and all encompassing. Ample room can be found for everything, no matter how strange or unusual, as long as it benefits the work of the government. This applies even more to the Imperial House: from the viewpoint of preserving its sacred character, the further removed from the ordinary, the more effectively the essential purpose of the Imperial House will be served. I am not one to fret over the fate of high priests, princely prelates, and the like, but even so, I deeply regret their decision to descend to the world of ordinary mortals, and for the sake of the Imperial House, I hope they will resume their former status.

In this connection, I shall mention the Fujiwara family. Associated with the Imperial House for hundreds of years, the family has shared in its glory and decline, joys and sorrows, and furthermore enjoyed exclusive access to the highest offices in government. This practice has remained unchanged in times of war or peace. To commoners accustomed to seeing the Fujiwara as a family apart, it mattered little whether or not the members were intelligent. Of course, I am not saying that affairs of the state should always be entrusted to the Fujiwara, though I hope that they will remain in a position above other subjects even if family members are excluded from politics. Nor am I trying to make an arbitrary claim for the family. Rather, I am saying that respect for the Fujiwara is consonant with respect for the Imperial House because such an attitude is in accord with the idea of cherishing the old. This is the same feeling that impels a feudal retainer to respect his master's possessions because he respects his master as a person. Whether we are speaking of a sword or crested formal kimono, the retainer treats the object with respect because his master owns and uses it. And so we must say that respect is all the more due to the descendants of an incomparably illustrious family that has been intimately associated with the Imperial House for over a thousand years! To feel esteem for the Fujiwara is only natural, and since this sentiment has its source in the same emotions that honor and esteem the Imperial House, attaching importance to such a family lineage indirectly strengthens the foundation of the Imperial House.

At the time of the Restoration, various reforms were carried out in the domains, though the scale, import, and effect on the respective domain governments varied greatly. In one reform, as if by mutual agreement, daimyo purged senior councilors and other high-ranking retainers from their government. As a result, their own authority was severely diminished, and when the new central government subsequently abolished domains at one stroke, they found themselves in a precarious position. To quote a Chinese saying, "When the lips are ruined, the teeth will feel the cold." There were a number of reasons for the ease with which the government abolished the domains, but the loss of power by the close retainers of the daimyo, the very men who shared the vicissitudes of fortune through the years, was surely one cause. In view of what befell these daimyo, I see no harm in according the highest honors to the Fujiwara, a family that has faithfully served the Imperial House for years, so long as it does not abuse its status to gain political privileges. Not only is there no harm in this, such a practice will be of great importance in preserving the Imperial House.

Some people accuse the nobility of acting as a protective wall surrounding the Imperial House, but since such remarks are vague, without any clarification, I shall assume that they have not thought the matter through. In my opinion, as I have already explained, the nobility rightly serves as a protective wall for the Imperial House. Nobles are descendants of feudal daimyo and court aristocracy; they may not be particularly intelligent or virtuous, and a few are quite rich, but some commoners are just as rich, if not richer.

What do I mean, then, when I say nobles not particularly distinguished in wealth or moral character constitute a protective wall? I am simply referring to their lineage. The present nobility may not be endowed with exceptional intelligence and virtue; some are probably below average. In riches, too, they probably have nothing to boast about, but when we look into their antecedents and the achievements of their ancestors, we find that they are beyond comparison with other families. People today see the present generation of nobles as representatives of distinguished ancestors, and regardless of personal character or wealth, pay them respect in much the way they cherish the distant past. And since the propensity to cherish old families naturally redounds to the Imperial House, the assertion that the nobility acts as a protective wall is far from baseless. From a purely up-to-date rational point of view, honoring nobles, who have themselves done nothing, seems inexcusable. But no one should consider this a cause for alarm since there is not the faintest chance that they will take advantage of their prestige or fame to interfere in politics. We should respect them for what they are—a wall that protects the Imperial House.

If the benefit in preserving the old nobility is indeed as I have stated, to my mind, creating new nobles is unwise. Members of the old nobility are useful to the nation solely because of their ancient lineage; they are rare and valuable like curios and antiques, and hence, their singular worth. Letting people join their ranks because of a recent achievement would rob the old nobility of the aura of antiquity, and this, I feel, is not to the advantage of governing the nation. Rationalists may object to the phrase "aura of antiquity" and argue that lineage or personal accomplishment makes no difference; nobles are nobles, why distinguish between the old and the new?

To refute their objections, I shall give an example that should prove that, even today, the Japanese make a distinction between the old and new nobility. For the sake of argument, let us assume that people are correct in saying there is no difference between the old and new nobility. Then, let us suppose that several years hence, the Imperial House undertakes the important ceremonial procedure involved in selecting an empress. In choosing from among eligible young women, those responsible will not look abroad, since there has never been intermarriage between our Imperial House and foreign royalty; someone from the Japanese nobility will be chosen. The question is, what kind of nobility? If ancient precedent is followed, a daughter from the Fujiwara family or from an old and established military or aristocratic family will undoubtedly be chosen. This is because the historical antecedents of such a family will impress and satisfy the Japanese people, who have always regarded the empress as the mother of the country.

Now let us say there is a young woman who comes from a family newly appointed to the higher ranks of the nobility. She is possessed of superior intelligence and exceptional beauty—qualities to be found in one out of ten women. She is eminently qualified to be empress; on the surface, there is not the slightest objection. Yet, would the Japanese people be satisfied and look upon her with awe as the mother of the country? I will leave the final judgment to those who object to making a distinction between the old and new nobility, but I am quite certain that, along with the rest of the people, they will say "No," unless they are totally devoid of normal human feelings. And why? Because even though the family undeniably belongs to the nobility, it does not have a distinguished historical pedigree; hence, no matter how elevated the family's title, the people will demur at accepting the daughter as the mother of the country.

Those who claim there is no difference between the old and new nobility are speaking from pure reason, whereas those who would demur at the choice are speaking from the heart. Reason never trumps emotion. All the people recognize that the old nobility is important because it nurtures and strengthens their feelings for the past and naturally serves as a protective wall for the Imperial House. They also know full well that the old nobility's value lies solely in its historical pedigree and not in its intelligence or family wealth. Let us consider it a blessing then that we have nobility descended from court aristocrats and military houses with rich historical associations. Their aura of antiquity will help preserve for the ages the ineffable aura that distinguishes the most precious of treasures in Japan—the majestic and sacrosanct Imperial House. I pray from the bottom of my heart that even as a temporary expedient nothing new is added that will impair the distinctive character of the old nobility.

As to the second way of preserving the sanctity of the Imperial House, the emperor should regard all Japanese equally, bestowing his grace and beneficence on officials and commoners alike, firmly take hold of (*shūran*) the hearts and minds of all the people, and encourage them to participate in the furtherance of rapidly advancing civilization. From the first, I have firmly maintained that the Imperial House transcends the world of politics and that the emperor bears no responsibility for the good or bad points of the government in power. I have also believed that the Imperial House is not the Imperial House of a particular government but of the entire nation and that it should not discriminate between officials and the people at large.

To all outward appearance, the government may seem closer to the Imperial House, and in a confrontation with the people, it could well be perceived as enlisting the support of the Imperial House. But this would be a gross misunderstanding. Even supposing the Imperial House to be actually close to the government, a government is in power only temporarily; each time the officials change, perforce, policies also change. This will become even more pronounced after a national assembly is established in the near future and gradually begins to function as planned. Governments change regularly, so is there any reason that the Imperial House, which has lasted for thousands of years, would attach itself to something impermanent, much less share in its reversals? Nor can one rule out the abhorrent possibility that, if worse comes to worst, the Imperial House will be praised or maligned along with the government. I would find this utterly unacceptable. Therefore, I hope with all my heart that the Imperial House will take an impartial and nonpartisan stance and resolutely stay independent of politics. Its innate and sole purpose is to reign from on high over the nation as the fount of grace and favor; under no circumstances should the Imperial House be the object of popular resentment.

At the same time, when we examine the practice of contemporary politics, we find that even a purportedly flawless government enjoys, at most, the support of little over half the people; the minority cannot help but be dissatisfied. Worse yet, the average human being is selfish, superficial, and prone to blame others without examining his own conscience. Even when a court judgment adheres to the written law and leaves no room for argument, the losing party will think of a pretext and grumble and complain in private. A law, of necessity, serves the purposes of one segment of the people and leaves the rest at a disadvantage. A reduction in taxes causes barely a murmur, whereas an increase or imposition of a new tax raises a hue and cry. This is particularly true in Japan, where advances in civilization have led to an unending rise in government expenditures and long-term trends make this unavoidable. Again, as human intelligence develops apace and people become more adept at argumentation, inevitably, there will be disputes about financial policy. But airing grievances of this kind is a given in this world of mortals. The proper function of politics is to resolve the difficulties skillfully, and with the support of the satisfied majority, restrain the disappointed minority and secure temporary peace and stability.

The foregoing account may give the impression that politics is intolerably troublesome, but in an emergency, men of suitable character will always come forth to lead. Undeterred by obstacles, they will resolutely take charge of the political situation, gladden some of the citizens, strike fear in others, win friends here and make enemies there. To their right, they will hear a chorus of approval, to their left, slander and condemnation. In turn elated or dejected, safe or endangered, they will not have a moment's respite, yet will find their work rewarding. In extreme cases, they may even become sick, but even then, they will not hesitate to sacrifice their lives. Such men we call statesmen (*seijika*).

From the lofty standpoint of the Imperial House, it is most fortunate that politicians of such stature appear in the world below. All mundane matters can be entrusted to them; as such, they will be praised or censured. Those with popular support will be given the right to govern, but as soon as they lose favor, they will be replaced. Some will be political enemies and some will be political allies; at times bitterly resented, at times resenting others, they will have to endure many trials and tribulations. Yet, throughout, the Imperial House alone will stand serenely apart and regard all men with impartial benevolence. In the eyes of the Imperial House, the Japanese are all loyal good people, neither friend nor foe. No matter how urgent the situation, I, for one, would never tolerate having the Imperial House praised or censured along with the government that happens to be in power. The reason? Because the Imperial House is the undefiled wellspring of grace and beneficence, and never an object of grievance and resentment. Independent and above the fray of politics, impartial and nonpartisan, its appointed task is to secure the complete and boundless trust and respect of the people.

Barely twenty years have passed since the Restoration and traces of the feudal ethic of loyalty binding lord and retainer remain. Because of this, the Japanese people still trust and revere the emperor in a nonrational way, and despite their annoyance with government laws and regulations, bear not the slightest grudge toward the Imperial House, nor would they think of complaining about their painful lot. Survivors from the feudal era are dying out, however, and with each succeeding generation, "civilized men" (*bunmei-ryū no danshi*) will be increasingly cold-hearted and drawn to legal theory. Each time a new law is passed, they will scrutinize the text and argue over its meaning. If they start saying that the Imperial House is the ultimate source of the law, what can one do? I fear disrespectful talk of this kind will secularize the Imperial House and have the gravest repercussions. Men concerned with governance will be thrown into a panic, pro-emperor moralists will "gnash their teeth and clench their fists in indignation," all and sundry will lament that the situation is beyond help. This is exactly the sort of development that worries me deeply.

A person's life is not limited to his lifetime. For is there anyone who does not think of what will happen after he dies? People who are concerned for their descendants and pray for the stability of Japanese society should think calmly and selflessly about the future, and this, without reference to the sanctity of the Imperial House as our country's most precious treasure. And when they look at society today and come to the conclusion that, however peaceful at present, there will certainly be instability a hundred years hence, they should not dismiss this lightly. People may laugh at me for being overly cautious, but let them laugh. After I am dead and gone, they will see whether I was right or wrong.

When I say the Imperial House transcends politics, I do not mean that it is inert and does nothing. Far from it. In his position as the most exalted, the emperor does not directly deal with politics but reigns over the entire nation, including, of course, the government. Indeed, one could say the government presides over the portion of peoples' lives that is tangible and concrete, while the Imperial House presides over the portion that is intangible—their hearts and minds. Because the Imperial House presides over the people in this manner and is ever the fount of their conduct, every move and gesture on its part immediately affects the country.

Needless to say, this is no simple matter. When we survey the present situation in Japanese society, that is, the way people act and think, we realize that in a world of ever advancing civilization, standards in scholarship and education must be raised, techniques in commerce and industry improved, the people's moral sense nurtured, the dissemination of religious teachings encouraged. In more minor matters, the arts and skills unique to Japan must be fostered and preserved. All of these affect the rise and fall of our country, and if the Imperial House bestows its favor and beneficence upon the furtherance of such endeavors, the benefits will be immeasurable. In the field of learning and education, the Imperial House could give preferential treatment to scholars, in commerce and industry, award honors to men of achievement. It could give public recognition to filial children and virtuous women, accord special consideration to learned priests and prelates, extend patronage to masters of the *koto*, chess, calligraphy, painting, and other arts. Gestures of this kind will not only renew national pride and spur the progress of civilization, but also will win the overwhelming gratitude of the people, and as a matter of course, strengthen the majestic and sacrosanct foundation of the Imperial House.

What I propose is no private musing, nor a particularly novel idea. The same suggestions have long been made by Western intellectuals and duly heeded by their monarchs. One hears of many instances in which monarchs encourage even the smallest matters related to learning, commerce and industry, and confer honors on men of distinction, both in official and in private circles. By nature, the monarch regards his country as one family, and he treats all like equal family members, dispensing his grace and beneficence to all the people to win their hearts and minds. I not only admire the scale, but I continue to be amazed by the skill with which the monarch performs his royal functions. The principle of looking upon the nation as one family and treating the people equally is firmly established, so he makes no distinction between officials and commoners. If he is closer to the government and acts in its favor, those outside of government will feel that, despite being his children, they are not treated accordingly and are prevented from approaching their father, the monarch. He can ill afford to lose the allegiance of the majority of his subjects, so he never discriminates between those in government and those not. Again, the monarch honors famous and accomplished persons, including those in the arts. He does this without any hesitation, because a person renowned in the arts is not alone, but surrounded by people who feel morally indebted to the artist or associate with him socially; thus, when the head of the group is honored, his disciples and friends feel they, too, have been honored, and are deeply moved by the royal beneficence. In truth, the royal gesture is like "rain or dew that alights on one spot, yet brings moisture to the whole." This practice is especially effective because the artist so honored almost always belongs to the higher than average social class. This is undoubtedly what is meant by the proverb, "Feed the hen and the chickens will gather, call the mother cow and the calves will follow."

Such a practice is common in Western countries, and on close inspection, we cannot fail to be impressed by the skill with which the monarchs carry out their plans. In Japan, needless to say, the Imperial House regards the country as one family, and throughout history, has been the head family (*sōke*) of all the people. The Imperial House cherishes everyone in the same way, not because this is strategically wise, but because such an approach accords with human sentiment and reason. At this present stage of civilization, the emperor casting his effulgent rays across the entire country to promote social progress and reform, and at the same time firmly taking hold of the hearts and minds of the people will surely be to the long-term advantage of the Imperial House.

It is not without reason that I prattle on about the role of the Imperial House in furthering civilization. Thus far, I have based my argument on the simple fact that human beings cherish the old and remember the past with fondness. The sentiment is sound and harmless, but a strong attachment to the past can easily turn into unyielding narrow-mindedness. In extreme cases, people will ignore the changing times, or worse, oppose the very idea of renewal and enlightenment. With this in mind, I stressed the importance of human propensity to revere the old in preserving the majesty and sanctity of the Imperial House, while at the same time I also expressed my heartfelt hope that the grace and benevolence of the Imperial House will help advance human culture, and that it will not only be the supreme ruler of Japan but also be the center of its civilization and enlightenment. I trust I have made my humble opinion clear.

At the risk of repeating myself, in ending this essay, I would like to make a final point. Needless to say, my essay focuses on honoring and revering the Imperial House. I have insisted throughout that the Imperial House should transcend the world of politics, but readers who have not fully understood my argument may complain that this would render the emperor an empty vessel—a mere figurehead. So, perhaps, I should make myself clearer: I uphold the principle of revering the Imperial House in every particular [way], and not only pray for its everlasting happiness but also sincerely hope that its sacredness will help ameliorate tensions in the secular world.

By maintaining its distance from the world of politics, the Imperial House, in my view, will ensure its own everlasting happiness and keep intact its limitless merits and virtues. And when I say that the Imperial House should stay outside of politics, I mean to say that it should not be involved with politics, and not that it should abandon the government. The Imperial House reigns over the myriad things in Japan for the ages; this of course includes the government. Indeed, is there anything exempt from the dominion of the Imperial House in our realm? By staying outside of politics, the Imperial House does not become a figurehead. Instead, it firmly grasps the handle of a great vessel—our nation—and looks upon the entire country as family. But if all of Japan is seen as a nation possessing only one vessel in one segment called politics, if the emperor is deemed a figurehead because he is not directly involved with politics, and if someone tries to make the emperor a real political power by attaching him to a government of unstable power and these entities act jointly, the immediate effect may be impressive, but in the long run of thousands of years, the effect will clearly be detrimental.

At present, in government, as well in private circles, there is not a single person of learning who does not honor and revere the emperor. The sentiment is genuine beyond all doubt and comes from the bottom of the heart. Yet, if such people truly revere the emperor, they must think of ways to render homage. The results may not be apparent for three or five years, or even ten. Nevertheless, as one who sincerely hopes that future progeny will have no cause for regret, I urge these people to give the matter their thorough consideration, and abandoning all thoughts of immediate loss or gain, reflect upon the situation many times.

Commentary

In "Revering the Emperor," Fukuzawa places an even greater emphasis on the role of the emperor than he did in his previous writing. Its very title suggests, and was intended to suggest, that he was a devoted supporter of the emperor. "*Sonnō*" means "revering" or "honoring" the "emperor." The phrase was familiar to all Japanese as a part of the slogan "honor the emperor and expel the barbarians" (*Sonnō joi*) that had been used by the pro-emperor forces in the Restoration. The essay was timely; it was published in October 1888, just five months before the promulgation of the Meiji Constitution. Government leaders had decided that the Constitution would be presented as a gift from the emperor to the Japanese people. In stressing the importance of the emperor, Fukuzawa was urging his readers to accept the establishment of a constitutional monarchy.

In another judgment, Fukuzawa appraises the role of reason in world affairs and concludes is that it is small.

> We ... survey the world and say we live in the age of reason, but such views apply to only a limited segment of human affairs. The masses of people in this world are like bits of flotsam tossed about in a restless sea of emotions; people who act according to reason are but one or two out of ten.

Fukuzawa tries to achieve a delicate balance between emotion and reason in the essay. He had to weigh in on the side of reason; his basic rationalism required that he do so; he could not invoke myth to buttress his argument. Yet, to reach his readers, he had to appeal to emotion, since he felt that 80 to 90 percent of the people were like bits of flotsam tossed about by their emotions. The coloration of the 1888 essay suggests that he felt the majority of Japanese had not progressed much beyond the Tokugawa level. They had a modicum of education, they had become literate, but they were far from being fully rational.

We note three salient points about the essay's setting: (1) Fukuzawa's appraisal of his readers' beliefs and the fashioning of an argument that would appeal to them; (2) the recognition that the authority of the emperor was still great; (3) the use of new intellectual tools to conceptualize the emperor's role, in particular, Walter Bagehot's "rational use of the irrational" in *The English Constitution*.

The belief-system of most Japanese of his day, Fukuzawa seems to suggest, was an ill-woven tapestry with Shinto and Buddhist strands (and some Confucian threads as well). Soon after the Restoration the government had decreed that Shinto be separated from Buddhism. Despite this, in the minds of most Japanese, the two were still commingled and a normal part of the routine of life. Japanese were taken to a Shinto shrine as infants, married according to Shinto rites, buried with Buddhist rituals, and felt no sense of contradiction. Within these practices, the variation, of course, was immense. A Shinto priest might cite Japanese creation myths. A Buddhist priest would read the sutras favored by his sect. Some villagers might practice both, even though acquainted with only a few strands of the entire tapestry.

The Shinto strands might include the oldest Japanese chronicle, the *Kojiki*, which tells of Amaterasu, the Sun Goddess and ancestor of the imperial lineage, who lived on the Plain of High Heaven and presided over a multitude of nature deities or *kami*. They would certainly include the two most famous shrines— Ise, dedicated to Amaterasu, and Izumo, to Ōkuninushi no mikoto, another important deity. Shinto beliefs might also touch on gods of the seas, mountains, and waterfalls. Even old gnarled trees were often thought to be manifestations of the indwelling forces of nature, and festooned with straw ropes. There were innumerable national, regional, and local gods. Historical figures like Sugawara no Michizane and Katō Kiyomasa were posthumously enshrined and worshipped as *kami*—as gods of a sort. Finally, the emperor, because of his lineage, figured importantly in the Shinto myth. Even while alive, he was viewed as a living god, an *ikitsugami*.

For the light that it sheds on Fukuzawa's essay, we might note that even a century later a belief in *kami* persists among many Japanese. People offer prayer-slips or tablets sold at the shrine office and attach them to prayer-racks or to the branches of shrine trees. In 1975, the following prayers were posted at the Yoshida Shrine in Kyoto: "May my husband recover from cancer." "May Sachiko love me." "May my daughter enter the Kodomo no Ie Kindergarten." "May I be admitted to the Department of Electrical Engineering at Kyoto University." A century earlier, what Max Weber termed the "garden of magic" was certainly more luxuriant than it was in postwar Japan. Fukuzawa understood the place of religion in his times.

Of course, the typical Shinto worshiper does not have the *Kojiki* in mind. Most probably, he has not read it. He simply throws a coin in the grated box, bows his head, claps his hands, and pulls the bell rope. Sometimes, he does not know the name of the shrine's god. Rather than possessing a set of clearly defined beliefs, he practices a faith. He is not sure that his prayers will be answered. If asked whether the emperor is descended from the Sun Goddess, he would smile at the strangeness of the question and merely shake his head.

Fukuzawa ignores most of the tapestry, picking up on only a few patches. He emphasizes the moral authority of the emperor in Japanese affairs, his unbroken imperial lineage, and his effulgent presence—of which more later.

As to the emperor's utility or influence, the 1888 essay closely follows the 1882 essay. Fukuzawa likens the emperor to a "neighborhood boss," who can step in and with a few words end a fight between hotheaded youths. Or to a doctor, who uses "a wondrous treatment that is nonrational" on a patient whose ills are not physical. In politics, he observes, the animosity between rival politicians may reach "a fever pitch such that the parties are ready to resort to physical force or deadly weapons." But invoke the Imperial House, which presides high above the world of politics, and like a miracle, "the fever immediately subsides and health is restored."

In yet another homely analogy, which may have appealed to rural readers, Fukuzawa compares the emperor to a thousand-year-old pine tree in a remote farming village. Reason dictates that the tree be felled, the valuable wood sold, and the land it shaded used for crops. But whenever the village elders meet, human feelings trump reason.

> The ancient pine tree is known throughout the neighboring provinces as something unique; it is at once an ornament of the village and the pride and joy of the villagers. ... the villagers swell with pride, feeling that they alone possess such a tree.

In the end, the tree is left untouched.

Fukuzawa also introduces Western ideas in his analysis of the imperial institution. From the mid-1870s, possibly on the advice of foreign teachers at his school, he had begun to read contemporary Western works such as John Stuart Mill's *Utilitarianism*, Alexis de Tocqueville's *Democracy in America*, Herbert Spencer's *Sociology* and *First Principles*, and Walter Bagehot's *The English Constitution*. Of these, Bagehot's book was particularly important. Fukuzawa had briefly cited it in his 1882 essay on the Imperial House, but by 1888, he had more fully assimilated his ideas.

Walter Bagehot (1827–77) was the chief editor of *The Economist* for seventeen years. His most famous book, *The English Constitution*, was published in 1867.

Disraeli's Reform Act of the same year extended the vote to most males, including workers. To adjust to this change, Bagehot added a sixty-six page introduction to a second edition of his work, which was published in London in 1872. Fukuzawa owned a copy of this edition.[8]

In principle, Bagehot approved of the Disraeli government's reform, but he felt that the majority of British voters were as yet insufficiently educated to understand or participate in the actual workings of a parliamentary government. He therefore proposed that their attention be directed instead to the attractive, if somewhat mysterious, figure of the monarch who would serve as a "dignified" facade, concealing the true functioning of the cabinet government. When he wrote of republics in the following passage, was he thinking of the United States or France?

> To state the matter shortly, Royalty is a government in which the attention of the nation is concentrated on one person doing interesting actions. A Republic is a government in which that attention is divided between many, who are all doing uninteresting actions. Accordingly, so long as the human heart is strong and human reason weak, Royalty will be strong because it appeals to diffused feeling, and Republics weak because they appeal to the understanding.[9]

Of England, he writes:

> The nation is divided into parties, but the Crown is of no party. Its apparent separation from business is that which removes it both from enmities and from desecration, which possesses its mystery, which enables it to combine the affection of conflicting parties, to be a visible symbol of unity to those still so imperfectly educated as to need a symbol.[10]

The mystery surrounding the crown is a key to Bagehot's thought. The "greatest power" of the English constitutional monarchy is that:

> It acts as a *disguise*. It enables our real rulers to change without heedless people knowing it. The masses of Englishmen are not fit for an elective government; if they knew how near they were to it, they would be surprised, and almost tremble.[11]

The separateness of the crown, its aloofness from the political issues of the day, provides a quasi-religious or magical sanction for government. He continues:

> Above all things our royalty is to be reverenced, and if you begin to poke about it you cannot reverence it ... Its mystery is its life. We must not let in daylight upon magic. We must not bring the Queen into the combat of politics, or she will cease to be reverenced by all combatants; she will become a combatant among many.[12]

Bagehot also wrote of countries where the constitutional form of government is new.

> Among a people well-accustomed to such a [constitutional] government ... [the prime minister] may be bold; he may rely, if not on the parliament, on the nation which understands and values him. But when that [constitutional] government has only recently been introduced, it is difficult for such a minister to be as bold as he ought to be. He relies too much on human reason, and too little on human instinct. The traditional strength of the hereditary monarch is at these times of incalculable use.[13]

This passage surely caught Fukuzawa's eye. In many ways he must have felt that Japan was behind but similar to England, a country he much admired. The Japanese emperor, like the British monarch, would serve as a national symbol. The emperor would bring the nation together. But he would be able to fulfill these functions only if he stood above the fray of politics, only if the people held him in reverence.

Japan also resembled England in terms of the social distance between the ruler and the people. To preserve that separation, Fukuzawa argues in favor of keeping the old Japanese nobility—the Fujiwara family and the like—as a protective "wall" between the emperor and the people. As with the Imperial House itself, it was the existence of the nobles as venerable social entities that mattered, and not their present-day characteristics.

Bagehot's analysis emphasized the personal dimension. As noted, the appeal of the personal explained why nations with kings have an advantage over republics. Bagehot stressed personal actions as a powerful force within society. After the assassination of President Abraham Lincoln, he wrote, "They say that the Americans were more pleased by the Queen's letter to Mrs. Lincoln than at any act of the English Government."[14] Bagehot so clearly separated the individual from the institution that at moments he could even denigrate the occupant of the throne. In his book, he once referred to Queen Victoria and the Prince of Wales as "a retired widow and an unemployed youth," and in private once spoke of the queen as a "meddling fool."[15]

In Japan, in contrast, while imperial births, marriages, and deaths are matters of considerable public interest, there is less emphasis on personality as such and more on religion. Shinto rites are an integral part of succession ceremonies. The English sing "God save the Queen," but they would find it utterly strange to think of the queen as a deity. In Japan, although the *kami* were very different from the Christian God, it was not strange. Also, unlike Bagehot, Fukuzawa never separated the person from the institution, never mentions the merits or demerits of this or that emperor, and from the late 1870s, never belittles the imperial institution.

On reading the essay, we are struck by the gap between the "coloration" and the logic. The "coloration" is evident in the very first line: "The Imperial House of our great nation of Japan is majestic and sacrosanct (*songen shinsei*)." *Songen* may be translated simply as "majestic" or "august" or "dignified." *Shinsei* is more problematic. The ideograph *shin* can be read as "*kami*," which means a Shinto god or spiritual entity; it can also mean "sacred," "sacrosanct," "holy," or "venerable." The second ideograph, *sei*, can mean "saint," "sage," "great master," or "sacred." When the two ideographs are combined, the word has distinctly religious overtones. Only at the extreme end of the range of possible interpretations, can it be read in a secular sense to mean "pure" or "inviolate. " On one occasion, Fukuzawa applies the term to European monarchs, who clearly were not Shinto gods. But the application runs counter to the root meaning of the ideographs.[16]

In writing of the Imperial House in 1882, Fukuzawa used the phrase *songen shinsei* sparingly, but in the 1888 essay he uses it repeatedly. The later essay also contains many other passages that may have been inserted, in some measure, to appeal to the Shinto beliefs of his readers. To mention a few:

> The further removed from the frenzy of politics, the more exalted is its [the Imperial House] majesty and sanctity, and the greater its power to moderate and restrain ... any loss or infringement of its majesty and sanctity will immediately cast society into darkness.
>
> In changing from one great leader to majority rule ... we must look elsewhere [than law or reason] for an entity possessed of a strange and wondrous power that has a soothing and calming effect.
>
> Try one thing and another, but the only thing that satisfies people in boundless ways and resonates with boundless significance is the effulgent glory of the Imperial House.
>
> From the very beginning, I have upheld the sanctity of the Imperial House and looked to its never-ending continuance ... I thus hope that it will cast its sacred rays (*kōmyō o terashite*) from a place high above politics, ensuring an eternal spring ...

Can these passages with their reverential coloration be interpreted in a secular manner? Perhaps. But the real question is how Fukuzawa intended them and how the readers of the essay saw them in 1888. It is likely that they would have interpreted them, as he intended, in a familiar Shinto light.

The logic of the essay is at odds with its coloration. Fukuzawa begins by asking why the Imperial House is sacred. Many Japanese, he comments, would respond by saying, "the Imperial House is sacred because it is the Imperial House." He dismisses this tautological view offhand; it may have sufficed in the simpler world of the past, but the times are changing and it will not do for the future. Instead, he fastens on the antiquity of the imperial lineage as the true explanation for the people's reverence toward the Imperial House. It is the oldest family in Japan, older than the Fujiwara, older than the oldest temples and shrines, so old that it has no surname. It is connected with Japanese history at every important juncture. The emperor, consequently, has acquired a "sentimental value" that differs from an economic value, which depends on the labor involved.

His argument is weak, but it is the only one that he has. The antiquity of the imperial lineage may help explain why people with only a primary school education still revere it, but it offers absolutely no grounds for the continuation of that sentiment. Two decades had passed since the Restoration, and what was old was mostly in disrepute. Nor does reverence grow out of need. Separated from myth, the argument for the antiquity of the Imperial House carries little weight.

A decade earlier, Fukuzawa had suggested that people believe in the god of the Asakusa Shrine because others believe in it, whereas they care less for the gods of lonely roadside shrines.[17] In "Revering the Emperor," in spite of the coloration, he comes close to telling his readers that there are no rational grounds for venerating the emperor. People believe in the emperor out of habit and because others do.

Toward the end of the essay, Fukuzawa further undermines his already weak argument by adding a generational logic. He states that the present generation accepts tradition and with it the Imperial House, but he predicts that the next, more rational generation will not. As the "feudal ethic" weakens, the new generation of "civilized men" (*bunmei-ryū no danshi*) will not accept the emperor simply because he stands at the end of an ancient lineage. They will be "cold-hearted and drawn to legal theory." To gain their continued support, the emperor must justify his worth. He must be impartial and nonpartisan, and "resolutely stay independent of politics." He must support the arts and sciences and the progress of civilization. In short, the emperor must comport himself like an ideal European monarch. To reinforce this point, Fukuzawa adds, "the same suggestions have long been made by Western intellectuals and duly heeded by their monarchs."

Coloration and logic thus clash. The coloration in the essay appeals to the older generation of Japanese who were still emotionally attached to the emperor and to some degree still lived in a "garden of magic." Fukuzawa tries to win over these readers by suggesting that he shared some of their beliefs. (This contrasts with Bagehot, who wrote for those who like himself could understand the true nature of politics.) Fukuzawa also hopes that his readers will be caught up in the momentum of reading, and unmindful of the coloration, accept his rational conclusions. Fukuzawa wrote to persuade. But, in fact, the underlying logic of his argument differed little from the detached secular views he held during the 1870s.

7

The Future Course of the Diet
(*Kokkai no zento*), 1892

Introduction

"The Future Course of the Diet" presents what might be termed Fukuzawa's third model of history. The first model was slow change over centuries—the model he used in *Conditions in the West*.[1] The second model in 1879 was rapid change over decades caused by technology. But even in 1879, he may have felt that he was giving too much credit to the external factor of Western inventions. So, in 1890, he sketched out a third model that stressed changes during the Tokugawa past. He did not abandon the West; rather, he identified positive features of the era that were like those that had occurred earlier in the West.

The swift transition from Tokugawa to a very different Meiji Japan poses a conundrum: usually, historical changes are less abrupt. Even in revolutions, the interests of key segments of the population are better addressed. This is not to imply that the Tokugawa era was static. Yet, viewed in a comparative perspective, the pace of change seems slower than that of late feudal Europe. Any century of, say, French history saw greater institutional changes, at least in government, than the two and a half centuries of Tokugawa rule. Or so it can be viewed. When the Meiji revolution occurred in 1868, it was as if a coiled spring had been loosed: overnight Japan changed from a feudal land ruled by samurai warriors to a modernizing state.

The changes had two dimensions. One was the confluence of internal forces: political, economic, intellectual, and social, which are standard in all histories. The other was the Western impact from outside: first military and diplomatic, then, overlapping these, scientific, industrial, and cultural. The overthrow of the Tokugawa regime led to the sudden introduction into Japan of a broad range of Western cultural elements. During this period, Japan was more heavily influenced by these elements, we would contend, than any other non-Western land. The establishment of the Diet only twenty-two years after the Restoration illustrates both the power of internal factors and the impact of the Western model.

Fukuzawa wrote "The Future Course of the Diet" in December 1890, less than a month after the opening of the Diet on November 25. His stated purpose is to confute those foreign critics who predicted that Japan's new Diet would fail. Foreigners, he laments, are woefully ignorant of Japan's history.

> Western intellectuals expect our Diet to fail, or in the event that it succeeds, will consider this a wondrous stroke of luck. They know that Japan has adopted a constitutional system of government less than thirty years from the time of the Restoration; in their view, the sudden switch from what they imagine to have been monarchic despotism to constitutional rule is like sowing the seeds of Western civilization on soil barren of the basic elements and expecting them to grow and bear fruit immediately.

Even some Japanese, Fukuzawa writes, are alarmed by the changes that came so suddenly, but if they give some thought to the historical facts, they will quickly shed their doubts about the Diet's future. Foreigners require more information; provided with ample facts, they too will "realize that while Japan is geographically a part of East Asia, its people are not the East Asians they have long imagined, and will clearly understand why the establishment of the Diet is no mere accident and will shed any doubts as to its future."

In point of fact, it is highly doubtful that Fukuzawa wrote the essay to persuade foreigners. True, most foreigners were ignorant of Japanese history. As Fukuzawa indignantly observes in the essay, some foreigners have even placed bets on the outcome of Japan's experiment with electoral politics. But as far as we know, Fukuzawa made no effort to have his essay translated into English, though he could have done so easily. We are forced to conclude that he wrote it for domestic consumption, to reassure his Japanese readers that the future of the Diet would be as "smooth sailing as a ship borne by a gentle tailwind."

Translation

Since the promulgation of the Constitution, in 1889, many of our editorials on politics have dealt, directly or indirectly, with the Imperial Diet. In particular, "The Future Course of the Diet," "Brief Comments on Public Security" (*Chian shōgen*), "The Origins of Difficulties with the National Diet" (*Kokkai nankyoku no yurai*), and "Concerning the Land Tax" (*Chisoron*) have caught our readers' attention. Requests for copies have poured in from all over the country, but with the supply of paper already exhausted, we have been unable to meet the demand. For this reason, we have decided to publish the four editorials together in a book.[2] At a time of intense interest in politics, we will be delighted if the book, in some small way, helps to elevate the tone of public debate.

June 1892
Tokyo Kyōbashi-ku Minaminabe-chō 2 chōme
Jiji Shinpōsha, Journalists

The adoption of a constitutional system of government and establishment of the Diet has been a change of the greatest magnitude, an event unprecedented in Japan, the question of their future of grave concern not only to Japanese but also to foreigners, who have hitherto shown little interest in our affairs. Indeed, rumors from abroad cannot be lightly dismissed. Intellectuals assert that representative government in Western countries has a long history, evolving over centuries of strife and turmoil, prosperity and decline, and that only now has attained its final form, indeed, some countries having yet to reach this state. The Japanese, the people of an East Asian (*tōyō*) country, have been in contact with Western civilization for barely thirty years, and despite the antiquity of their country, they are extremely immature in their understanding of civilization; for these people to switch suddenly from monarchic despotism (*kunshu sensei*) to constitutional government (*kunmin dōchi no rikken*), in which ruler and people share in government, is easier said than done. Some even say that the establishment of the Diet is but a momentary attack of political fever, which can only harm the country. Others, in contrast, say Japan's progress in recent years has been extraordinary, and that inasmuch as the multitude of decisions wondrously expressed the will of the people, the structural reform in government should be seen as yet another wonder. Also, they say that if Japan, by any chance, succeeds in this great undertaking, not only will the country benefit but a new dimension will be added to political discourse among Western scholars, who witness this unexpected achievement and cite it as an event unparalleled in history. Indeed, there are reports that the difficulty in deciding between the two opposing views has led some intellectuals to place bets on whether the Japanese Diet will succeed or fail.

Needless to say, I, too, have no special foresight and find it difficult to predict the future. Nevertheless, I have looked closely into the history of Japanese society and thought about the future of the Diet in light of political and human affairs in the past, and I can affirm with utmost certainty that it will succeed. Before going into this, however, I shall first explain the difference between monarchic despotism and constitutional government. Under despotism, a single ruler takes personal control over all matters and makes all the decisions. His will is law: if he changes his mind, so, too, does the law. Laws are good when the ruler is wise, and bad when he is foolish. People live in peace under a wise ruler, but as soon as a foolish ruler succeeds him, they live in fear of their lives. Since safety and danger are unpredictable, people are in a constant state of apprehension and snatch happiness from moment to moment. Such is the reality of life under monarchic despotism.

Putting aside Europe's past history for the moment, when we look at our neighbors China and Korea, we see a political system of unmitigated despotism under which a ruler's wisdom or folly immediately affects the fate of his subjects. They may enjoy prosperity and happiness for a time, but then be suddenly cast into abject misery. Not without reason did an ancient sage say that in governing a country, the faults of the ruler must first be corrected. By contrast, under a constitutional government, in which ruler and people share political power, ultimate power rests in the Constitution. The citizens dare not defy it, not even the ruler can go against it. Both ruler and subjects have set up a kind of absolute authority, as it were, and having agreed to abide by its sanctions, are mutually restrained from acting as they please. Ruler and subjects are in opposition, and following the scientific laws of nature, if one side expands, the other must contract. Since the two sides are unable to act as they wish, neither side is excessively pleased or excessively aggrieved; a happy medium is reached and balance is maintained in politics.

When the ruler does not possess absolute power and the freedom to act as he pleases, a benevolent ruler is unable to bestow his grace and favor as he likes in the conduct of government, and a tyrannical ruler is unable to give full rein to his cruelty. Under a constitutional system of government, a ruler's wisdom or folly, benevolence or cruelty, has little effect; as a result, his subjects may not enjoy an abundance of royal grace and favor, but neither will they suffer extreme hardship. Pain and pleasure are evened out, and on his own, each individual must secure the well-being and happiness of his family. In Western countries with a constitutional government, a ruler may be wise or ordinary, but this does not particularly affect national power because, over the centuries, this form of government has become customary; the ruler almost unknowingly restrains himself, and the people, for their part, are content to live with no more than their due share of self-rule.

For these reasons, Western intellectuals expect our Diet to fail, or in the event that it succeeds, will consider this a wondrous stroke of luck. They know that Japan has adopted a constitutional system of government less than thirty years from the time of the Restoration; in their view, the sudden switch from what they imagine to have been monarchic despotism to constitutional rule is like sowing the seeds of Western civilization on soil barren of the basic elements and expecting them to grow and bear fruit immediately. Or, it is like an actor in a play who discards one mask for another and suddenly changes from a youth to an old man. They think that the Japanese have approached the matter much too casually and are naturally dubious.

This is only to be expected, for even among the Japanese the principals—those who merely look at the surface of things—are alarmed by the recent course of events. So how can we reproach foreigners, who have so little to lose or gain in the matter! People have every reason to be doubtful, and with this in mind, I have decided to give a brief sketch of the origins of political and human affairs that are distinctly Japanese, and to clarify certain facts that do not appear in traditional histories. Provided with this information, perhaps intellectuals, both in Japan and abroad, will shed their doubts and understand that the establishment of constitutional government and the Diet is no accidental stroke of luck.

I can see why intellectuals in Japan and abroad have misgivings about the future of the Diet and hold a diversity of views. In a word, this is because they feel that human beings cannot tolerate so sudden a change as a switch from an East Asian type of monarchic despotism to a Western type of representative government. In human affairs, there is bound to be a disruption that threatens public peace when something goes from one extreme to another. A human being can tolerate a gradual change from winter to spring, but not an overnight change from midwinter cold to the sweltering heat of midsummer. I fully understand how these intellectuals feel. But was government in Japan in fact a purely East Asian monarchic despotism, with the ruler acting arbitrarily, as defined by the term? And did the Japanese people submit passively to oppressive rule, without ever showing the spirit of self-governance? These questions are surely worthy of study by scholars.

To state my own views, Japan is geographically situated in East Asia and neighbors China and Korea; in politics and human sentiments, however, Japan bears no resemblance to these countries. To all outward appearances, Japan was undeniably a country ruled by a despot, but the more we search into the reality of the situation, the more we find that this was not the case. If the government was despotic in name but not in reality, there must have been an essential factor in governance that explains this. This was none other than the fact that both ruler and people were unable to act as they pleased, each restraining the other, without being fully aware of it, and in time both became accustomed to staying within their respective spheres. The wording of the law may have been simple and incomplete, but custom always trumped the written law and no one dared to go against it.

In short, government in Japan was far from a so-called East Asian despotism. Setting aside Japan's ancient history, this kind of governing custom was nurtured from the time of the founding of the Kamakura bakufu [in the twelfth century] and, especially, during the two hundred and fifty years of Tokugawa rule. And because the custom was firmly rooted, the new government was able to abolish feudal domains soon after the Restoration, put in place a centralized prefectural system, and establish the constitutional government and Diet we have today. Thus, even if the form and structure of the Diet is modeled on the West, its underlying spirit has had a long history and in no sense emerged overnight.

Foreigners claim that the government in Japan was a type of East Asian despotism. We can hardly reproach them since they know nothing about our history. Strangely enough, many Japanese hold the same view, but this, too, is only natural and has its reasons. To explain, the stated aim of the Meiji Restoration was to clarify the relationship between sovereign and subject, but the real aim of the men now in government was to overthrow the Tokugawa bakufu. When an adversary has been defeated, human nature and political expedience compel the victor to point out his opponent's evils and boast of his own achievements. The entire Tokugawa era, from the largest to the smallest features, was summarily condemned, and just when the good points were being concealed and the evils cited, Western civilization was introduced to Japan. This was most fortuitous, for now Western civilization could be used as the criterion to judge the government and customs of the Tokugawa era head on: the arbitrariness of the bakufu, the servility of the people, the oppressive social system, its excesses, its backwardness, its abuses, and so on. Every evil in the human world was attributed to Tokugawa rule, the extreme cases singled out and the virtues of the whole completely ignored, and, in consequence, Japan was seen as a country with a purely East Asian type of despotism.

On behalf of Japan, I must protest this long-standing, false charge. Of course, I am not saying that I yearn for the Tokugawa past and want to turn my back on the present. On the contrary, I have always advocated progress and development, but we cannot understand the new without knowing the old. Today's great event, the opening of the Diet, has not unduly alarmed the people because of

The Future Course of the Diet (Kokkai no zento), 1892

certain political and human factors that date back to our past. So perhaps, a brief explanation of their origins will be of some use to scholars concerned with these issues.

When we look at Japan's history, we note that political power was detached from the Imperial House and entrusted to a succession of military governments. Affairs of the state were the exclusive domain of the military overlord; there was an Imperial House, but it was as if it existed and did not exist. In fact, the Imperial House did exist, for unless the military overlord was given the title of shogun by the emperor, he lacked the authority and respect required to unite the people. The title was essential: even if the shogun had military control over the entire country, he still had to acknowledge the emperor as his superior and accept his own vastly inferior position.

Thus, both the emperor and the military overlord could not act as they wished; the most exalted was not necessarily the strongest, the strongest was never able to aspire to the position of the most exalted. Not only were they mutually constrained from attaining power to their complete satisfaction, as a political strategy to control the people, the military overlord had to look up to the emperor at the same time he looked down at those below him. Even though the Imperial House did not concern itself with politics, the shogun still had to act with self-restraint, and, in particular, think of ways to bring together the hearts and minds of the people. The Hōjō, for example, did not come to power on its own military strength, so successive heads deliberately chose not to ask the emperor for honorary court titles to avoid the envy of others. The fact that the Hōjō had real power and ruled the country effectively in a manner commensurate with its humble rank proves that a balance between political power and family position was maintained and the family was never despotic in ruling the people.

Military government in the past is said to have been despotic, but as we see, their deference to the Imperial House was, to some extent, a moral obligation. The fate of a military house also depended on maintaining the people's allegiance. Surely, this fortunate convergence of circumstances enabled it to practice self-restraint and care for the people, without neglecting affairs of the state. In this, the Imperial House served as a kind of indirect inducement for the military government to refrain from acting like an absolute despot. This is why Japan did not have the likes of Shi Huangdi, the founder of the Qin dynasty, or Emperor Yang of the Sui dynasty. When the ruler on high does not exercise absolute power, there is room for the subjects below to exercise a measure of self-governance as a matter of course. The Japanese should not to be compared with the people in China and Korea, who groan under tyrants and have never known how to act on their own.

Japan entered a new phase during the Tokugawa era, when the principle of the balance of power (*kenryoku heikin*) was upheld not only in politics but also in minor matters concerning commoners. With no one in the entire country excessively proud or dissatisfied, with every aspect of society organized according to the principle of the golden mean, the people enjoyed two hundred and fifty years of unbroken peace, and, by coincidence, the same principle served to encourage competition in the literary and military arts as well as in a multitude of crafts and skills. Along with the advance in culture, the people's sense of self-governance also grew apace and led to the realization that a country did not necessarily have to be ruled by a despotic government. Beyond a doubt, these factors dating back to the past, and, more particularly, to the Tokugawa era, prepared the ground for the establishment of the Diet barely twenty-three years after the Meiji Restoration.

The history of the world is old, and upheavals [are] more frequent than periods of peace. Japan under Tokugawa rule was the sole exception. A country of thirty million lived in peace for two hundred and fifty years; there was no one brandishing a dagger, and people in every stratum of society kept to their station in life and at the same time worked to advance culture. What the Tokugawa accomplished is unmatched in the world, and if this owes to the careful forethought of the dynastic founder Ieyasu, he must be seen not merely as a man of Japan but a hero whose achievements are without equal in world history. Whether or not Ieyasu alone deserves all the credit, the results of his achievements did not disappear with the downfall of the Tokugawa bakufu, for, with the changing times and new opportunities for action, it has become increasingly clear that his legacy has helped ease the way for the establishment of the Diet.

To explain what I mean by the balance of power during the Tokugawa era, I shall quote from a set of eighteen statutes that Ieyasu drew up, in Genna 1 [1615], soon after he unified the country. The statutes, which were posted in the Shishiiden Hall of the Imperial Palace in Kyoto, stated, among other things, that he, the shogun, had control over the three princely and five regent houses, all the nobles and daimyo, and that he would not report to the Imperial House on matters of government and would bear sole responsibility for the peace of the country and any military disturbance that might occur. The document closed as follows:

> With fear and trepidation, I present the eighteen statutes to His Imperial Majesty.
> In compliance with imperial orders, these statutes make clear the reasons the

military house should take charge of the government and maintain the peace of the country. I shall make bold to post them in the Shishiiden Hall. I hereby comply with imperial orders.

First Year of Genna.

Ryōin Bettō. Ieyasu seal.[3]

By force of intelligence and courage, Ieyasu had subjugated rival warlords and gathered all power into his hands. He feared no one in the country, yet, to his regret, he was obliged to put himself in the position of a subject vis-à-vis the Kyoto Imperial Court. This is precisely what I meant when I said earlier that the strongest was not necessarily the highest and that even the shogun's power was checked by the Imperial House and unable to reach its fullest expression. This relationship is the first example of the balance of power. The same principle applied to the relationship between court nobles and daimyo: nobles were high in status but low in income, while daimyo were lower in status but higher in income.

In China and Korea, the heads of past governments have frequently been chosen from the royal family or from maternal relatives. For example, in China, the present government is controlled by members of the royal family, and in Korea, by the queen's relatives. Their lineage is lofty to begin with, and when one adds to this the power that comes with political office, the heads of government may be satisfied to their hearts' content, but more often than not, the custom gives rise to abuse and insurrection. In contrast, the Tokugawa set up a system whereby men of low rank were appointed to the highest positions in government, and important daimyo and relatives of the shogun were not allowed to participate in bakufu affairs. This was clearly spelled out in the "One Hundred Statutes to be Stored at Kunōzan," the last will and testament written by Ieyasu.[4]

> There are many hereditary (*fudai*) vassals, but among these, the houses which have served me from the time I was based in Mikawa Province are Torii, Itakura, Ōkubo, Toda, Tsuchiya, Honda, Sakakibara, Ishikawa, Kuze, Abe, and Katō. Their descendants are to be chosen on the basis of talent to assist the shogun in government affairs and given the title of senior councilor. No matter how superior they may be, men from "outside" domains are not to be appointed to government office.[5]

All the daimyo houses listed by Ieyasu are of lower rank, with only a few having domains larger than 100,000 *koku*. They were popularly known as the "office-holding houses," and descendants who showed ability were always appointed senior councilors. In the years that followed, samurai from other families were also appointed, but they were usually from daimyo houses with assessed revenues ranging, at most, from 50,000 or 60,000 to 100,000 *koku*. With the exception of Ii [Naosuke] and Sakai [Tadatsumi], who were appointed great councilor (*tairō*), no one from a large domain was ever named to that office.

Politically, senior councilors (*rōjū*) wielded unlimited power over the daimyo and bannermen (*hatamoto*); no one was exempt from their firm control, not even daimyo related to the Tokugawa House or those with large domains. But since they came from domains no larger than 60,000 or 70,000 *koku*, they were not the equals of the so-called eighteen great domains in terms of military might. Also, in the eyes of the three collateral houses of Owari, Kii, and Mito, the lineage of the senior councilors was no more distinguished than that of their own retainers. Thus, when their actions were restrained by the senior councilors, it was as if the masters were following the orders of their retainers.

Nevertheless, so great was the force of law and custom that no one challenged the system. Daimyo with large domains and military forces might have considered the senior councilors their inferiors, but not for a moment could they infringe on their political authority. By virtue of their political power, the senior councilors controlled the daimyo, as a grown-up would a child, but in military strength and status, they were vastly inferior and could never hope to approach them. Each side was both strong and weak, satisfied and not satisfied, and restricted as they were by bakufu regulations, neither side could act high-handedly. In sum, an intricate balance of power was put in place. A configuration of this kind would have never occurred to the Chinese or Koreans; in East Asia, Tokugawa Ieyasu alone had thought of the idea.

During the first years of the Tokugawa era, arable land was less extensive than it is now, and the rice yield was correspondingly small. One statute in the aforementioned "One Hundred Statutes" reads: "Of the total amount of 28,190,000 *koku* of fiefs (*chigyō*) in Japan, 20,000,000 shall be given to loyal daimyo and 8,190,000 shall be directly controlled by the bakufu." In other words, the country was divided into three parts, with the Tokugawa bakufu holding roughly one-third and the remaining two-thirds allotted to three hundred daimyo. Treated as one body, the daimyo might be expected to compete with one another for a greater share of power, but here, too, the principle of balance of power worked to eliminate undue competition. For instance, in one corner of western Kyushu, Higo, an important domain, was placed next to Satsuma, a strong domain; Hizen and Chikuzen were placed next to each other, with Kurume close by. [In western Honshū] Geishū [Aki] was placed to the east of Chōshū, and Awa next to Tosa. Another strategy was to split a domain into two separate domains, as with Bizen and Inaba, Tsuyama and Echizen, Sanuki and Mito, Uwajima and Sendai, Oshi and Nakatsu. These daimyo houses were kin and bore the same name, but having been divided, each could claim to be the main branch and disagree on other internal matters as well. The conflict between the daimyo houses in Tsugaru and Nanbe in northwest Honshū was particularly acrimonious.

Besides relocating domains, the bakufu implicitly exerted further control by placing the domains of Tokugawa relatives in strategic areas and interspersing territories under its direct control throughout the country; nothing was left to chance. Even the placement of samurai residences in Edo was subject to strict rules; one has only to look at an old map of the city to see the meticulous precautions that were taken.

Daimyo in Japan were not without ambition, but strategically placed to keep a close watch on each other, they were in effect powerless. Because of this mutual restraint, the bakufu did not need a particularly powerful military; it merely had to supervise a "self-propelling machine" (*jidōki*). In internal organization, too, the bakufu applied the principle of balance of power. Senior councilors held the ultimate power; even junior councilors (*wakadoshiyori*), the next rank down, were not allowed to interfere. Yet, inspectors (*metsuke*), who reported to junior councilors but not to senior councilors, had the right to bring charges against the senior councilors. Not only that, but when inspectors made a joint appeal directly to the shogun, the senior councilor in question could be removed from his post. Working under the inspectors were the traveling inspectors (*kachimetsuke*), and under these, the inspectors of commoners (*kobitometsuke*). Although the latter were minor functionaries subordinate to the traveling inspectors, they had the right to bypass their immediate superiors and appeal directly to the *metsuke* inspectors to impeach them. Regional intendants (*daikan*), who supervised bakufu territories, and *yoriki* and *dōshin*, policemen who served the city magistrates, could secretly augment their income and live beyond their station in life, but in the world of officialdom, they were of extremely low rank and had little prestige. An intendant oversaw bakufu lands amounting to tens of thousands of *koku*, but once he returned to Edo, he paled into insignificance. In an audience with the superintendents of finance (*kanjō bugyō*), for instance, he had to behave like a retainer in the presence of his master. *Yoriki* and *dōshin* who were assigned to the Great Guard unit (*ōbangumi*) and Body Guard unit (*shoinbangumi*) had no perquisites and were poor, but in social status they belonged to the higher echelons of town officials and accordingly took pride in this distinction. Many other similar examples can be found in bakufu organizations. Indeed, the more one looks the more one is impressed by the thoroughness with which the principle of balance of power was maintained.[6]

The domains followed the bakufu's example, and apart from minor differences, organized their government on the same principle. Thus, over the course of several hundred years, the principle of one element counterbalancing the other became ingrained in the minds of the Japanese, and as this idea was passed on from generation to generation, everyone knew that in politics, full and limitless satisfaction did not exist. This is probably what is meant by the popular saying, "The moon can be dimmed by a passing cloud and flowers scattered by the wind," or the poem that speaks of "flowers in the wind and evening rain."

To turn from the internal organization of the bakufu to relations between samurai and commoners, the upper ranks of samurai were extremely powerful and occupied a status high above commoners, as if they were a race apart. In matters concerning commerce and the production of goods, however, they had no say at all. For example, the yearly finances of daimyo domains were largely entrusted to rich merchants in cities (notably Osaka), and when daimyo needed ready cash, they borrowed from these merchants and repaid the loan with domain products (rice, in nine out of ten cases). Merchants not only received interest on the loan, but also had total control over the sale of the rice, the rate of exchange for money remitted to Edo, and the final market price. Brooking no interference from the government, they reaped sizable profits. If a daimyo took advantage of his political power and reneged on his payment, one would expect the merchant to have no recourse. But rich merchants formed a close-knit group, and if the unscrupulous daimyo asked another merchant for a further loan, he would be refused out of hand. In matters concerning money, even a powerful daimyo had to follow rules imposed by merchants. I am quite sure the elderly among us remember how daimyo in the Kansai area treated Osaka merchants with respect, as they would a samurai, and at times even granted them yearly rice stipends (*fuchimai*).

As for samurai of lower rank, they had to make do with their hereditary stipends and were strictly forbidden from engaging in trade. Their houses were tax-exempt, but they were not allowed to lend the premises to tradesmen to conduct business. Poorer samurai occasionally engaged in handicrafts and similar work at home, but since this was done in private, they were helpless when a merchant took all the profits. A samurai's true duty lay in the pursuit of the literary and military arts; the precept to "know shame and not seek monetary gain" had been taught for generations and had become their second nature. If a samurai secretly dealt in commercial goods, borrowed or loaned money, he was immediately ostracized by his fellow samurai. In extreme cases, a samurai would be ashamed of any wealth he had and boast that he was poor.

One might think a merchant would envy a samurai for his status and honor, but he secretly pitied him for his penury, his rigid and restricted way of life, and avoided any contact. In brief, in Japanese society, the poor had high status and the wealthy low status. Wealth did not lead to high status, high status did not stave off poverty. Rich or poor, highborn or lowly, everything evened out, with no one completely satisfied and no one completely dissatisfied.

The laws decreed by the Tokugawa were unquestionably despotic in nature. But they pertained solely to those aspects of the central government that affected its survival, such as barrier stations in strategic sites, limits on building castles in the domains, forced residence of daimyo families in Edo, and the ban on transporting arms into Edo. These regulations concerning public security were extremely stringent, and anyone committing a crime against the state was severely punished. In contrast, laws pertaining to regional systems and customs were exceedingly lenient. If someone tried to evade the officials at barrier stations, he was not detained so long as he did nothing particularly harmful. As for offenses like gambling, prostitution, sexual misconduct, adultery, brawling, verbal disputes, indecent behavior, thievery, fraud, bribery, and the like, the law was as expansive as the ocean. Letting the ebb and flow of the mundane world take its course, seeing and yet not seeing, the government enforced the law in only the most flagrant cases. Law during the Tokugawa era was like a person who has a document attesting to a loan but rarely demands payment. A literal interpretation of the law would have forbidden this and prohibited that; in actuality, minor offenders were left to go unpunished, which was much the same as borrowing money without being asked to return the loan. However, once a crime was judged to imperil the public peace or infringe on bakufu authority, the offender was swiftly and mercilessly punished according to the "Honorable Laws."

From the viewpoint of commoners, a literal interpretation of bakufu law may have been intimidating, but in fact they had nothing to fear and could freely make their way in the world without worrying about whether they would lose their life or possessions. To be sure, during the Tokugawa era, there were evils like extortionate taxes, mandatory loans, and bribes openly demanded by government officials. Samurai were said to kill commoners with impunity, and foreigners who heard of this assumed that life and property were unprotected in Japan. But this is to look at only one aspect of things, to pick out a single flaw and ignore the virtues of the whole. Past or present, has there ever been a government entirely innocent of bribery? Indeed, one could say that Japan was unique in the relative absence of bribery and indifference to monetary gain, both in the government and the country at large. Despite the growing demands of more complex human affairs, this holds true even today, to say nothing of the Tokugawa past! There may have been venal officials in the lower ranks of the bakufu, but if we examine conditions in the domains, we will find that most of the rough-hewn and guileless samurai were scarcely aware of what bribery entailed. The accusations of mandatory loans, too, are no more than petty arguments fashioned by immature scholars. The greater part of loans was requisitioned to succor the poor, which was never the government's duty to begin with, and, on balance, government coffers suffered and people gained. In the domains, too, the situation was much the same. As for samurai killing commoners because of disrespectful behavior, this was officially permitted. To quote again from the "One Hundred Statutes":

> Samurai are the presiding officials of the four classes. Peasants, artisans, tradesmen, and their ilk must not be disrespectful toward samurai. A disrespectful person is a rude and impudent boor. A samurai may put to death anyone guilty of rude behavior. Among samurai, too, distinctions exist between direct and rear vassals, superior and subordinate, master and retainer. The rule regarding rude behavior applies to them as well.

A samurai thus had the prerogative to kill a commoner, as did a samurai of higher rank vis-à-vis one of lower rank. The wording of the statute strikes fear in our hearts, but were many commoners actually cut down for no reason? Emphatically no. To prove my point, I shall refer to a domain I happen to know quite well. The domain, with an assessed holding of 100,000 *koku*, had one thousand five hundred samurai families. Counting household heads, retired men, second and third sons, those entitled to bear swords came to about three thousand. These samurai dealt with farmers, artisans, and tradesmen on a daily basis, but during the two hundred and fifty-three years of Tokugawa rule, from 1614 to 1867, there was only one instance of a samurai killing a commoner for disrespectful behavior.[7] Multiply three thousand by two hundred and fifty-three, and we arrive at a ratio of one samurai out of seven hundred and fifty-nine thousand striking down a commoner, a truly negligible figure. Give or take a little, I daresay the same ratio obtained in other domains. Forbearance was a defining characteristic of Japanese samurai; taught by parents and constantly reminded by elders, the injunction never to draw a sword without cause was bred into their bones. The law permitted a samurai to kill a commoner, but social custom proved more powerful, and restrained reckless and violent behavior.

In light of what I have said thus far, the assertion that Japanese during the Tokugawa era lived under despotic rule and were controlled by despotic laws is completely unfounded. No despot ruled from on high, and despotic laws were applied only in the most egregious cases. The majority of people lived under the law but knew nothing about it; as long as the government did not misuse the so-called Honorable Laws, there was no fear of being ensnared in its web; both high and low could trust to ordinary human nature (**common sense**) and live free from worry.

To be sure, during the two hundred and fifty-three years of Tokugawa rule, there were repressive regulations and instances of high-handed behavior by officials. But an occasional stain in one spot does not sully the whole. When the good is weighed against the bad and the honest against the corrupt, we find that, on average, the founding principles of the government stayed intact. Furthermore, during the same era, the civil and military arts were encouraged and the majority of Japanese pursued their material interests unhampered by arbitrary laws. They were also aware that the body of existing laws was merely a formality and in no way affected their well-being. And as this truth was deeply impressed on the minds of the people, from high to low, respecting the law and not trifling with it became a custom and eventually served as an essential factor in building the new Japan. I am quite certain that no one will disagree with my assertion that this owes to the merits and virtues of the Tokugawa system of government.

Local systems during the same era differed from domain to domain, but in general, people were allowed to handle local affairs on their own, with little interference from the government. As stated in the "One Hundred Statutes":

> One: Even if something is found to be in error, if it has been in place for the last fifty years, it must not be changed.
>
> Two: Some lowly commoners in counties, villages, and hamlets have long-standing associations with their place of residence. They are to be appointed to office. Itinerants who have come from afar are not to be appointed. This ruling is to be conveyed to administrators of fief lands, governors of provinces, lords of castles, lesser officials, and needless to say, bakufu intendants.

Clearly, old customs and practices were to be preserved and villagers expected to manage local affairs.

County and village officials were appointed by commoners or domain officials and in keeping with local custom. In some areas, the residing bakufu intendant selected the headman (*shōya*) from a list of three men submitted by the villagers. (This is no different from the way the House Speaker of the Diet is chosen today.) The titles of village officials differed from area to area: *shōya, ōjōya, nanushi, toshiyori, kumigashira, ginmiyaku, hyakushō sōdai,* and so on. Their duties also differed, but all were designated village officials and their salaries paid by the villagers. The officials mediated between the villagers and domain government, attended to the collection of yearly taxes, and took responsibility for public works such as building or repairing roads and bridges. (In many cases, villagers were ordered to work without pay.) Expenses were borne by villagers. In Edo, too, townsmen or samurai households were held responsible for building and repairing the roads and bridges in their ward. Of the many bridges scattered throughout the city, twenty-six surrounding Edo Castle and three spanning the Ōkawa River were handled by the superintendents (*sakuji bugyō*) and commissioners of public works (*kobushin bugyō*), one hundred and twenty by city magistrates, and the rest by local townsmen.

In each village, neighborhoods were organized into units of five households (*gonin-gumi*). Units were not always limited to five; at times, there were as many as seven or ten. The members of each unit formed a tightly knit group and helped one another at weddings, funerals, festivals, and in emergencies like fires, floods, and illness; in their daily association, they were more like close kin. Sharing the expenses incurred on these occasions meant that villagers had a kind of insurance to deal with the uncertainties of daily life. Institutions like hospitals and poorhouses did not exist in Japan at the time, but of the various reasons for the relative absence of grinding poverty among the people, the most significant was the existence of these five-household units. In truth, the units served as the basis for commoner self-governance and as such were accorded the greatest importance by the bakufu.

New laws introduced during the Kansei year period [1789–1800] greatly reduced expenditures in Edo, and each year 70 percent of the surplus money was deposited at an office that handled emergency funds. The "Seventy-percent Fund," as it was called, was used to help the city poor and victims of fires, floods, and other unforeseen disasters. The office also collected interest on the loans it made, owned rice granaries, and rented out substantial pieces of land. It was supervised by government officials but financially independent and given complete control over the use of the money. By the middle of the Keiō year period [1865–8], the office had actually accumulated as much as 2,700,000 *ryō*, an enormous sum. Because of an unstable political situation, the bakufu was suffering huge financial losses at the time, but committed to the principle of local self-governance, it did not touch the money even once, proof enough that the government was not despotic. In contrast to this, the leaders of the Restoration, who accused the bakufu of oppression and decried its despotic rule, behaved shamefully: they no sooner entered Edo than they stripped the residents of their right to self-governance, seized the aforementioned money, and let two or three officials squander it as they pleased. They ought to have blushed with shame vis-à-vis the deposed bakufu.

During the same era, each town and village maintained a band of guards to watch for fires and thieves. In emergencies, the head or hired help of a household assisted the guards in patrolling the neighborhood at night. All these preventive measures were left to the people, relieving government officials of extra work and expenses. In regard to the publication of books, scholars were required by law to submit their writings to the Shōheikō, the highest seat of learning in the government. Novels and plays such as Takizawa Bakin's *The Lives of Eight Heroes* and Tamenaga Shunsui's *The Plum Calendar*, colored woodblock prints, and the like were of no interest to the government and so were merely inspected by city magistrates. Another example of self-governance was the handling of court cases. As noted earlier, village officials mediated between commoners and the domain government. One of their duties was to handle appeals submitted by villagers. In general, these were amicably resolved, without resorting to formal procedures. The plaintiff usually deferred to village officials and accepted their decisions, thus sparing the courts extra work and making for convenience all around. Aside from minor differences, this was the custom throughout the country, with the spirit of self-governance prevailing in every town and village in Japan.

The following is from an essay about Edo city magistrates written by my friend Komiyama Yasusuke:

> Under the old bakufu, residents of Edo naturally depended on the judgment of the city magistrates in matters concerning their welfare, but they were on familiar terms with their commoner ward head (*nanushi*) and felt much closer to him. The system at the time was much like self-rule, with the ward head bearing responsibility for all the affairs in his ward. For example, when a written appeal was rejected (Commoners were allowed to submit appeals in a box at the city magistrate's office, that is to say, the court, and when an appeal was rejected, a note to that effect was written on the back of the appeal.), a notice on the back of the appeal would instruct the ward head and household head (the plaintiff) to discuss the matter with members of his five-household unit, and in the event of an impasse, appear in court on the seventh day. A public notice issued by one city magistrate, in the second month of Kyōhō 2 [1717], contains instructions

that individual appeals concerning verbal fights, drunken behavior, arguments between parent and child or husband and wife, disagreements between servant and employer, are to be handled by the household head and ward head, and that only in unresolved cases are the plaintiff and defendant to appear in court. Also, if the parties feel the household head and ward head have been unreasonable, they may make an appeal. This public notice reflects the general practice at the time. The ward head conducted business in the front hall, or *genkan* of his residence, and was popularly known as the "*Genkan*." Disputes and altercations in the ward were all handled in the hall. Anyone guilty of misconduct was duly admonished, and depending on the circumstances, miscreants were sent to court at an appropriate time. Over the years, these practices served as precedents, and out of respect for the ward head, not many went against his decisions. The head would occasionally take advantage of his position and make improper demands on ward residents, but in most cases, he was punished. In Edo, the ward head was elected by household heads and confirmed by government officials. Because he was entrusted with public matters, he was known as the "entrusted ward official (*otanomi nanushi*)."

The system of local self-governance was distinctive to Japan and long familiar to the people. The Restoration, however, destroyed everything at one stroke, and the old system of self-governance was affected to some degree. People were temporarily at a loss, but then a new system of local government was instituted, with the express purpose of reinforcing the base of popular self-governance. It was as if a Japanese enamored of things Western decided to tear down his old-fashioned Japanese-style house, but worried lest a purely Western house prove uncomfortable and a Japanese-style house inconvenient, decided to build one that combined Western and Japanese features. The system of self-rule during the Tokugawa era suited a monarchic government but not a constitutional government; naturally, adjustments had to be made, but old or new, self-rule is self-rule. And it is precisely because the habit of self-rule was ingrained in the people that the new system functions smoothly and suits constitutional government admirably. In the human world, something cannot be created out of nothing; only the form can change. I thus earnestly hope that those in power, together with those who established the present system of local government, do not complacently think that they have created something anew, but will proceed with uttermost circumspection in replacing the old for the new.

As noted earlier, during the Tokugawa era, rulers from shogun to local daimyo lived under a system based on the balance of power and were unable to act to their full satisfaction like despots. Not only that, but Ieyasu, who honored Confucianism and believed in Buddhism but did not necessarily follow their teachings, drew up a set of house rules that he himself followed: he exhorted members to be loyal to the emperor, filial to parents, faithful to principles, to know what it is to feel shame, and to practice self-restraint. He particularly emphasized self-restraint, a principle that would prove distinctive to the Tokugawa family; in the passages dealing with morals in his many writings, he unfailingly stressed the importance of "overcoming the self and knowing contentment." Indeed, the first statute in the first fascicle of the "One Hundred Statutes" stated: "Before all else, shun what pleases you and strive to do what displeases you." Samurai from Mikawa were widely respected and feared at the time, but their singular character owed entirely to Ieyasu's moral example and training.[8] A great many heroes and brave men emerged at the end of the period of Warring States, but it was Ieyasu alone who won the staunch allegiance of his followers though they had little hope of reward. They would subsequently serve as faithful retainers of the Tokugawa, not solely because they were awed by Ieyasu's military prowess but because, just as the disciples of Confucius esteemed their master, they admired Ieyasu's moral stature.

Japanese samurai have long been known in the world for their rough and simple ways and their strong sense of honor. The warrior ethos was especially encouraged and nurtured during the Tokugawa era. In this respect, it is no exaggeration to say that Ieyasu was not only the founder of a government but the spiritual leader in revitalizing the country's social and moral climate. Successive generations of shogun and daimyo followed the injunctions and teachings of this great spiritual and military leader; despite holding positions of unchallenged power, they did not dare abuse their office. In China, by contrast, many rulers let their favorites run the government at will, concubines brought the country to ruin, emperors ordered the execution of a minister in a fit of rage, drank to excess, and extorted money from their subjects. A ruler's single-minded determination can raise or ruin the country, but nothing of the sort occurred in the entire course of the Tokugawa era. On occasion, shogun and daimyo had their favorite retainers and concubines, but these were no more than passing diversions. We never hear of the government being disrupted on this account, still less of retainers being wantonly killed or commoners being robbed of their possessions. As a people, the Japanese would not have permitted such a thing. If we looked closely enough, we might find that over the course of two hundred and fifty odd years, some of the three hundred daimyo indulged in wrongful behavior, but compared with China, the harm was inconsequential.

In sum, whether shogun or daimyo, rulers in Japan were despots in name only and unable to exercise arbitrary rule. The rare tyrant confined his wayward behavior and taste for luxury to his personal life and never let this interfere with the conduct of government. Also, since despotism was politically impracticable, a ruler's intelligence or lack thereof had little influence on government. A wise ruler did not necessarily make for good government; a feeble-minded ruler did not necessarily exclude effective government. Among the fifteen shogun of the Tokugawa family, Ieyasu, the first, Iemitsu, the third, and Yoshimune, the eighth, were unquestionably able, with many praiseworthy achievements. Of the rest, on average, half were intelligent, the other half, or even more, were feeble-minded and self-indulgent. Despite this, politics remained the same throughout the period, with no appreciable change. In other words, a stupid ruler was unable to give full rein to his foolish and capricious behavior in politics, thus clearly proving that despotism was more apparent than real.

What was true of the central government was true of domain governments: a daimyo could be intelligent and his government inert and ineffective; conversely, a daimyo could be feeble-minded and his government active and effective. It might seem strange that a daimyo and his government bore little relation to each another, but this did not matter since the actual power was held by the elders, who in turn were implicitly restrained by the general opinion of samurai in the domain. It was as if the elders entrusted by the daimyo to run the government were accountable to domain samurai; for every official decision, good or bad, they were the ones who were blamed or praised, never the daimyo. At times, a wise daimyo would work closely with his capable councilors and put domain affairs in good order, but this was exceedingly rare; over the years this occurred on an average of one time out of ten million and so was hardly typical. The Japanese people honored and revered their feudal lord not for political reasons, but because they genuinely felt that way and knew that his subordinates ran the government. Circumstances differ, of course, but the situation is much the same in Britain, where the people deeply respect and honor the royal family, but know beyond all doubt that the real power of government rests with the House of Commons.

I shall mention yet another curious fact about feudal rulers in Japan. Shogun and daimyo alike led lives of utmost refinement and were treated in every way with great courtesy. This became more pronounced during the two hundred and fifty years of Tokugawa rule and gradually led to the neglect of their education and a tendency on their part to shun the world and stay within the quiet confines of their residences. In extreme cases, they were not allowed to handle money, some actually ignorant of what it was. These so-called princely lords of the palace, who seemed to belong to a different species, were utterly incapable of talking about ordinary human affairs.

Meanwhile, middle and lower-ranking samurai in the domains were developing the mental and physical traits inherited from their forebears and making progress by the day. This was especially true from the Genna year period [1616–24], when, finally relieved of fighting wars, they were able to pursue scholarly interests. During the years from the Genroku year period [1688–1703] to the end of Tokugawa rule, book learning in Japan reached close to its peak: beginning in the Hōreki year period [1751–64], many samurai, no longer content to limit their studies to Chinese learning, began reading Dutch books and taught and discussed Western medicine and science. Instead of talking only about the military arts, they discussed politics, edited history texts, and wrote books on political economy, for the most part without the help of Buddhist clergy. Writing on these subjects flourished as never before during these years. On the one hand, weak and inept shogun and daimyo were unable to exercise personal control over the government and were in fact disinclined to do so; on the other hand, samurai were accumulating political experience and becoming more adept at analyzing politics. Japan was poised for political change; it was only a matter of waiting for the right moment.

The opening of Japan presented the samurai with the right opportunity to act; without question, this marked the beginning of political change in the country. What followed, however, was nothing so simple as fervid calls for "revering the emperor and expelling the barbarians." The samurai took advantage of the momentous turn of events to further their long-held aims; the call for expelling foreigners was only a temporary expedient. They, of course, knew only too well about incompetent feudal rulers and detested autocratic rule. But old customs die hard; more particularly, the moral duty to observe the distinction between superior and subordinate was engraved in the minds of the Japanese, so the samurai accordingly mapped out a plan: they would first invoke the sanctity of the Imperial House, and then, acting in the name of their respective domains, rally the nation to "revere the emperor and expel the barbarians," and decisively bring down the bakufu.

The samurai succeeded in overthrowing the bakufu, but they had no intention of founding a new bakufu since they knew that feudal rulers were not to be trusted; they were confident that they possessed the skills and experience to govern the country. They had also become acquainted with conditions in the civilized countries of the West, listened to Westerners, read their books, and discovered that a country did not have to be ruled by an absolute monarchy: there existed a form of government in which ruler and people shared political power and an elective assembly that represented the will of the people. Having honed their political skills and learned of political practices in Western countries, these samurai were not only loath to establish another bakufu and work under a despotic government, but the thought had never occurred to them. They eagerly embraced the idea of a Western-style deliberative assembly, abandoned their frenzied calls to expel foreigners, and forthwith adopted a policy of opening the country and promoting progress and reform.

[In April, 1868,] immediately after the restoration of imperial rule, the samurai issued the Charter Oath in the emperor's name. One of the five guidelines in the Oath stated, "Deliberative assemblies are to be established and all matters of state decided by popular discussion." The guideline reflected the prevailing trend in the political world and was by no means accidental. (By then, information on Western medicine, science, and military arts had become available in translations from Dutch works. A book entitled *Conditions in the West* had also been published. This was a survey of governments and human affairs in Western countries, essentially a record of what the author heard from Americans and Britons, and partial translations of books published in their countries. It contained information that was completely new to the Japanese and was read by virtually everyone in the political world. Sales, including pirated editions, reached more than one hundred and fifty thousand. The same author published another book entitled *An Encouragement to Learning*. Consisting of seventeen chapters, this work sold more than one million copies. The popularity of the two books reflects the keen interest in Western civilization at the time.) From today's perspective, the developments I have described seem unplanned and yet inevitable. Indeed, many admit to having acted without really knowing why. Events had swept over Japan like a swiftly flowing river, the people carried along willy-nilly, bobbing up and down like so many specks of dust.

The forces for progress and reform were now at the peak of power; the old feudal system had no chance of surviving. The new government ordered the abolition of domains and overnight unified all three hundred. The establishment of a firm and flawless foundation for the government of the great nation of Japan was an achievement of enormous significance, conclusive proof that samurai activists were not seeking to expel foreigners or to punish the bakufu. They had overthrown the bakufu not because they opposed the institution as such, but because they opposed the system of monarchic despotism it represented. This is borne out by the fact that when they abolished the domains, they treated the culpable House of Tokugawa in the same way that they treated the domains commended for their role in its overthrow. All the domains suffered the same fate; guilt or merit was not ascribed to a particular house or individual;

The Future Course of the Diet (Kokkai no zento), 1892

the political enemy of the new Japan created by samurai was none other than monarchic despotism.

There is a letter written by Saigō Takamori, on the nineteenth day of the seventh month, early in the Meiji era. Addressed to his friend Katsura Shirō, the letter reveals the great resolve of the samurai as they took up their tasks at the time.

> The mornings and nights have taken on an autumnal cool. I rejoice that you continue to be in the best of health. I am happy to report that the situation in the country has improved markedly. The domains that hitherto wavered have finally bestirred themselves, and beginning with Owari, five or six domains, including Awa and Inaba, have submitted memorials [to return domain registers]. Despite minor differences, they have even urged the government to abolish domains and establish a centralized prefectural system. In fact, many domains to the east of western Honshū have given every indication that they are ready to adopt the form and structure of a prefecture (*gunken no teisai*). The daimyo of Chōshū has already resigned from his post as governor and is said to have drafted a letter expressing his wish to become a commoner. At this point, if [Satsuma, Chōshū, Tosa, and Higo,] the four domains which took the initiative to return domain registers, do not relinquish their domains, they will not only be ridiculed by everyone in country but be seen as deceiving the imperial court. The country could well be thrown into confusion, and concerned men will start arguing among themselves. To add to this, foreigners are evidently saying that Japan is a country where the emperor's authority is not firmly established, the government fragmented, and that nothing resembling a clearly defined national polity exists. At a time when Japan must take an assertive stance against the nations of the world but is powerless to do so, the government must resolutely issue orders to revive the old prefecture and county system (*gunken seido*). Both our families have been indebted to the House of Shimazu for several hundred years, and seeing our domain abolished will cause us great pain, but given the forces at work in society, a centralized prefectural system will inevitably be established within the next ten years. This turn of events is beyond human control. Our domain took the lead in returning domain registers, and so drew the attention of the entire country. But if we start arguing now, the whole purpose of overthrowing the bakufu on behalf of the emperor will not be fully achieved. More particularly, the benefits likely to accrue from no longer allowing samurai to own land—which they have been permitted to do since [Minamoto] Yoritomo's time—will be rendered meaningless. There should be no objection to this, but if the old system under the bakufu is discarded all at once, trouble may break out in some of the domains. But please rest assured that the imperial court is determined to stand firm and is ready to use military might to abolish domains. Given the

trends of the times, there is no justification for private ownership of domain lands. While there is no immediate threat of strong opposition, we have no way of knowing what kind of conflict will ensue if we make the wrong move. I have now given you a brief description of the present situation. I shall keep you informed. Written in haste, I am humbly yours,

Saigō Kichinosuke

Nineteenth day of the seventh month

To Katsura Shirō[9]

Saigō's letter elucidates the true intent of the Restoration and makes abundantly clear that the abolition of domains, the establishment of a centralized prefectural system, and the principle of equal human rights lay at its very heart, and that the leaders were determined to abolish the old system of absolute monarchy even if it meant displacing the age-old principle of moral obligation binding lord and retainer.

During the following decades, all manner of changes occurred: retainers of the Chōshū daimyo, who had been effusively praised by Saigō for his decision to resign from the post of governor and assume commoner status, along with the samurai from other domains who had played an important role in the Restoration, were appointed to the new nobility. Their pride and joy in their elevated status was shameful, an affront to Saigō, and to some measure ran counter to the spirit of the Restoration. The creation of a class of new nobles was as meaningless as child's play, a sop to male vanity; one can only hope that the members will reflect upon this and eventually have a change of heart. In political discussions, too, samurai were divided between those who favored a popular assembly and those who opposed it. At times, things seemed to go forward, at times, to go backward. If we look at only one aspect of evolving developments, we are often baffled, but taken together the perturbations were but momentary ripples on the water's surface. Nothing could stop the course of events: the Diet was established as promised and the spirit of the Restoration given concrete form.

It should come as no surprise then that the Diet is nothing less than the embodiment of the spirit of the Restoration. People point out that parliaments in the West were mainly formed under popular pressure and not by peaceful means, whereas in Japan alone, the Diet was established not only amidst peace and harmony between people and government but was actually initiated by the government. Some find this strange, even suspect, while others secretly take pride in what they consider a clever sleight of hand. Still more dubious are foreigners, who have no particular interest in our country and fail to examine the circumstances leading to the Diet. This is perfectly understandable, but if they took the trouble to look into the history of Japanese politics—what I have just described—perhaps their doubts will be dispelled. The Japanese people are not lukewarm about politics; in changing from monarchic despotism to participatory government, some turbulence is to be expected. East or West, human nature is the same, but in Japan, the turbulence that would normally accompany the founding of a national assembly occurred at the time of the Restoration and is already a thing of the past. As I explained earlier, the Restoration was not simply a movement to overthrow the Tokugawa bakufu but also an effort to root out monarchic despotism. For this reason, men took up arms and shed blood. A war had been fought, and it was because of the war that samurai, that is to say, the Japanese, were able to fulfill their cherished hopes without further opposition.

Judging from the history of other nations in this world, people who overthrow a government and successfully establish a new one often have to contend with outbursts of lingering resentment. I will not go into the long rivalry between the Minamoto and the Taira families, since this belongs to the distant past, but in the early days of Tokugawa rule, dispossessed samurai [still loyal to the Toyotomi] put up fierce resistance in Osaka. Even today, in France, years after the abolition of the monarchy, a royalist party is bent on restoring the house of the former emperor Napoleon. Worse, not a few are said to long for the Bourbon dynasty, which ruled a hundred years ago. But this is human nature and perhaps unavoidable.

In Japan, the Restoration saw the collapse of a government that had ruled for two hundred and fifty years and the abolition of three hundred feudal domains, yet despite the unprecedented reversal in fortunes, once achieved, not a dissenting voice was heard in the entire country. People were taken aback by the abrupt change in the personal circumstances of the shogun and daimyo, but took their leaders' fall from power in stride, as though this was only to be expected. No one thought this unusual or sad, much less a cause for anger or indignation. Like a springtime dream, the past had vanished without a trace. The people's emotional detachment is surely without parallel in the world, past or present. This alone should prove that the Restoration was not a personal vendetta against a feudal ruler but an attack on the despotic system he represented. Given the people's state of mind, does it not stand to reason that no turmoil accompanied the establishment of the Diet, an institution diametrically opposed to despotism?

Some people insist on setting up two opposing sides—one, the present government they deem despotic, the other, commoners who believe in political freedom—and predict an inevitable clash. But this is pure fantasy, the result of a superficial knowledge of Western history and ignorance of the actual situation in Japan. The government is far from despotic; its leaders, moreover, are men who strove to their utmost to overthrow a despotic political system. Having destroyed one despotic government, they would never build another one, for they realize only too well that the peace and security of Japan depend not on a feudal ruler but on an elective national assembly. They also know, and are convinced beyond doubt, that in the past, the reins of government were never held by the feudal ruler but by his subordinates. In a word, the leaders in government are the advance guard of freedom and reform and are personally in charge. Thus, no matter who the commoner advocates of political freedom may be, the facts simply do not warrant a clash between the two forces working for political freedom.

Admittedly, during the last twenty years or so, some in government may have taken advantage of their position and abused their political power. The stubborn and incompetent may have misunderstood the true spirit of the Restoration, and having overthrown one despotic government, misguidedly hoped to establish another one. The old-fashioned and shallow-minded may have been misled by the phrase "imperial restoration," and disrespectfully dreamed of having the sacred person of the emperor involved in secular affairs of the state. People took notice of this, and disgruntled, accused the government of autocratic practices, the unfair dominance of men from certain domains, and unrealistic policies that disregarded the national polity. But these were minor disturbances in the world of political discourse, with little effect on larger trends. They were like today's political parties or members of the same party, each with contending views but in complete agreement on the country's goal for progress and reform. For the past twenty years, the government and people may not always have been in accord, but they will never come to blows over the theoretical benefits of the Diet. And why? Because both the government and people of Meiji Japan have broken free of despotic rule and taken the road to progress. For reasons I shall explain later, I am confident that the Japanese, in their accustomed manner, will amicably resolve matters concerning future Diet politics.

As I stated in a previous passage, under constitutional government, in which ruler and people share political power, a certain kind of absolute power must restrain both sides and prevent them from reaching the height of satisfaction or descending down to the depths of dissatisfaction. Also, if a constitutional government under a ruler is to function properly, the people may honor and cherish the ruler as they would a god or parent, but they must also accept the fact that he is not concerned with secular affairs of the state and under no circumstances is to be resented or held responsible for what happens. Furthermore, inasmuch as the written law cannot cover the myriad complexities of human affairs, people who live under constitutional government must accept the rule of custom that arises from everyday life and not rely exclusively on the written law. At the same time, when they take action under the protection of law, they must remember never to exceed its limits. Again, under a constitutional government free from interference by a despotic ruler, people must be given the right to self-determination in certain areas of public life, including, of course, where they live and how they make a living.

These, then, are the indispensable elements of a constitutional political system under which ruler and subject rule jointly. If someone were to ask me whether these elements are to be found in the customs of Japanese citizens, I would proclaim loudly, "Yes, and abundantly so." For leaving aside the ancient past, during the two hundred and fifty years of Tokugawa rule, the principle of the balance of power was applied on a large scale in the organization of government, extending widely over relations between samurai and commoners, and to minute matters concerning the people at large. Satisfaction countered dissatisfaction in equal measure; no one, whether high or low, rich or poor, strong or weak, attained full and complete satisfaction. Yet, each person possessed something he could be proud of and rested secure with his lot in life. This habit of mind was transmitted over the generations, becoming second nature.

The organization of the Diet has been formalized in the Constitution and, needless to say, national sovereignty rests in the Imperial House, undisturbed through all ages. But contrary to what some head-in-the-cloud theorists think, the Imperial House must not be implicated in petty matters of secular politics so they may secretly be dissatisfied. Again, before the opening of the Diet, the government rarely deferred to the people and forcibly enacted ill-conceived policies, but also won recognition for its many admirable achievements. Now, the government must submit all matters to both Houses for approval. This frequently entails a great deal of time, work, and inconvenience for the government, yet strangely enough, the credit may well redound to the Diet. Diet members, too, who waited so long for the Diet to open, may often be disappointed and dissatisfied because even as they realize that their political power derives from the people who elected them, they are unable to use the authority of the institution to influence policies as they like.

The principle of countering power with power applies not only to the government but also to relations between political parties and among members of the same party. In truth, the more human culture advances the more contentious the arguments: win on one issue and lose on another; yesterday's subordinate becomes today's superior, whose orders must be followed; the elderly must be ever on the alert, the young, mindful of undue pride. This ceaseless interplay of power is unavoidable in the world of politics; no one, be it A, B, C, or D, can hope to be fully satisfied. At such a time, the only way to attain peace of mind is to recall the old cliché that "the moon is often hidden by a cloud and flowers scattered by a wind." On no account, should one resort to extreme measures to salve a moment's discontent or anger. In this respect, we Japanese are unmatched in our ability to maintain calm; foreigners are simply not equal to us in this. A few Japanese may persist in behaving waywardly, or in a fit of exuberance for the new, attempt something outrageous, but in general, the Japanese have been brought up to maintain their composure. Anything out of the ordinary is momentary, a mere ripple on the surface of political waters. Viewed from one angle, a ripple may look dangerous, but there is really no cause for alarm.

It is said that an essential point of a constitutional monarchy is to honor and cherish the ruler but not to ascribe political responsibility to him. Awareness of this moral duty is distinctive to the Japanese; from remote antiquity, everyone has known that the Imperial House is sacred and inviolable (*shinsei ni shite okasubekarazu*). In fact, during the age of military government, the moral obligation binding ruler and subject was defined even more explicitly: not only did people revere the sanctity of the Imperial House, but retainers and commoners regarded the feudal shogun and daimyo as beings akin to gods or parents. Several shogun and daimyo during the Tokugawa era were said to be despotic, but this was more apparent than real, for we never hear of a samurai or commoner openly resenting a superior for a misstep in government. The master was ever the fount of beneficence, never the object of malice or resentment. This habit of mind was deeply ingrained in the Japanese and became second nature; in honoring and cherishing the Imperial House today, we are merely following our human nature. Our everyday speech and behavior is unconsciously based on this, the depths of our feelings such that we are at once aware and not aware of the emperor's presence. Whether the government is constitutional or not, the Imperial House is the Imperial House for the ages; however incompetent the government, no one would think of holding the emperor responsible. There are many monarchies in the world, but in firmness and stability, not one compares with the Imperial House of our great country of Japan. On this score, too, people should know that we do not lack the indispensable elements of constitutional government.

Again, it is said that people who live under constitutional government should not rely on the letter of the law but appeal to common sense. Many countries have a constitutional government, each with its own set of written laws. The laws, however, are insufficient for performing the complex and endless work of government in a fair and just manner; indeed, relying exclusively on the written law may even lead to an impasse. Law is important, true; a single legal document safeguards the lives of the citizens. But we should resort to it only in an emergency: under ordinary conditions, both the government and people should be able to live under the law and yet remain unaware of its workings; only when they form the habit of speaking and acting naturally, without breaking the law, can constitutional government be considered healthy and sound.

Consider Britain. The real power of the British government resides in the House of Commons, but the monarch has the prerogative of appointing members to the House of Lords. Thus, if the monarch is dissatisfied with the decisions of the House of Commons, he can always create new lords, and by giving them seats in the House of Lords, control the lower house. The right is clearly stipulated in the British Constitution; yet, in the last century or so, no monarch has been known to exercise this right. If, by any chance, a monarch were actually to do so today, people from every walk of life would be outraged and probably not permit it. In other words, the British people live under the law but do not allow it to be carried out. Or to give another example, under the British Constitution, the monarch has the prerogative to declare war or conclude a truce and has supreme command over the military. Under the **Mutiny Act**, however, laws pertaining to the military are subject to a yearly parliamentary review, so if Parliament decides not to renew a certain law, the monarch, despite having supreme command, is left without a military, as it were. A curious situation, to say the least, but this, too, has never come to pass.

I shall next quote a passage from *The English Constitution*, a book by [Walter] Bagehot, published in 1878 [sic: 1867].

> When the Queen abolished Purchase in the Army by an act of prerogative (after the Lords had rejected the bill for doing so), there was a great and general astonishment. But this is nothing to what the Queen can by law do without consulting Parliament. Not to mention other things, she could disband the army (by law she cannot engage more than a certain number of men, but she is not obliged to engage any men); she could dismiss all the officers, from the General Commanding-in-Chief downwards; she could dismiss all the sailors too; she could sell off all our ships of war and all our naval stores; she could make a peace by the sacrifice of Cornwall, and begin a war for the conquest of Brittany.

She could make every citizen in the United Kingdom, male or female, a peer; she could make every parish in the United Kingdom a "university"; she could dismiss most of the civil servants; she could pardon all offenders. In a word, the Queen could by prerogative upset all the action of civil government within the government, could disgrace the nation by a bad war or peace, and could, by disbanding our forces, whether land or sea, leave us defenceless against foreign nations.[10]

I could give many more examples of oddities of this kind in the British government. Indeed, a close look at the government would suggest that an absolute monarchy is possible and a purely republican form is also possible. By disposition, however, the British allow neither. Put bluntly, do they think that having no law is better than carrying out every single law? In many respects, the American Constitution resembles the British system. The president has the right to ask Congress to reconsider a vote, but if both houses have a two-thirds majority in favor of it, Congress can bypass the president and enact a law. On this point, the president would seem to be powerless, but since he controls the executive branch of the government, even if a law is passed, he can delay or hasten its implementation, without interference from Congress. This might suggest that there is no clear locus of real power, yet after long years of custom, the government runs smoothly.

The American Constitution was framed more than a hundred years ago, and with the vicissitudes of time, some of the statutes are no longer appropriate to the present age and some of the wording is less than complete. To give an example or two, the Constitution states that Congress has the right to declare war but says nothing about concluding peace. Thus, once war is declared, the president, as commander-in-chief of the armed forces, mobilizes the military and wages war as long as he sees fit and Congress is unable to stop him. Again, Congress must approve of the issuance of government bonds, but since there is nothing in the Constitution about paper currency, the president can order the issuance of paper currency [without approval from Congress] as part of his executive powers. Government bonds and paper currency differ in name, but since they have the same nature, denying one right to the president but permitting the other is strange indeed.

Many other statutes would be unsuitable today if they were carried out according to the letter of the law. As a people, however, Americans are not inclined to dwell on particulars. Frank and large-minded, they go about life trusting in ordinary human nature. Without questioning the wording of the Constitution, they let politics proceed as it should, and the government functions smoothly.

It is as if an executor reading the will of the deceased knowingly interprets the unfavorable parts to the advantage of the heirs. According to an American joke, if candidates for Congress were required to pass a test in grammar and **spelling**, Congress would be forced to shut down. The joke undoubtedly refers to the tendency among members of Congress to misconstrue the syntax deliberately and interpret the Constitution to suit their own purposes, and that if they had to interpret the Constitution literally in accordance with the grammar of the text, Congress would not last another day.

In Japan, too, if the Constitution were interpreted strictly according to the letter of the law, both the government and people would confront one another and to their mutual distress, eventually clash. An acquaintance with no connection to the government has recently told me that while both the government and people are tolerant in most matters, they can be quite merciless and unyielding when something touches on the Constitution. For example, if someone on one side prepares his case thoroughly and insists that a certain statute means such and such, he will naturally give offense and someone on the other side will oppose him with a different interpretation. In one extreme case, a person apparently threatened to submit the matter to the Throne (*jōsō*). I was stunned to hear this, for even though the term appears in the Constitution, the procedure should never be used, not even once in a hundred years. One would think that this is understood, but this is not the case, because ignorant and inexperienced politicians and their ilk are carried away by their enthusiasm for the Constitution. Both sides are to blame.

Given the political reality today, an unreasonable person in government or otherwise might possibly make a deliberate attempt to provoke a clash for the sake of a momentary thrill, despite being fully aware of the consequences. Worse, he may even attempt something that precipitates a national crisis. But as I mentioned earlier, the Japanese, by good fortune, lived under the Honorable Laws of the Tokugawa bakufu for two hundred and fifty odd years, and though controlled by a despotic political system, never suffered the iron hand of a despot. They knew that, beside the strict and oppressive written law, there existed the lenient rule of custom, and that people can live undisturbed outside the confines of the written law. The spirit of tolerance is not easily lost in thirty or fifty years. Even if officials and commoners in today's political world fight over the meaning of the written law and someone resorts to unreasonable means to win, his victory will be short-lived. People will appeal to common sense, and in the end, this winner will be abandoned by society and condemned to live in isolation. In other words, under our constitutional form of government, there is no room for unreasonable men to act unreasonably. Someone may act unreasonably for a while, but the harm will be superficial and limited, for deeply rooted in our society is an abundance of the spirit of steadfast tolerance.

It is said that people freed from monarchic despotism and living under a constitutional government should be prepared to exercise self-governance (*jichi*). This, too, is nothing new to the Japanese. As I mentioned, during the more than two hundred and fifty years of Tokugawa rule, commoners might have been barred from direct contact with the central authorities but they were amply experienced in local self-rule and never subject to government interference. Since the Restoration, however, a reversal in government policy has led to needless expenditures in human labor and money, though more recently, possibly due to a measure of self-reflection, the authorities have started to encourage greater self-governance at the local level. Self-rule in a feudal age and self-rule in a modern age naturally differ, but the underlying spirit is the same. If the government rights past wrongs, refrains from meddling, and puts an end to the baleful feudal custom of officials scorning commoners, people will be able to assert anew the spirit of self-rule and take no small pride in being the essential elements of a constitutional government.

While our National Diet assumed its completed form in 1890, its real birth was not in 1890 but in 1868, the year of the Meiji Restoration. To say it was born that year is to say that it was conceived during the centuries of Tokugawa rule; labor was induced by the opening of the country in 1854, and delivery was quickened by the arrival of Western civilization. Because its antecedents were of long duration, because its growth within the womb was complete, and because its birth occurred at full term, the infant, the National Diet, is healthy and should enjoy a long, long life. I trust that all knowledgeable men will not differ in their diagnosis.

What I have stated in this essay is clearly borne out in our history, and if the Japanese people gave my words some thought, they would immediately agree. Foreigners, however, will not be persuaded so easily. They have little access to information about Japan, and just as Japanese have difficulty learning about the true character of foreigners, foreigners are apt to glean bits and pieces of information about us and leap to conclusions. This is why, at the risk of boring my Japanese readers, I have written about the Tokugawa era to bring out facts that do not appear in historical records. I thus hope that intellectuals abroad will make a careful study of our country's human and political affairs in recent centuries, for once they realize that while Japan is geographically a part of East Asia, its people are not the East Asians they have long imagined, and will clearly understand why the establishment of the Diet is no mere accident and will shed any doubts as to its future.

The foundation of our Diet is solid, its future as smooth sailing as a ship borne by a gentle tailwind. But just as a ship cannot rely solely on the wind, the government and the people will have to cooperate and pursue a steady course if Japan hopes to maintain parliamentary government and join the ranks of civilized nations. Not only should the government and the people help one another in harmony, but they should also reflect upon their actions and practice self-restraint when necessary.

Judged in this light, the government has acted with courage and resolution in undertaking many programs. Immediately after the Restoration, it prohibited the wearing of samurai swords; allowed commoners to bear surnames and ride on horses; abolished daimyo domains and instituted the prefectural system; established prefectural assemblies and a centralized postal service; laid down telegraph lines and railroads; expanded shipping; modernized and strengthened the army and navy; and reformed the legal, tax, and monetary systems. In all this, the government was eminently successful.

But at the same time, the government, despite claiming to be the center of talented and knowledgeable men, embarked on some foolish collective actions, the consequences of which are evident to this day. The mistakes did not harm the national polity, but the waste of money and effort frequently incurred public criticism. For instance, the government floated bonds abroad, for what purpose is still unclear; it issued government bonds to start enterprises to no avail; it excavated mines to little profit; it heedlessly printed paper currency, causing turmoil in the market; its efforts to rectify this led to the bankruptcy of commercial firms; the treasury monies it lent to a certain company and individual disappeared; it promoted education ill-suited to the people and squandered public and private funds; it unnecessarily hired officials of high and low rank for personal reasons, adding to cumbersome paperwork. Contrary to long-standing political practice, it meddled with religion and destroyed historic and sacred sites on the pretext of separating Shinto from Buddhism. Hostile to Buddhism—in effect Japan's state religion—it tacitly supported Shinto and had the temerity to persuade the Imperial House to change the funeral rites it had observed for hundreds of years. It frequently interfered with the traditional practice of popular self-governance, and even as it called for equality, condoned the feudal custom of officials looking down on commoners. Its decision to create a new class of nobles with honorary ranks and titles was as frivolous as child's play and further estranged the people. Worse, the government used police power for political ends. This might be forgiven if something positive resulted from detaining people, searching their houses, and prying into their secrets with impunity, but often enough police were led astray by their overheated imaginations, and people complained. For instance, in December 1887, the police ordered a group of people to vacate a house in Tokyo on the grounds that they were secretly plotting to instigate a rebellion and hence endangering public peace. We have no way of knowing whether the charge was justified and a rebellion was actually foiled, but as I think upon it calmly, I cannot help feeling that the order was probably unnecessary. Although there is no point in saying anything now, I find this incident deeply regrettable.

In view of the situation in Japan today, advocates of popular rights and government officials must work together for reform and progress and move forward side by side. Officials serve the government that happens to be in power and differ only temporarily in status. Just because they are higher in status, one should not see them as enemies. Rather, officials and popular rightists should associate with one another with tolerance and ease, the older teaching the young, and the young learning from the older. They should lay aside all selfish thoughts of fame and fortune, and unite for the greater good of the country, thereby securing their own happiness and the happiness of their descendants.

But this is hardly the case at present. Men in government were freed from the shackles of monarchic despotism, and during the first years of the Restoration, absorbed the spirit of consultative government. But at times they have been led astray, perhaps, by the need to keep up appearances, and have lost sight of this spirit's original intent. Drawing a line between those in government and not, they act as though they are the masters of the house and the people the visitors. Treating each other cordially but shunning visitors, dispensing favors and wielding influence like despots, they have forgotten how men of virtue should act in associating with others. They stray from the true purpose of government and disdain those below them. Given human nature, this is unavoidable, but even so, all too few are experienced in the conduct of government and ignorant of the precept to overcome the self and know one's place in life. I should add that many of the popular rightists fail to impress me.

In a sense, the Restoration took advantage of the trends of the times. Those who saw the trends and acted are now the leaders in government; they were like speculators who acquire great wealth by seizing the right moment, and though none of this requires hard work, no one else can claim the profits since they were the ones who knew when to act. The men of the Restoration seized the right moment, but they also experienced untold hardships and saw many fellow activists die. Present leaders are among those who survived, and so, despite some excesses, perhaps the wiser course is to forgive them. And it was because those very leaders realized that the original spirit of the Restoration forbade the unlimited exercise of power that we have the Diet today. The people no longer have cause to complain; the only question is the scope of the assembly's power and the government's intentions.

The conduct of government is extremely complex: the present government was established barely twenty odd years ago, and since then, it has had to contend with all manner of historical precedents, a tangle of relationships, a host of unforeseen issues. Thus, for now, both sides should simplify procedures and focus on the issues that are clear-cut in their merits and demerits. Then, as the government and the Diet express their opinions candidly, the government's intentions will naturally become known and the scope of parliamentary power will be more clearly defined. They should proceed with caution in all things, and in their eagerness to attain a state of perfection, should not act with undue haste. Among the impressive array of talented members are many hotheaded men who have been seething with discontent even before the opening of the Diet. They view the government as their sworn enemy and disapprove of every measure taken in the past twenty years; attacking this and that, from one to a hundred, they see only the shortcomings and failures. Instead of thinking of the good of the country and clarifying what is right or wrong, they are more intent on taking revenge on the government. Already, some people are secretly worried that members have forgotten the true colors of the institution and spend too much time debating the minutiae of parliamentary power. I grieve to hear this, and by way of criticism, I can only say that this is because the worthies in the Diet lack self-respect and self-restraint.

Japan today is not the secluded Japan of the past but a nation that takes its rightful place among the nations of the world. Thus, when the Diet and government debate and enact affairs of state, they should consider not only the smaller benefits that directly affect the Japanese but also think of ways to strengthen the country over the long term and raise its good name in the world. But if officials, high and low, are more intent on defending their positions, and Diet members all too eager to attack them, both sides will be too busy thinking of ways to win and will neglect the important and far-reaching policies on which the country was founded.

Did they plan to do this all along? Men in politics today, officials and non-officials alike, were once feudal samurai or educated commoners who shared the same outlook on life. As such, are they not like the faithful retainers of old who were ready to die for their masters in battle? Of course, I am not proposing that they give up their lives in the line of duty. Rather, I am saying that they should serve their country in the spirit of retainers who put their masters first; casting aside petty resentments, selfish thoughts of private virtues, fame, and gain, they should fix their eyes on this great nation of ours—Japan—and endure annoyances and renounce all hope of achieving fame and honor to their fullest satisfaction. I pray for this with all my heart.

During the past twenty years or so, relations between the government and the people have not always been pleasant. Yet, viewed from the perspective of the larger trends in the country, the perturbations are as one short breath and will hardly affect the fate of politics in Japan. We can never tell what changes the Diet will bring about, but I, for one, firmly believe that our constitutional government, with its strong and solid foundation, will last far into the distant future.

In general, the maintenance and preservation of the things in life depends on one's peace of mind. Fear gives rise to dark and menacing thoughts: fear of illness invites illness. The shallow-minded who distrust their own government are likely to do harm. This is to say nothing of foreigners! With only a superficial knowledge of political conditions in Japan, who knows what conclusions they will draw. Thus, for several days, I have taken up my brush like an anxious old woman to give a measure of assurance to people in this country and abroad.

Commentary

If Fukuzawa's 1875 *An Outline of Theories of Civilization* is taken as a thesis, in several respects "The Future Course of the Diet" can be viewed as its antithesis. In *An Outline of Theories of Civilization,* he depicted Tokugawa society as suffering from an "imbalance of power" (*kenryoku no henchō*), with each person looking up to the next higher authority. At every level, the scales were "tilted to one side," resulting in a culture of dependence. In "The Future Course of the Diet," he characterizes the same period as having "a balance of power" (*kenryoku no heikin*), a diametrically antithetical phrase. He finds not a tilted society but an equilibrium of checks and balances. He contends that Tokugawa Japanese were distinguished by self-rule, self-respect, and a measure of independence. In both pieces of writing, the conditions during the Tokugawa are critical to his argument, but in the 1890 essay, they are the opposite of those in the 1875 work.

The two pieces of writing also differ in their historical references. In *An Outline of Theories of Civilization,* Europe was the model for historical change.

Fukuzawa almost unreservedly accepted the ideas of Western scholars, occasionally mentioning a Buckle or Guizot by name. His signal contribution was to fit Japan into an early slot along the European historical continuum; his view of Japan was explicitly comparative. In "The Future Course of the Diet," he is still using European criteria, but his focus is on the Japanese past. Rather than describing Europe, he turns to the configuration of forces in Tokugawa society to explain Japan's acceptance of representative institutions. He sees Japan's modern history as an outgrowth of its pre-modern history. Western intellectuals are not his mentors but his intended audience, or so he states; their lack of understanding of Japan frames his argument. In the essay, he promises to provide the historical details that will convince even ignorant foreigners of the timeliness of a national assembly for Japan.

Fukuzawa's view of East Asia also changed. In *An Outline of Theories of Civilization*, Japan, China, and Korea differed in several regards, but all three faced the common threat of Western imperialism. In "The Future Course of the Diet," the differences are critical: China and Korea have changed little; they are still in the grip of monarchic despotism, whereas Japan, which never had monarchic despotism, has advanced and is fully prepared for representative government.

Why did Fukuzawa's views change so markedly between 1875 and 1890? One explanation is that Japan itself had been transformed. In 1875, Japan was still backward and in need of change. *An Outline of Theories of Civilization* emphasized that point by comparisons with the West. But by 1890, Japan had changed much more than had seemed possible. Also by then, Fukuzawa had become conservative in the sense that he wished to keep the post-Restoration changes that had prepared the ground for the new Constitution and Diet.

The dramatic change within Japan demanded a new theory. In both *Conditions in the West* and *An Outline of Theories of Civilization*, historical change was a slow process occurring over centuries. But change had happened faster in Japan. In his 1879 works, *Renewal of Popular Sentiments* and "On a National Assembly," he explained this with a new theory based on inventions and their social consequences. But to explain Japan's leap to a constitution and elective national assembly, the adoption of new inventions was not enough; Fukuzawa was compelled to go back, as noted earlier, to pre-Meiji Japan. That is, by 1890, the problem is not to overcome the drawbacks of Tokugawa society, but to build on its strengths.

In the essay, Fukuzawa does not abandon altogether the idea that Japan had been feudal. He praises the Meiji leaders for destroying feudal institutions; he approvingly quotes a letter by Saigō Takamori, which speaks of the need to overcome the age-old lord–vassal (*shujū*) relationship. But by 1889 and 1890, he sharply distinguishes between Japanese feudalism and that of medieval Europe.[11] In his view, the Tokugawa era, though feudal, was an age of learning and letters, an age in which Japan moved forward on every front. Having made great strides, it was able to accept Western ideas and practices. In contrast, he implies, medieval European feudalism lacked such positive factors. Probably no European "feudal monarchy," to use Joseph Strayer's term, would have responded as quickly and effectively had it been suddenly confronted by a more politically and technologically advanced civilization. At least, Fukuzawa seems to suggest that this was the case.

Fukuzawa begins the present essay by describing Tokugawa government and society as an intricate network of checks and balances, a system so effective that it preserved peace for two hundred and fifty years. The founder of the system, Tokugawa Ieyasu, he declares, is "a hero whose achievements are without equal in world history."

Under the Tokugawa system, the emperor, at the apex of the society, gave the shogun legitimacy, but the emperor's unassailable position was balanced off by the shogun's military and political power. This balance prevented a despotic ruler, such as the first Qin emperor of China, from ever emerging in Japan. Likewise, court nobles surrounding the emperor balanced off, in some sense, the daimyo lords. The collective autonomy of the two hundred odd daimyo, who actually ruled two-thirds of the land in Japan, limited bakufu power. Small "collateral daimyo"—those who were vassals before 1600—had little power of their own, but, as bakufu officials, they restrained the larger "outside daimyo." The strategic placement of daimyo long loyal to the Tokugawa also blocked the power of "outside" lords. Checks and balances were ubiquitous at other levels, as well. Domain elders controlled the daimyo. Lower samurai had a larger role in domain governance than their rank merited, constraining higher-rank retainers. Such offsets existed at every level in the system. In sum, whether shogun or daimyo, rulers in Japan were despots in name only and unable to exercise arbitrary rule.

But most important was the balance between samurai rule at the top, and commoner self-rule in villages and city wards at the bottom. Merchants may have been of lowly social status, but they ran their businesses independently and exercised great influence over domain finances. Village and city wards were largely self-governing. A variety of local organizations, such as the five-household units, strengthened local self-governance. Fukuzawa describes the local scene in detail, and concludes that "local self-rule was from olden times a system peculiar to Japan, and one to which its people were long accustomed." He likens this perfectly balanced and long-evolving system to a "self-propelling machine."

Custom, too, was vital. Tokugawa laws were harsh in form, but good sense prevailed in their application. Barriers were located at strategic points of entry to the Edo heartland, yet when bakufu security was not affected, people passed through easily without incident. By law, a samurai could cut down a disrespectful commoner. But in the domain of Nakatsu, he recounts, this happened only once. Fond of mathematical exposition, Fukuzawa multiplied the three thousand Nakatsu samurai by the two hundred and fifty-three years of the Tokugawa period, and arrived at a figure of only one such incident in seven hundred and fifty-nine thousand "samurai years." Laws were strictly applied only when the security of the regime was affected. Most laws were like IOUs for which claims were never pressed. A thick wall of custom protected the people, and a few exceptions apart, they lived without fear in a society that enjoyed centuries of peace.

Nor was Tokugawa Japan unique in relying on custom. To help his readers understand this point, Fukuzawa cites Britain, where the monarch can appoint new members to the House of Lords and thereby override the House of Commons, but is restrained by custom from exercising that prerogative. Similarly, and here he quotes Bagehot, the ruler can begin or conclude a war, or disband the army, but by custom does not. Good sense, not the letter of the law, has made Britain what it is. In the United States, too, law covers only a part of the workings of government. As head of the executive branch, the president can delay the implementation of laws passed by Congress. While only Congress can issue government bonds, the president has the authority to issue paper money, which is not dissimilar. In practice, however, the president usually refrains from taking action. These customary practices do not daunt Americans, whom Fukuzawa had observed during his 1867 trip to the United States. "Frank and large-minded, they go about life trusting in ordinary human nature. Without questioning the wording of the Constitution, they let politics proceed as it should, and the government functions smoothly."

Fukuzawa goes on to assert that in a society so perfectly balanced and guided by custom, the character and self-awareness of the Japanese people gradually changed.

> During the two hundred and fifty years of Tokugawa rule, the principle of the balance of power was applied on a large scale in the organization of government, extending widely over relations between samurai and commoners, and to minute

matters concerning the people at large. Satisfaction countered dissatisfaction in equal measure; no one, whether high or low, rich or poor, strong or weak, attained full and complete satisfaction. Yet, each person possessed something he could be proud of and rested secure with his lot in life. This habit of mind was transmitted over generations, becoming second nature.

At each level of society, individuals were responsible for their own lot and exercised a measure of self-rule (*jichi*). Little by little they were transformed. Self-rule may not have been recognized formally, but it was integral to the system. Accompanying it, and necessary to it, were habits of self-respect, responsibility, and tolerance.

Fukuzawa acknowledges that progress during the early Meiji years was not always smooth. The centralization of government destroyed the Tokugawa system of checks and balances. A few Meiji leaders failed to understand the changes of which they were a part and clung to despotic practices. But the habit of self-rule, and the self-respect that it engendered, survived to provide an underpinning for new institutions, namely, the prefectural assemblies in 1878, the newly reorganized villages of 1878, and the Diet in 1890. Fukuzawa's conclusion was that "self-rule in the feudal age and self-rule in a modern age naturally differ, but the underlying spirit is the same."

A telling argument for the universal acceptance of the 1868 revolution is that no one considered a return to the old regime. This is most unusual, Fukuzawa notes. In the early Tokugawa years, retainers loyal to the memory of Hideyoshi had put up armed resistance to the Tokugawa regime. In post-revolutionary France, "a royalist party [was] bent on restoring the house of the former emperor Napoleon," and some even wanted to restore the Bourbons. But in Meiji Japan, despite "the collapse of a government that had ruled for two hundred and fifty years and the abolition of three hundred feudal domains ... not a dissenting voice was heard in the entire country." "Like a springtime dream, the past had vanished without a trace."

Fukuzawa compares the advent of the Diet to the birth of a healthy infant.

> While our National Diet assumed its completed form in 1890, its real birth was not in 1890 but in 1868, the year of the Meiji Restoration. To say it was born that year is to say that it was conceived during the centuries of Tokugawa rule; labor was induced by the opening of the country in 1854, and delivery was quickened by the arrival of Western civilization. Because its antecedents were of long duration, because its growth within the womb was complete, and because its birth occurred at full term, the infant, the National Diet, is healthy and should enjoy a long, long life.

Should we accept Fukuzawa's view of the Tokugawa past? How much self-rule or *jichi* was there in the Tokugawa era? Was it actually as widespread as he claims? Didn't the self-rule of a peasant member of a five-household group differ greatly from that of a samurai? Didn't a samurai holding even a minor domain office possess self-awareness very different from that of a gate guard at the daimyo's castle?[12]

Furthermore, can we equate Fukuzawa's concept of Tokugawa "self-rule" with the Western idea of "independence?" No one in Tokugawa Japan thought of himself as a self-contained entity endowed with human rights in the Western sense of the term. Is not such awareness crucial? Can Tokugawa "self-rule" substitute for "personal independence" within a Western-style parliamentary system? If self-rule had to be transformed into independence, then the birth of the Diet, even using the most elastic of definitions, was in 1890, not in 1868, as Fukuzawa claimed. That said, while none of these questions negates the importance of Fukuzawa's insights about the Tokugawa social system, they compel us to turn our attention to the early Meiji.

We may further question whether the government and nascent political parties in fact wanted the same thing. In one respect they did: both were willing to have a national assembly. The government could have prevented its formation, at least for a time, but it did not. Fukuzawa was right on that count. But in another respect, the two sides were far apart: the parties wanted power, and the government was not about to hand over power to irresponsible party politicians. Itō's framing of a Prussian-type constitution, with limited Diet powers and a limited electorate, kept most of the levers of power in the hands of the government. The Meiji Constitution gave the parties only a modicum of power, which was all that was possible in that age. Despite the aspirations of party leaders, a window for a vastly more liberal system was never open.

Fukuzawa understood this. He recognized that the new Diet was a far cry from British Parliament that he had earlier held up as a model. Despite this, he does not seem to have been dissatisfied with Itō's framing of the Constitution. He had little regard for the leaders of the political parties, and did not want to see them take power. That an elective assembly had been formed at all was a momentous event; parallel to his view of the Meiji Restoration, he was confident that responsible politicians would appear in time. In short, he saw the new Constitution and Diet as an opening to the future. Even though power, or most power, remained in the hands of the government, he looked forward to a future in which the Diet would gradually extend its sway.

Fukuzawa died in 1901 at the age of sixty-six. Though sick and frail, he no doubt approved of the formation of the Seiyūkai Party by the oligarch Itō and party politicians in 1900. He would certainly have approved of the appointment of Hara Kei, a commoner and party president, as prime minister in 1918, and the enactment of universal manhood suffrage in 1925. Had he been asked about civilian control of the military, or the "imperial" appointment of prime ministers, in retrospect obvious shortcomings in the Meiji Constitution, he would have probably replied that these, too, were matters for later governments to handle.

He titles his essay "The Future Course of the Diet," but the essay actually seeks to explicate the historical foundations of the Diet. Looking back at the institutions of Tokugawa rule, he wrote: "I firmly believe that our constitutional government, with its strong and solid foundation, will last far into the future."

Notes

Chapter 1

1 Fukuzawa Yukichi, *An Outline of a Theory of Civilization*, 22 (revised trans. David Dilworth and G. Cameron Hurst), New York, 2008. We have used the edition of *Fukuzawa Yukichi zenshū* (hereafter FYZ) published from 1958 to 1971 by Iwanami Shoten, Tokyo. The passages from *Bunmeiron no gairyaku* are in FYZ IV, 20–1. Fukuzawa doubtless thought that Western culture, however complex, was one culture. But he was also aware that the theories of Samuel Augustus Mitchell, John Hill Burton, Thomas Buckle, and François Guizot were not the same. For this reason I translate the title of his 1875 book as *An Outline of Theories of Civilization*.
2 Albert M. Craig, *Civilization and Enlightenment: The Early Thought of Fukuzawa Yukichi*, 163–4, Cambridge, MA, 2009. See this book for a fuller analysis of civilization as the idea was developed in the West and adopted by Fukuzawa. The Japanese edition was published as *Bunmei to keimō: Shoki Fukuzawa Yukichi no shisō*, trans. Adachi Yasushi and Umetsu Jun'ichi, Tokyo, 2009.
3 Fukuzawa was fascinated by American history. He presented a sketch in the first volume of *Conditions in the West*, and included both the *Declaration of Independence* and the *United States Constitution*, but he felt that the absence of feudal lords and kings made the history of the United States less relevant to Japan.
4 For the Tokugawa application of Chinese history to Japan, see Asai Kiyoshi, *Meiji ishin to gunken shisō*, Tokyo, 1968, in particular chapter 1. Also see Kōno Yūri, *Taguchi Ukichi no yume*, Tokyo, 2013, for a careful analysis of *hōken* and *gunken* in Meiji thought. Fukuzawa avoided using *gunken* to describe Japan's modern centralization because of the word's association with dynastic China. No model, he thought, for a modernizing Japan!
5 J. Thomas and T. Baldwin (eds.), *Lippincott's Pronouncing Gazetteer*, revised edition, 1288, J. B. Lippincott & Co., Philadelphia, 1866.
6 FYZ I, 346.
7 FYZ I, 355; John Ramsey McCulloch (or M'Culloch), *A Dictionary, Geographical, Statistical, and Historical of the Various Countries, Places, and Principal Natural Objects in the World*, vol. II, 288, London, 1866. The original edition was published in 1841. Fukuzawa used the 1866 edition, edited by Frederick Martin and published by Longmans, Green, and Co. It differs slightly from the earlier one.
8 McCulloch 2, 288; FYZ I, 355.

9   McCulloch II, 288; FYZ I, 357.
10 McCulloch II, 290; FYZ I, 361.
11 For Russia, Fukuzawa's two sources were George Ripley and Charles A. Dana (eds.), *The New American Cyclopedia* (hereafter NAC), vol. I, D. Appleton and Company, New York, 1866; and Julius Eckardt, *Modern Russia*, Smith, Elder, and Co., London, 1870.
12 William C. Taylor, *The History of France and Normandy*, 22–3, Charles Desilver, Philadelphia, 1856, in Pinnock's School Series; FYZ I, 557–61.
13 Rutherford Alcock, *The Capital of the Tycoon*, 109, Harper and Brothers, New York, 1863.
14 William Griffis, *The Mikado's Empire*, 434, 293, Harper and Brothers, New York, 1876. Griffis also wrote:

> Much, also, has been said and written in praise of Japan for her abolition of the feudal system by a stroke of the pen, and thus achieving in one day what it required Europe centuries to accomplish. An outsider ... may be so far dazed as to imagine the Japanese demi-gods in statecraft, even as American newspapers make them all princes. To the writer who has lived in a daimio's capital before, during, and after the abolition of feudalism, the comparison suggests the reason why the Irish recruit cut off the leg instead of the head of his enemy. Long before its abolition, Japanese feudalism was ready for its grave. The overthrow of the shogun left it a headless trunk. To cut off its leg and bury it was easy.

15 Charles H. Eden, *Japan, Historical and Descriptive*, 19, M. Ward, London, 1877.
16 Erwin Baelz, *Awakening Japan: The Diary of a German Doctor*, 16, Bloomington, IN, 1974.
17 NAC, vol. VII, 669.
18 FYZ I, 561.
19 NAC, vol. VII, 669–70; FYZ I, 561–4.
20 Taylor 188; FYZ I, 565.
21 NAC, vol. XIV, 72; FYZ I, 568–9.
22 Feudalism remained important to Fukuzawa until the abolition of daimyo domains in 1871. Needless to say, the Japan of 1866, when he wrote about the Netherlands and England in the first volume of *Conditions in the West*, was quite different from the Japan of 1870, when he wrote about Russia and France.
23 Alexander Fraser Tytler, *Elements of General History, Ancient and Modern*, 130–1, J. F. Brown, Concord, NH, 1851; FYZ I, 356.
24 Tytler, 131, 146; FYZ I, 356–9.
25 Tytler wrote: "The crimes of Henry were expiated by his misfortunes. His only son was drowned in his passage from Normandy." Having read Tytler, Fukuzawa was aware of Henry IV's crimes, but in describing them, he changed expiation to "retribution": "That his only son had drowned on the high seas was a retribution (*mukui*) for the crimes he had committed against his older brother." (Tytler, 131;

FYZ I, 360.) I have found the right sources for the texts Fukuzawa used in writing about the Netherlands, Russia, and France. For England, I have located some texts, but others remain uncertain.
26 McCulloch II, 292.
27 FYZ I, 361.
28 McCulloch II, 293.
29 McCulloch II, 293; FYZ I, 361.
30 FYZ I, 363.
31 McCulloch II, 294; FYZ I, 363.
32 McCulloch II, 295.
33 FYZ II, 366.
34 John Hill Burton, *Political Economy for Use in Schools and Private Instruction*, 18, William and Robert Chambers, London, 1853.
35 Sir William Blackstone's book (1766) was repeatedly republished (1770, 1772, 1774, 1775, 1778). A one-volume abridgment of the original four volumes was published in 1856. Fukuzawa most probably used this. See Robert Malcolm Kerr, *The Student's Blackstone: Selections from the Commentaries on the Laws of England*, John Murray, London, 1858.

Chapter 2

1 Fukuzawa Yukichi, *The Autobiography of Fukuzawa Yukichi* (Kiyooka Eiichi trans.), revised trans., Lanham, MD, 1992.
2 In speaking here of Fukuzawa's stance toward Confucianism, I mean his lack of interest in religion, his explanations of social functions in terms of human nature, the connections he made between education and morality, and so on. All of these tendencies may be labeled Confucian. But by 1875 Fukuzawa had rejected many of the other ideas at the core of Confucianism. I have benefited immensely from conversations with Watanabe Hiroshi, whose elucidation of the relation between Song thought and Tokugawa Confucianism is brilliant. As for Fukuzawa, we agree that Confucian teachings, as modified by Dutch studies, provided him with the platform he used to approach nineteenth-century European thought; we also agree that "civilization" did not just mean "current Western civilization." But Professor Watanabe, if I interpret his position correctly, feels that Fukuzawa's rejection of Confucianism was itself the affirmation of Confucian rationality. I feel that Fukuzawa's rationality during the 1870s had gone beyond Confucianism in any meaningful sense. In his *Plan* for *An Outline of Theories of Civilization*, Fukuzawa wrote: "Until now learning in Japan has been stupid. The Confucian classics are either guidebooks for slaves or instructions for the rearing of slaves."

And even earlier, while studying Dutch medicine during the late 1850s, Fukuzawa looked down on students of Chinese learning. See Sashi Tsutae, "Shippitsu memo mitsukaru," *Mita hyōron*, August–September 1991.

3 Miyazaki Fumiko, "*Banshoshirabedokoro-Kaiseijo ni okeru baishin shiyō mondai*," in *Tokyo Daigakushi kiyō*, second issue, Tokyo University. Fukuzawa's new rank of *hon'yakugata* was fairly low in the hierarchy of bakufu ranks.

4 FYZ XX, 10. M. William Steele has made a slightly different but complete translation of the memorial. "Fukuzawa Yukichi and the Idea of a Shogunal Monarchy: Some Documents in Translation," in *International Christian University Publications III, Asian Cultural Studies*, Special Issue No. 7, March 31, 1997.

5 FYZ XVII, 31.

6 Ibid., 56.

7 FYZ Supp. vol., 20.

Chapter 3

i When we kill animals and plants and destroy their power of generation in order to consume them as food, their original power is transformed into a power by which humans beings live and breathe. A man, thus fortified, is able to carry, in the course of one day, a pair of traveling cases weighing 46 pounds for 24 miles. His energy is expended on carrying the load, and to replenish this, he must consume food. Phenomena of this kind are called the transformation or indestructibility of power.

ii It is said that Japanese warriors were brutal in past ages, yet one never hears of war being waged for plunder. The purpose or pretext for war was to rescue commoners from abject poverty. In this sense, war in Japan was decidedly different from war in Europe during the Dark Ages, where plunder and capturing prisoners were the sole objectives. This is why warriors in Japan were powerful, and commoners, meek and obsequious.

iii Although one speaks of civilization, in many cases one doubts whether this is truly civilization. Nevertheless, there is no denying that the tendency to discard the old for the new has been extremely strong. I myself am merely following common usage when I use the term.

iv There are people in the countryside who take pride in adopting new practices, such as using the solar calendar, putting up decorative pine trees at New Year's in the Western manner, and displaying the national flag on official holidays. Many are the owners of bookstores, Western-style eateries, shops specializing in imported goods, and other establishments opened since the Restoration. People feel secure when they find a suitable station in life.

v They are rich in virtue but lack intelligence and money.

vi Christians in the West contend that people without religious faith should not be considered human. It is different in Japan, where people who consider themselves scholars do not believe in gods and Buddhas, and also think that the more irreligious a person, the more refined he is. Westerners are not aware of this.

vii When so-called extremists undertake something, they never fail to issue a manifesto. Apart from minor differences, the authors of these manifestos assert that so-and-so did such and such, and having defiled Japan—the land of the gods—and betrayed their country, they will themselves take on the task of rescuing the people from misery. They never say a word about expanding people's rights. Judging from the way these extremists accuse others of betraying the country, it is clear that they think the sense of nationhood has been lost and concealed by others. Also, when they say they will rescue the people from misery, without mentioning the expansion of individual rights, they act as though they are the masters of the country. Instead of attending to their own rights, they are too busy minding the affairs of others, accusing the government of neglecting the people, and saying they will take care of them. From the ancient past to the present, the language used by samurai has been the same. Rather than getting the benefits of forming a political faction, they get only the harmful points.

viii In 1874, there were 84,689 rickshaws in Japan.

ix The haughty behavior of lowly officials is a habit formed by samurai over hundreds of years. The fault is due not to human weakness but to the trends of the times. An official does not go out of his way to act haughtily but unconsciously enjoys such an attitude.

x Having exhausted their political selves, *shizoku* are left with only their physical lives.

xi There is naturally a difference between a nation and its government.

xii It is said that during the last days of Tokugawa rule, an errand boy in service to foreigners acted rudely in the front entrance of a senior councilor's residence.

xiii The plan may seem ridiculous, but I mention it because some people actually think this way.

xiv The plan is just as ridiculous, though there are people who hope to win over *shizoku* with false promises of hereditary stipends. I mention it because an expanded version of this idea would amount to the same thing as the main point of my essay.

xv We should transform their power, not destroy it.

xvi Fruit is popular in the city and cheap sweet cakes in the countryside. City people eat food that is refined and contains carbon (*tanso*), so they prefer fruit, which has little carbon. Country folk like sweet cakes, which contain carbon. In days past, elegant ladies who lived in daimyo mansions preferred steamed cakes to fruit because their everyday food was delicate and sparse and had very little carbohydrates.

xvii There is a vast difference between telling people what to do and how it should be done.

xviii Merchants talk of "flooding the market." Men of learning usually ignore this, but it is the most important thing in the world of commerce.

xx In recent years, the establishment of a popular elective assembly has been heatedly debated, with some saying that it is too soon and others that it is already too late. They have yet to determine who is right or wrong because they have not looked into what constitutes a deliberative assembly. To try to determine whether something is right or wrong, without looking into its nature, is like arguing about heaven or hell without seeing it.

xxi Mental and physical power is substance. Good and evil, right and wrong are its forms or modes of function.

xxii Government laws are applied uniformly. The laws do not, of course, suit all of society. A law that suits the rich does not suit the poor, and a law that benefits the dull-witted is worthless to the intelligent. The essential purpose of government is to heed the wishes of the majority, and, in particular, the wishes of people with influence.

xix Conservative *shizoku* are a stubborn lot. By men concerned for the country, I mean the advocates of popular rights.

1 *Bunkenron* means "a discussion on the division of power" (between central and local government). (Please note that here and in the other commentaries quotations from the translated essays do not have endnotes.)

2 FYZ XVII, 199. Fukuzawa ends the letter saying, "I consider this essay to be a telling argument. In short, my purpose in writing it is to support and make full use of the *shizoku* class."

3 Tōyama Shigeki cites headlines from popular rights newspapers in 1876 that were often banned: "Freedom must be bought with fresh blood," "Overthrow oppressive government," "Assassinate cruel officials," "A murderous spirit is a basic element for establishing the nation." In contrast to these, Fukuzawa's essay strikes us as utterly moderate. Tōyama Shigeki, *Meiji ishin*, 330, Tokyo, 1956.

4 The essay is in FYZ IV, 231–93.

5 English words that Fukuzawa renders in katakana are set in boldface type. Fukuzawa's prose is fluent and lucid, but paragraphs occasionally run to more than a page. For clarity's sake, these have been divided.

6 One *koku* of unmilled rice equals 5.1 American bushels. *Koku* was the unit used in assessing domain revenues and samurai stipends.

7 Fukuzawa read the American edition of Alexis de Tocqueville's *Democracy in America* (*The Republic of the United States of America and Its Political Institutions, Revised and Examined*, translated by Henry Reeves [Reeve], with an Original Preface and Notes by John C. Spencer, Two Volumes in One, A. S. Barnes, New York, 1873) from June 24 to July 25, 1877, marking passages with small pieces of paper. In distinguishing between "government" and "administration," he drew on pp. 88–9 in the section "Political effects of the system of local administration in the United States" in chapter 5 of the first book. He presumably read a partial translation of the

section by Obata Tokujirō (1842–1905), which was published in issue 34 of a small family magazine called *Katei sōdan* on December 23, 1876, as well as other partial translations by Obata from the first book: "Liberty of the press in the United States" in chapter 11, published as *Jōboku jiyūron* in 1873; "Public spirit in the United States" in chapter 14, published in issue 23 of *Katei sōdan* on November 19, 1876; "Notion of Rights in the United States" in chapter 14, published in issue 29 of the same magazine on December 8, 1876. Obata, who was from a high-ranking samurai family in Nakatsu, studied at Fukuzawa's school, and later became a close associate. I thank Professor Nishizawa Naoko of Keiō University for the information about Obata.

8 The quotation is from pp. 89, 92 in "Political effects of the system of local administration in the United States" in chapter 5 of the first book of the American edition. Rather than translating back from the Japanese, I have used the American edition of Reeve's 1873 translation of *Democracy in America*.

9 The passages quoted are from the section "Public spirit in the United States," in chapter 14 of the first book, 262–4. I have used Reeve's translation. Obata's translation is elegant and accurate, but in one instance, it differs: "The country is lost to their senses, they can neither discover it under its own, nor under borrowed features" is rendered as "Ah, where is the country? We look for it but cannot see it; we incline our ears but cannot hear it. We search for it in the soil but the country is not there. We search for it in its culture but the country is not there."

10 For a more detailed analysis of de Tocqueville's influence on Fukuzawa, see chapter 4 in Anzai Toshimitsu, *Fukuzawa Yukichi to jiyū shugi: kojin, jichi, kokutai*, Tokyo, 2007. See also Matsuda Kōichirō, "Fukuzawa Yukichi to Meiji kokka," in Karube Tadashi, et al., *Nihon shisōshi kōza*, 4, Kindai, Tokyo, 2013.

Chapter 4

1 The essay marks Fukuzawa's first support for central government by a nationally elected body. As to the authorship, in the preface to the first 1898 edition of FYZ, Fukuzawa states: "I shall add a few words to clarify a small matter. Several of my publications in their original editions carried other names than mine, or sometimes it was announced on its title page that I formed the idea and other men set it down. These uses of other men's names was made necessary by the circumstances of the time." *Preface to the Collected Works of Fukuzawa Yukichi* (Kiyooka Eiichi trans.), 96, Tokyo, 1980. These words apply to many works where the title page states: "Fukuzawa Yukichi *ritsuan*, somebody else *hikki*." Since "On a National Assembly" was not put out under Fukuzawa's name, he could quote passages from his *Renewal of Popular Sentiments* and acknowledge "Fukuzawa-sensei" as the source of the information.

2. Perhaps Fukuzawa overstates when he writes: "I felt I had set fire to a field of grass and the fire was getting out of my control," in *The Autobiography of Fukuzawa Yukichi* (revised trans.), 319–20.
3. In *Renewal of Popular Sentiments* (*Minjō isshin*), Fukuzawa presents his new theory of history in considerable detail, listing specific dates and figures for a variety of inventions, innovations, and publications. The detailed factual material and the interpretation clearly come from an English source. I would guess it was a publication of the mid-1870s, but thus far I have not found it. For the data, see FYZ V, 24–30.
4. The essay is in FYZ V, 63–92.
5. The original phrases are: "Unbending strength, resoluteness, simplicity, and reticence are close to benevolence." "It is rare indeed for a man with cunning words and an ingratiating face to be benevolent."
6. One of the precepts of the Five Human Relationships in Confucianism enjoined a married couple not to be "overly familiar with each other or behave in an unseemly manner."
7. Pei Gong: Liu Bang, founder of the former Han dynasty.
8. Fukuzawa Yukichi, *Minjō isshin*. The author most likely is drawing from the 1879 edition. This passage is found in chapter 5.
9. *Injun*: a compound of *in* (to rely) and *jun* (to follow what went before).
10. Fukuzawa Yukichi, *Minjō isshin*. The authors most likely are drawing from the 1879 edition. The passages are found in chapter 5.
11. Fukuzawa uses "vote of credit" rather than "vote of confidence," the more commonly used phrase at present.
12. FYZ IV, 580.

Chapter 5

1. The essay first appeared from April 5 to April 14, 1882 as editorials in the *Jiji shinpō*, the newspaper Fukuzawa founded that year. We chose the essay for its analysis of the tension between the political parties and the government during the early 1880s.
2. The essay is in FYZ V, 235–55.
3. *Nanjū* is a compound of "difficult" and "slow down."
4. *Tama o futokoro ni suru*. The treasure refers to the national goal and, by implication, its implementation.
5. Fukuzawa refers to the Rikken Teiseitō (Constitutional Imperial Government Party), founded on March 18, 1882. The other parties founded the same year are the Rikken Seitō (Constitutional Party; February 1) and the Rikken Kaishintō (Constitutional Reform Party; April 16). The Jiyūtō (Freedom Party) was founded in October 1881.
6. Fukuzawa refers to the Rikken Teiseitō. In the March 31 and April 1 editorials of *Jiji shinpō*, he criticized the party and urged it to reconsider its name.

Chapter 6

1. Fukuzawa, *Outline of a Theory of Civilization*, 190.
2. FYZ V, 212–19.
3. We chose the 1888 "Revering the Emperor" (*Sonnōron*) rather than the 1882 "The Imperial House" (*Teishitsuron*) because it speaks more directly to the 1889 Constitution. Both essays first appeared as a series of newspaper editorials in the *Jiji shinpō*: "The Imperial House" from April 26 to May 11, 1882, and "Revering the Emperor" from September 26 to October 6, 1888. The 1882 essay is in FYZ V, 257–92.
4. FYZ V, 261.
5. Ibid., 265.
6. Ibid., 280.
7. The essay is in FYZ VI, 3–29.
8. Walter Bagehot, *The English Constitution*, Reprint of 1867 edition, ed. Miles Taylor, New York, 2001.
9. Ibid., 41.
10. Ibid., 45.
11. Ibid., 51.
12. Ibid., 54.
13. Ibid., 51–5.
14. Ibid., 41.
15. *The Economist*, 71, October 22–28, 1894.
16. FYZ VI, 13. The passage reads: "The historical antecedents of Western monarchs do not bear comparison with those of the Imperial House of Japan. Nevertheless, the majestic and sacrosanct (*songen shinsei*) authority of their [the Western monarchs] office has in many instances helped reconcile the conflicting emotions of subjects and subdue social unrest."
17. FYZ IV, 451–2.

Chapter 7

1. The essay first appeared as twelve editorials in the *Jiji shinpō* between December 10 and 20, 1890. It was published as a book with three other essays in 1892. Fukuzawa was fifty-five years old in 1890. Of the four essays, this essay speaks most directly to the topic of government.
2. The essay is in FYZ VI, 33–70.
3. Ryōin Bettō: an honorary court title conferred by the emperor. Doubts were cast on the authenticity of the document listing the eighteen statutes (*Kōbu hōsei ōchoku jūhakkajō*), and in 1904, three years after Fukuzawa's death, it was conclusively proven to be a forgery. See Tomita Masafumi's Afterword in FYZ VI, 595.

4. Ieyasu was initially buried at Mt. Kunō in Shizuoka City. The document *Kunōzan hōzōiri hyakkajō yuijō* has also been proven to be a forgery.
5. "Outside" or *tozama* daimyo were those who pledged allegiance to the Tokugawa after Ieyasu's decisive victory in the Battle of Sekigahara in 1600.
6. English terms for officials are taken from Conrad Totman, *Politics in the Tokugawa Bakufu*, Appendix B, 270–7, Berkeley, CA, 1967.
7. Fukuzawa refers to Nakatsu, his home domain in Kyushu.
8. *Mikawa bushi* were samurai who served Ieyasu from the time he was based in Mikawa province before his rise to national power.
9. Saigō's letter was actually written on the eighteenth of the seventh month, in 1871, four days after the issuance of the edict declaring the abolition of domains and the establishment of a centralized prefectural system. Banno Junji, *Saigō Takamori to Meiji ishin*, 148, Tokyo, 2013. The eighteenth of the seventh month in 1871 is September 2 according to the solar calendar, hence "autumnal cool." Tomita Masafumi notes in the Afterword to Fukuzawa's essay that the letter quoted by Fukuzawa differs in places from that in *Dai Saigō zenshū*, vol. II, and speculates that Fukuzawa used a copy. See FYZ VI, 595. Katsura Shirō Hisatake (1830–77) was a high-ranking samurai from Satsuma and a close friend of Saigō. He joined the Satsuma Rebellion and committed suicide after Saigō's death in the Battle of Shiroyama.
10. Rather than translating back from the Japanese, I have used the original passage on p. xxxviii of Bagehot's Introduction to the second 1872 edition of *The English Constitution*, which Fukuzawa owned.
11. Fukuzawa changed his mind about Japanese feudalism in 1889. In that year, he published a series of editorials on the Constitution in the *Jiji shinpō*, which were published as a book titled *The Origins of the Diet* (*Kokkai no engi*). He wrote: "When translating the word *hōken* into a foreign language, for want of a better term, we use 'feudal system.' When foreigners hear the term 'Japanese feudal system,' they think of Europe in the past. I find this truly intolerable. The two systems are not to be compared. In our civilization, from ancient to recent times, the Tokugawa represented a peak. Even looking back from the present day, it had much of worth. Putting aside a detailed discussion to another day, we must not mistake facts because of translation-words. We must ask foreigners to take special care." FYZ XII, 26–7.
12. In his article, "Fukuzawa Yukichi to Meiji kokka," Matsuda Kōichirō calls Fukuzawa's roseate account of pre-Meiji society a "Tokugawa monogatari," and doubts that Fukuzawa believed what he wrote about the distinctly Japanese sense of self-rule. Karube Tadashi, et al., *Nihon shisōshi kōza-kindai*, 4, 102–3, Tokyo, 2013.

Index

Note: Roman numerals in parentheses following a page number refer to Fukuzawa's marginal notes (pp. 212–14).

administrative power (*chiken*)
　of local government 64–8, 70
　vs. political power 53, 60, 62, 64–8, 70–1, 75–6, 84, 214 n.7
agriculture 5, 38, 48, 74. *See also* farmers
Aikokusha (Patriotic Party) 78
Akechi Mitsuhide 21
Alcock, Sir Rutherford 10
All the Countries of the World (*Sekai kunizukushi*; Fukuzawa Yukichi) 18
Amaterasu (Sun Goddess) 159, 160
anti-government party (*hiseifutō*) 82, 85, 86–7, 107
　commoners and 191–2
　public opinion and 119–21
Asakusa Shrine 164
assemblies, elective x, 214(xx), 215 n.1
　central government and 23, 93, 112
　centralization and 54–5
　communication and 76, 78, 112, 128
　debates on 190
　establishment of 78, 111
　former samurai and 48, 75–6, 187–8
　Fukuzawa's opposition to 27, 29
　inefficiency of 94, 119
　local 3, 29, 30, 75–8, 112, 128
　local government and 54, 63
　people and 93–4
　political conflict and 30, 116, 127–8
　political rights and 112–13
　prefectural 30, 76, 78, 85, 98, 112–13, 116, 119, 127–8, 206
　self-rule and 206
　in the West 32, 190
assembly, national (*shūsho kaigi*) 3, 24, 27, 77–107, 207. *See also* Diet, National
　arguments against 80, 82–6, 98, 105–6
　arguments for 81, 85–6, 89, 91–4, 106–7

　debate in 104–5
　delaying of 76, 82–6, 89, 91
　Imperial House and 134–5, 153
　inefficiency of 83–4
　local assemblies and 76, 113
　majority rule and 140
　petitions for 78, 127
　political unrest and 116–17, 124
　promise of 109, 110, 129, 130

Baelz, Edwin 11
Bagehot, Walter 79, 159–62, 165, 195–6, 205
balance of power (*kenryoku heikin*) 170–8, 202–6
　domains and 176–8, 186, 204
　government officials and 177–8
　the people and 170, 171–8, 184, 193
　in political parties 193–4
banking 53, 56, 95
Beale, Dorothea 18
Blackstone, Sir William 18
"Brief Comments on Public Security" (*Chian shōgen*; Fukuzawa Yukichi) 168
Brief Comments on the Times (*Jiji shōgen*; Fukuzawa Yukichi) 80, 133
Britain. *See* England
Buckle, Thomas 4, 203, 209 n.1
Buddhism 96, 115, 133, 149, 159, 184, 199
Burton, John Hill ix, 4, 16, 18, 209 n.1

centralization 13, 17, 21–3, 27, 47–8, 54–5, 209 n.4. *See also* government, central
Charles I (England) 15
Charter Oath (1868) 23, 92, 188
China

220 *Index*

centralization in 209 n.4
despotism in 91–2, 170, 171, 173, 174–6, 185, 203
government of 101–2
history of viii, 3, 21, 38, 80
learning from 5, 7, 20, 85, 187, 212 n.2
Western colonialism in 80, 102
Chōshū domain 20–3, 36, 92, 189, 190
Christianity 133–4, 162, 213(vi)
cities 5, 12, 46, 47, 178. *See also* Edo; Tokyo
  vs. countryside 39, 40–1, 44, 53, 66, 213(xvi)
  government in 53, 68, 138–9, 177, 182, 204
citizens (*kokumin*) 36, 55, 170, 193
  Imperial House and 145, 146
  laws and 61, 195
  rights of 62, 66, 111, 122, 129
civilization 211 n.2, 212(iii)
  competition and 147–8
  conflict and 136, 137, 153
  development of 3–6, 72, 94–5
  extravagance and 50, 153
  extremism and 89, 103
  forms of government and 6, 18, 56
  Imperial House and 147, 149, 152, 155, 156–7, 164
  majority rule and 140–1
  spirit and 4, 79
  Western 3–4, 79, 101, 102
class 72–3. *See also* commoners; farmers; merchants; nobles; samurai; *shizoku*
Collected Works (Fukuzawa Yukichi) viii
Commentaries on the Laws of England (Blackstone) 18
commerce 155, 156, 214(xviii). *See also* merchants
  development of 94–5
  foreigners and 51
  government and 55, 57, 58
  politics and 33, 36, 37
  samurai and 31, 38, 48, 74, 178–9
commoners
  anti-government 191–2
  education of 114–15
  government and 56, 57, 58, 65, 66–7, 87, 118
  as government officials 67, 68

Imperial House and 147, 150, 152, 156, 194
  laws and 179, 193, 205
  Meiji Restoration and 90, 199
  national assembly and 85, 98, 140
  vs. nobles 151
  political rights of 111, 112
  politics and 32, 35, 47–8, 71, 78, 85, 112, 113–15, 127–8
  samurai and 44, 47, 73, 178, 179, 180, 194, 205, 212(ii)
  self-governance by 69–70, 174, 182–3, 204–5
communication 39, 40
  assemblies and 113, 128
  railroads and 22, 46, 84, 101, 199
  telegraph and x, 22, 79, 84, 94, 101, 199
competition
  amelioration of 138–9, 142, 147–8
  balance of power and 174, 176
  conflict and 118, 138, 139
  economic 59, 71–2
  Imperial House and 139–40
  of political parties 100–1, 103–5, 137
  political power and 97–8
"Concerning the Land Tax" (*Chisoron*; Fukuzawa Yukichi) 169
Conditions in the West (*Seiyō jijō*; Fukuzawa Yukichi) 17–18, 20–2, 78, 209 n.3
  on feudalism 7, 8, 9, 17
  historical model in x, 5, 6, 27, 167, 203
  popularity of 92, 188
  sources for ix, 6, 7, 16
  terms in 8–9, 12
Confucianism 115, 133, 159, 184, 216 n.6
  of Fukuzawa viii, 19–20, 211 n.2
Constitution, Meiji 197, 203, 207, 208, 218 n.11
  Diet and 168, 193
  drafts of 109–10
  as gift of emperor 157
constitutions 170
  English 159–61, 195–6
  French 38
  US 17, 32, 38, 196–7, 205, 209 n.3
Cornell, Sarah 4
countryside. *See also* farmers; government, local

associations in 69–70
vs. cities 39, 40–1, 44, 53, 66, 213(xvi)
newspapers in 43, 44
taxes in 47

daimyo 185–6. *See also* domains
   abolition of 93, 111, 150, 191
   bakufu and 11, 20–2, 89, 176–7
   commoners and 58, 113, 194
   Meiji Restoration and 13, 89–93
   nobles and 151, 175, 204
Democracy in America (de Tocqueville) 74, 160, 214 n.7
de Tocqueville, Alexis 55, 61–2, 74, 75, 79, 160, 214 n.7
Dictionary, Geographical, Statistical and Historical... (McCulloch) 8
Diet, National 167–208
   balance of power and 170–8, 184, 186, 193–4, 202–6
   foreigners on 168, 169, 171, 172, 191, 198–9, 203
   government and 201–2
   Meiji Constitution and 168, 193
   Meiji Restoration and 191, 198
   suffrage for 208
   Western influence on 168, 172, 188, 198, 207
Discussion of the British Parliament (*Eikoku gijiin-dan*; Fukuzawa Yukichi) 18
Disraeli, Benjamin 161
"Division of Power" (*Bunkenron*; Fukuzawa Yukichi) 30–74, 77, 78
   commentary on 29–30, 74–6
Domain Offices, Edict for (*Hanji shokusei*) 23
Domain Registers, Return of (*hanseki hōkan*) 13, 23, 189
domains. *See also* Chōshū domain; Higo domain; Mito domain; Saga domain; Satsuma domain; Tosa domain
   abolition of 23, 33, 42, 93, 111, 114, 150, 172, 188–90, 191, 199, 206
   bakufu and 20, 175
   balance of power and 176–8, 186, 204
   Meiji Restoration and 48, 90, 92–3
   rebellions by 20–2, 29, 30, 36, 75, 78, 79, 109, 127, 135

   relocation of 176–7
   samurai and 32, 120
Dutch learning viii, 19, 187, 211 n.2. *See also* Netherlands

economy, Meiji. *See also* commerce; merchants
   competition in 59, 71–2
   education and 73
   farmers and 113–14, 128
   inflation in 25
   rapid development of 94–5
   role of government in 57–9
Eden, C. H. 11
Edo 40, 88, 89, 120. *See also* Tokyo
   Fukuzawa in viii, 19
   mandated residence in 20, 177, 179
   self-governance in 182, 183–4
education 53, 157, 211 n.2
   development of 48, 94–5, 114–15
   of Fukuzawa 19–20
   government and 68, 69, 70, 199
   Imperial House and 155
   newspapers and 94–5
   political unrest and 115, 116, 128–9
   politics and 18, 85, 114–15, 129
   power and 31, 32
   for representative government 3, 5, 17, 18, 27
   of samurai 32, 49, 73, 187
   of shogun 186
   Western 90, 129, 156
Education, Ministry of 94–5, 114
Education, Regulations for Universal 114, 129
Education Act 94
Edward I (England) 9
Edward II (England) 14, 15
Elements of General History (Tytler) 14
Elizabeth I (England) 15
emperor, Japanese 103, 160, 197. *See also* Imperial House
   in constitutional government 192–3, 194
   direct rule by 78
   vs. Imperial House 162–3
   Meiji Constitution and 157
   Meiji Restoration and 90–3, 119, 124

role of 134–5
shogun and 21, 22, 194, 204
Encouragement of Learning, An (*Gakumon no susume*; Fukuzawa Yukichi) 18, 188
England
constitution of 159–61, 195–6
feudalism in 7, 8–9, 13, 210 n.22
form of government in 17, 83, 161–2, 195–6
Fukuzawa's sources for ix, 6, 188, 211 n.25
vs. Japan 11, 66, 85, 162
as model x, 98–103, 104, 107
monarchy in 13–16, 102, 161–2, 195–6, 205
Parliament of 15, 17, 18, 79, 89, 98–104, 106, 107, 161, 186, 205
political parties in 87, 99–101, 103
Revolution in 15
royal family in 186
English Constitution, The (Bagehot) 159, 160–1
English language viii, 10, 19, 20
Europe. *See also* West, the; *particular countries*
education in 90
feudalism in 6–10, 18, 204, 218 n.11
in historical models 27, 80
medieval 6–11, 27, 204, 212(ii), 218 n.11
as model 202–3
monarchies in 17, 163, 164
"expel the barbarian" movement 22, 34, 42, 119, 120, 124, 157, 187, 188
extravagance
civilization and 50, 153
competition and 138
of governments 40, 57, 58–9, 68–9, 88, 199
immorality and 88
of samurai 41
self-confidence and 50–1

Family Registration Law 149
farmers 39, 64, 115
associations of 69–70
economy and 113–14, 128
politics and 32, 35, 78, 85, 112, 114, 127–8
samurai and 47, 52, 180, 207
in Tokugawa period 24, 58, 69–70, 85, 207

feudalism (*hōken*; *fengjian*)
advancement from 3, 17, 21
in England 7, 8–9, 13, 210 n.22
in Europe 6–10, 18, 204, 218 n.11
foreigners on 10–11, 210 n.14
former samurai and 52, 82
Imperial House and 154, 190
Japanese terms for 8–10, 17
Meiji Restoration and 23, 24, 188, 190–1
monarchy and 6, 21, 204
in Tokugawa Japan 6–10, 11, 13, 27, 111, 203–4, 218 n.11
First Principles (Spencer) 160
foreigners
competition with 71–2
expulsion of 22, 34, 42, 89–90, 119, 120, 124, 188
extremism of 194
on feudalism 10–11, 210 n.14
government officials and 59–60
on Meiji government 168, 169, 171, 172, 189, 191, 198–9, 203
rebellions and 21, 51
as threat 51, 79
foreign relations
central government and 53, 189
competition in 71–2, 125, 130
opening of Japan to viii, ix, 22, 33, 71, 89, 90, 111, 140
treaties and 23, 51, 90, 106
Western imperialism and 78, 80, 102, 203
France ix, 6, 62, 167, 210 n.22
Constitution of 38
feudalism in 7, 9–10, 18
Fukuzawa's sources for 9, 10, 12, 13, 211 n.25
Meiji military reforms and 23
monarchy in 10, 12–13, 18, 61, 102, 191, 206
representative government in 17, 18, 89, 161
French Revolution 83, 105
Fujita Mokichi 77, 81
Fujiwara family 150, 152, 162, 164
Fukuzawa Yukichi. *See also particular titles*
autobiography of 19–20, 77
later essays of 27
life of viii–ix

memorials by 21, 22
politics of 19–25
sources used by ix, 4, 6, 7, 9–13, 16, 188, 210 n.11, 211 n.25
translations by ix–x, 12–13, 22
travels of viii–ix, 19
works by viii, ix–x
Fushimi-Toba, battle of 22, 23, 91
"Future Course of the Diet" (*Kokkai no zento*; Fukuzawa Yukichi) 167–208
commentary on 167–8, 202–8

Gaihen (supplementary volume of *Conditions in the West*) ix
Gaikokugata ix, 7, 20
George II (England) 16
Germany 7
Gotō Shinpei 111
government
administrative *vs.* political power of 53, 60, 62, 64–8, 70–1, 75–6, 84, 214 n.7
Chinese 101–2
in cities 53, 68, 138–9, 177, 182, 204
extravagance of 40, 57, 58–9, 68–9, 88, 199
forms of 6, 18, 56
Imperial House and 136, 140, 147, 153, 154, 157
military and 3, 23, 120, 124, 125, 130
people and 56, 57–9, 66, 91–2, 153, 154, 155, 201–2
reason *vs.* emotion and 136, 141, 142
responsibilities of 126–7, 130, 131, 137
Russian 101
government, central 215 n.1. *See also* assembly, national
competition and 57–9, 97–8
extravagance of 68–9
foreigners and 51, 59, 79
vs. local 53–5, 60, 62–3, 66, 70, 75–6
people and 56, 57, 66
political power of 53, 60, 62, 64–8, 70–1, 75–6, 84, 106, 214 n.7
government, local. *See also* assemblies, local
administrative power of 53, 60, 62, 64–8, 70–1, 75–6, 84, 214 n.7
vs. central 53–5, 60, 62–3, 66, 70, 75–6
district head of 63–4

foreign relations and 72
former samurai and 65, 74–6
reforms of 30, 184
in Tokugawa period 179, 181–2, 198
government, Meiji. *See also* Tokugawa bakufu
centralization of 47–8, 206
commoners and 58, 66–7, 87, 118
conflicts with 24, 29–30, 36, 85–6, 87, 107, 125–6, 129–31, 201, 207
crisis of 1881 in 109, 110, 130
economic role of 57–9
education and 115
emperor and 134–5, 149
employment in 48–9, 51, 75
extravagance of 40, 57, 199
former samurai and 48–9, 52, 82
inefficiency of 119–20
majority rule and 141
military power of 23, 120–1
national assembly and 107, 201
vs. people 97, 117–27, 191–2, 199
vs. political parties 110, 122–3, 127–31, 207
vs. popular rightists 66, 86–7, 106, 120–3, 200
reforms of 22–3, 24, 30, 78, 95–6, 109, 110, 127
religion and 96, 137, 149, 199
government officials
arrogance of 44, 45, 66, 83, 85, 198, 213(ix)
assemblies and 93, 111–12
balance of power and 97, 105, 177–8
commoners as 67, 68
dismissal of 117–18
education and 95
election of 98–9, 104, 107
employment of 48, 49, 75, 199
foreigners and 59–60
vs. government 117–18, 119
Imperial House and 123, 152, 156
local 44, 45, 63–4, 66, 181–2, 183
majority rule and 141
national assembly and 84
popular rightists and 121, 200
role of 56, 73
samurai and 31, 32, 38–9, 43, 44–5, 47, 57, 67, 175–6
senior councilors (*rōjū*) 175–6, 177, 213(xii)

as statesmen (*seijika*) 154
Tokugawa 32, 44, 71, 175–6, 177, 180, 181–2
government, representative viii, 6, 29, 62, 203
  balance of power and 192–3
  constitutional (*kunmin dōchi no rikken*) 82, 83, 167–72, 184, 192–3, 195, 202
  vs. despotism 169–72
  education for 3, 5, 17, 18, 27
  foreigners on 168, 169
  in France 17, 18, 89, 161
  institutions of 3, 27
  Meiji Restoration and 187–8
  parliamentary x, 15, 17, 18, 79, 83, 89, 98–104, 106, 107, 161, 186, 205
government sect (*seifushū*) 124
  vs. people's sect 117, 119, 129
Griffis, William 10–11, 210 n.14
Guizot, François 4, 203, 209 n.1

Hachiman Shrine 149
Hagi (Chōshū) 29, 36
Han dynasty (China) 91–2
Hara Kei 208
Henry I (England) 14
Henry IV (England) 14, 210 n.25
Henry VIII (England) 14–15, 17
Higo domain 176, 189
historical models x, 5, 6, 18, 27, 78–80, 167, 202–3
History of France and Normandy (Taylor) 9, 10, 12, 13
Hōjō family 173
Honganji Temple 149
human rights 18, 110–11, 127, 190, 207

Ii Naosuke 176
Imperial House 135–58. *See also* emperor, Japanese
  ancient lineage of 145–6, 148, 150, 160, 164
  balance of power and 173
  civilization and 147, 149, 152, 155, 156–7, 164
  commoners and 147, 150, 152, 156, 194
  in Constitution 193, 194
  domains and 189

  government and 123, 136, 140, 147, 152–4, 156, 157, 192, 199
  national assembly and 134–5, 153
  necessity of 136–43
  politics and 121–3, 140, 147, 151, 153–5, 157, 162–4, 173, 193
  preservation of 136, 147–58
  reason *vs.* emotion and 136, 138, 143, 145, 149, 156–8, 163–5
  religion and 133–5, 155, 159–60, 162, 163
  sacredness of 136, 143–7, 163–4
  samurai and 187
  shogun and 174–5, 204
  vs. Western monarchies 217 n.16
"Imperial House" (*Teishitsuron*) 134
imperialism, Western 78, 80, 102, 203
industrialization
  in Japan 27, 47, 48, 55, 57, 71, 73, 94, 155
  in the West ix, 5, 16, 167
Invitation to Learning (*Gakumon no susume*; Fukuzawa Yukichi) ix
Ise Shrine 39, 69, 159
Ishikawa Hanjirō 135
Itagaki Taisuke 24, 111, 127
Itō Hirobumi 23, 78, 107, 109, 207, 208
Itō Jinsai 115
Iwakura mission 23–4
Iwakura Tomomi 23
Izumo Shrine 149, 159

James II (England) 15
Jiji shinpō (newspaper) 110, 135, 169, 217 n.1, 218 n.11
Jiyūtō (Freedom Party) 216 n.5
John, King (England) 83

Kamakura bakufu 172
Katō Kiyomasa 159
Katsura Shirō 189, 190, 218 n.9
Keiō University x, 25, 79
Kido Takayoshi 23, 78
Kojiki 159
Kōjunsha (political association) 109
Komiyama Yasusuke 183–4
Korea 133
  despotism in 170, 171, 174, 175, 176, 203
  expeditions against 24, 30, 42
Kumamoto 29, 36

land system 24, 176
  taxes and 30, 78, 96, 113, 114, 116, 128
laws 51, 138, 154, 199, 214(xxii)
  citizens and 61, 195
  commoners and 179, 193, 205
  vs. customs 180, 181, 193, 195, 205
  Family Registration 149
  international 16
  Three New 30, 78
  Tokugawa 179, 180, 181, 182, 183–4, 197
Lincoln, Abraham 162
Lippincott's Pronouncing Gazetteer 7
literacy 5, 49, 115. *See also* education
Liu Bang (Pei Gong) 91–2
Lives of Eight Heroes (Takizawa Bakin) 183
Locke, John 18
Louis VI (France) 12
Louis IX (France) 12
Louis XI (France) 12

Magna Carta (England) 17, 79, 83, 106
Mary, Queen of Scots 15
Matsuda Kōichirō 218 n.12
McCulloch, John Ramsey 8, 9, 14–15, 16
Meiji Restoration (1868) ix, 22–5. *See also* Constitution, Meiji; economy, Meiji; government, Meiji
  commoners and 90, 199
  daimyo and 13, 89–93
  despotism and 172, 188–9, 191
  Diet and 191, 198
  domains and 48, 90, 92–3
  emperor and 90–3, 119, 124
  extremism in 90
  feudalism and 23, 24, 188, 190–1
  lack of opposition to 206
  leaders of 200–1
  local self-governance and 183, 184
  military and 23, 24, 92
  rapid change and 79, 94–6, 203
  religion and 159
  representative government and 111, 187–8
  samurai rebellions and 29–30
  "Seventy-percent Fund" and 183
  spirit of 190, 192, 201
  timing of 89–90, 91, 106
merchants 58, 115, 139, 214(xviii)
  foreigners and 59–60
  politics and 85, 112, 127, 204
  samurai and 178–9
Mikado's Empire, The (Griffis) 210 n.14
military
  balance of power and 176
  control of 195–6, 208
  of domains 92–3
  foreign 3, 16, 21, 22, 90
  government and 3, 23, 120–1, 124, 125, 130
  politics and 32, 37
  popular rightists and 41–2, 120
  rebellions and 21, 46, 47, 120, 126
  reforms of 23, 24, 84
  samurai and 32, 38, 52, 74
Mill, John Stuart 79, 160
Minamoto family 191
Minoura Katsundo 77, 81
Mitchell, Samuel Augustus 4, 18, 209 n.1
Mito domain 124, 176, 177
Miyazaki Fumiko 20
monarchy. *See also* Imperial House
  balance of power and 170, 171–8, 184, 193
  British 13–16, 102, 161–2, 195–6, 205
  constitutional 157, 161–2, 170, 194
  despotic 169–72, 203
  feudal 6, 21, 204
  French 10, 12–13, 18, 61, 102, 191, 206
  patriotism and 61, 62
  vs. representative government 3, 162
  shogun and 17, 22
  in Tokugawa period 17, 111, 184, 190
  in the West 15, 17, 27, 143, 156, 163, 164, 217 n.16
  Western thought on 160, 164
morality 151, 155, 185, 211 n.2
  balance of power and 173
  in education 114–15
  Ieyasu and 184–5
  Imperial House and 135, 136, 137–8, 149, 160, 194
  traditional *vs.* modern 41, 49, 61–2, 88
Mount Kōya monastery 149

Napoleon Bonaparte 191, 206
National Rights (*Tsūzoku kokkenron*;
    Fukuzawa Yukichi) 79
Netherlands ix, 6, 7, 17, 101, 210 n.22, 211
    n.25
New American Cyclopaedia (eds. Ripley
    and Dana) 9, 12, 13, 210 n.11
New School Geography (Mitchell) 4, 18
newspapers 43–4, 77, 114. *See also Jiji
    shinpō*
  assemblies and 83, 113, 128
  education and 94–5
  extremism in 214 n.3
  foreign-language 10, 11
  former samurai and 39, 40
  government and 66, 103, 104
  political unrest and 44, 118, 128
Nishizawa Naoko 215 n.7
nobles (*kizoku*) 9, 162, 175, 204
  new 149–52, 190, 199

Obata Tokujirō 55, 61, 215 n.7
Oda Nobunaga 21
Ogata Kōan viii, 19, 20
Ogyū Sorai 115
Ōkubo Toshimichi 23, 30, 78
Ōkuma Shigenobu 109
Ōkura Nagatsune 58
"On a National Assembly" (*Kokkairon*;
    Fukuzawa Yukichi) 77–107, 203
  commentary on 77–80, 105–7
"On People's Rights" (*Tsūzoku minkenron*;
    Fukuzawa Yukichi) 79, 105–6
"One Hundred Statutes to be Stored at
    Kunōzan" (Tokugawa Ieyasu) 175,
    180, 181, 185, 218 n.4
Origins of the Diet (*Kokkai no engi*;
    Fukuzawa Yukichi) 218 n.11
"Origins of Difficulties with the National
    Diet" (*Kokkai nankyoku no yurai*;
    Fukuzawa Yukichi) 168–9
Outline of Theories of Civilization
    (*Bunmeiron no gairyaku*;
    Fukuzawa Yukichi) ix, 4, 5, 79,
    133, 211 n.2
  historical model in x, 18, 78, 202–3

patriotism 61–2, 70, 74
Pei Gong (Liu Bang) 91–2

people, the. *See also* commoners; farmers;
    merchants
  assemblies and 93–4
  balance of power and 170, 171–8, 184,
    193
  in constitutional government 170
  government and 56, 57–9, 66, 91–2,
    153, 154, 155, 201–2
  political power and 70–1
people's sect (*jinminshū*) 117, 119, 129
Perry, Matthew viii
Plum Calendar (Tamenaga Shunsui) 183
police 46, 47, 109, 177, 199–200
Political Economy (Burton) ix, 16, 18
political ideas (*seiji no shisō*) 82, 83, 85,
    105
political parties viii, 78–9, 161, 208, 216
    nn.5–6
  alternation of 107
  balance of power in 193–4
  competition of 100–1, 103–5, 137
  draft Constitutions and 109
  in England 87, 99–101, 103
  Fukuzawa's dislike of x, 29, 134
  vs. government 110, 122–3, 127–31, 207
  political unrest and 124–5, 129, 192
political power (*seiken*) 30–1, 49, 99, 104,
    106
  vs. administrative power 53, 60, 62,
    64–8, 70–1, 75–6, 84, 214 n.7
  competition and 97–8
politics (*seiji*)
  balance of power in 174, 178, 194
  commoners and 32, 35, 47–8, 71, 78,
    85, 112, 113–15, 127–8
  competition in 95, 139
  conflict in 35, 142, 153–4, 160
  education and 18, 85, 114–15, 129
  extremism in 148, 213(vii)
  of Fukuzawa 19–25
  human rights and 111
  Imperial House and 121–3, 140, 147,
    151, 153–5, 157, 162–4, 173, 193
  samurai and 32–3, 36–7, 137–8, 187–8
  in US 32, 85
  Western theories on 58
popular rightists 78, 79, 111
  extremism of 85, 88–9, 213(vii)
  vs. government 66, 86–7, 106, 120–3, 200

monarchy and 103
national assembly and 83, 85–8
political unrest and 116, 127, 128
rebellions and 41–2
shizoku as 34, 43, 214(xix)
postal system x, 39, 79, 94, 101, 199
power 138, 214(xxi). *See also* balance of power; political power
administrative *vs.* political 60, 70–1, 75–6
balance of 202–3
government 53, 84, 96
military 16, 21, 22, 23, 37, 46, 47, 92, 120–1
of samurai 31, 33, 34, 60, 204
sources of 31, 212(i)
Prefectural Assemblies, Regulations for 112
prefectures 42, 45
establishment of 23, 111, 114, 172, 189, 199
printing x, 79, 94, 101
publication regulations 29, 43
public opinion 50, 107, 112
anti-government 119–21
on British Parliament 99–100, 101
competition for 104–5
on national assembly 80–1, 82, 84, 96–7, 127
newspapers and 43–4
rebellions and 42, 45

Qin dynasty (China) 91–2, 173
Qing dynasty (China) 80, 102

railroads 22, 46, 84, 101, 199
reason *vs.* emotion
government and 136, 141, 142
Imperial House and 136, 138, 143, 145, 149, 156–8, 163–5
monarchy and 161, 162
the past and 146, 147
value and 143–6
rebellions
causes of 36–45, 74–5
conservative *shizoku* and 29–30, 35–6, 45–7
by domains 20–2, 29, 30, 36, 75, 78, 79, 109, 127, 135

foreigners and 21, 51
Fukuoka 29
military and 21, 46, 47, 120, 126
popular rightists and 41–2
Satsuma 30, 75, 78, 79, 109, 127, 135
Taiping 21
reforms 33, 131
of government 20, 22–3, 24, 78, 95–6, 109, 110, 127, 150
military 23, 24, 84
social 44
tax 24, 30, 109, 111, 113, 114, 116, 127, 128, 199
religion. *See also* Buddhism; Christianity; Shinto
foreign influence and 51, 133
Fukuzawa and 19–20, 37, 211 n.2
government and 96, 137, 149, 199
Imperial House and 133–5, 155, 159–60, 162, 163
majority rule and 141–2
monarchy and 161
patriotism and 61, 62
in the West 12, 15, 135, 213(vi)
Renewal of Popular Sentiments (*Minjō isshin*; Fukuzawa Yukichi) 79, 94, 107, 203, 216 n.3
on British Parliament 99–103
"Revering the Emperor" (*Sonnōron*; Fukuzawa Yukichi) 133–65
commentary on 133–5, 158–65
Richard I (England) 15
Richard II (England) 14, 15
Richelieu, Cardinal 13
rights
human 18, 110–11, 127, 190, 207
political (*sansei no kenri*) 61–3, 66, 111–13, 127–9
Rikken Kaishintō (Constitutional Reform Party) 216 n.5
Rikken Seitō (Constitutional Party) 216 n.5
Rikken Teiseitō (Constitutional Imperial Government Party) 216 nn.5–6
Risshisha (popular rights party) 78
rōnin (masterless samurai) 9, 75, 90, 91
Russia ix, 6, 9, 18, 101, 210 n.11, 210 n.22, 211 n.25

Saga domain 22, 29, 36, 109
Saigō Takamori 24, 30, 78, 189–90, 204, 218 n.9
Sakai Tadatsumi 176
samurai. *See also* shizoku
   assemblies and 48, 75–6, 82, 105, 127–8, 187–8
   commerce and 31, 38, 48, 74, 178–9
   commoners and 44, 47, 52, 73, 178–9, 180, 194, 205, 207, 212(ii)
   disestablishment of 25, 38
   education of 32, 49, 73, 187
   emperor and 135, 137
   extremism of 213(vii)
   Fukuzawa as 19
   government officials and 31, 32, 38–9, 43, 44–5, 47, 57, 67, 175–6
   Meiji government and 48–9, 52, 82
   Meiji Restoration and 89–90, 93
   morality of 180, 185
   political unrest and 120, 124, 125
   politics and 32–3, 36–7, 137–8, 187–8
   power of 31, 33, 34, 60, 204
   the West and 11, 187
Sasaki Takayuki 78
Satsuma domain 20, 22, 23, 92, 112, 176, 189
   rebellion by 30, 75, 78, 79, 109, 127, 135
Seiyukai Party 208
self-governance (*jichi*) 69–70, 174, 182–4, 198, 199, 204–5, 218 n.12
"Seventy-percent Fund" 182
Shi Huangdi (China; Qin dynasty) 173
Shiji 91
Shinto 96, 133, 149, 199
   Imperial House and 134, 159, 162, 163
shizoku (military class, former samurai) 33–74, 213(x), 213(xiv), 214 n.2. *See also* samurai
   categories of 34–5, 74
   commoners and 44, 47, 73
   conservative *vs.* progressive 35, 37–8, 40–1, 42, 43, 45–6, 52–3, 60, 73, 74, 214(xix)
   definition of 9, 52, 74
   employment of 31, 34, 38–9, 46, 48, 49, 52, 57, 65, 74
   extravagance and 39–40, 41, 50–1, 66

   government officials and 44–5
   in local government 60, 65–6, 71, 74–6
   Meiji government and 34, 43, 48–9, 52, 66–7, 74, 82
   politics and 32–3, 36–7
   power and 31–5, 47, 74
   rebellions of 29–30, 35–6, 45–6, 47
   spirit of 47, 48
   unification of 52–3
shogun 173, 174–5, 185, 186, 191, 194, 204. *See also* Tokugawa bakufu
Smith, Adam 4
Sociology (Spencer) 160
Soejima Taneomi 111
songen shinsei (majestic and sacrosanct) 135, 143, 163
Sonnō joi (honor the emperor and expel the barbarians) 22, 34, 42, 90, 119–20, 124, 157, 187–8
Spencer, Herbert 79, 160
spirit (*seishin*) 4, 79, 82, 115
   of Meiji Restoration 190, 192, 201
   of *shizoku* 47, 48
spirit of the times (*toki no kiun*) 116, 117, 119, 125, 129
statesmen (*seijika*) 154
steam engine x, 31, 39, 48, 74, 79, 94
Strayer, Joseph 204
Student's Textbook of English and General History, The (Beale) 18
Sugawara no Michizane 149, 159
Switzerland 101

Taiping rebellion 21
Taira family 191
Takizawa Bakin 183
Tamenaga Shunsui 183
taxes 53, 153, 182
   assemblies and 30, 84, 127–8
   farmers and 47, 112, 113
   land 30, 78, 96, 113, 114, 116, 128
   reforms of 24, 30, 109, 111, 113, 114, 116, 127, 128, 199
Taylor, W. C. 9, 10, 12, 13
technology. *See also* railroads; telegraph
   in China 101
   national assembly and 84, 106
   rapid development and 79–80, 94–5
   representative government and 5, 27

steam x, 31, 39, 48, 74, 79, 94
  of warfare 12-13
  Western 22, 71, 90, 133
Teiseitō (Imperial Government Party) 134
telegraph x, 22, 79, 84, 94, 101, 199
Tenman Shrine 149
Thoughts on Raising Domain Productivity (*Kōeki kokusan-kō*; Ōkura Nagatsune) 58
Three New Laws 30, 78
Tokugawa bakufu
  balance of power in 170-8, 184, 186, 193, 202-6
  central government of 54, 71, 179
  corruption in 179-80
  daimyo and 20-1, 22
  despotism of 141, 181, 185-6
  domains in 176-7, 186
  extravagance of 40, 57, 88
  farmers in 24, 58, 69-70, 85, 207
  feudalism in 6-10, 11, 13, 27, 111, 203-4, 218 n.11
  Fukuzawa's support for 19-20
  internal forces in 167-8
  laws in 179, 180, 181, 182, 183-4, 197
  monarchy in 17, 111, 184, 190
  officials of 32, 44, 71, 175-6, 177, 180, 181-2
  opening of Japan and viii, ix, 22, 33, 71, 89, 90, 111, 140
  overthrow of 5, 33, 89-90, 91, 92, 102, 106, 167, 191
  political rights in 111, 127
  political unrest in 118-19, 120, 121, 123, 124, 125
  self-governance in 179, 181-2, 198, 206, 207
  vassals of 7, 9-10, 17, 20-1, 89, 175, 180, 204
Tokugawa Iemitsu 186
Tokugawa Iemochi 123
Tokugawa Ieyasu 7, 186, 204, 218 n.5, 218 n.8
  balance of power and 175-6
  statutes of 174-5, 217 n.3
Tokugawa Yoshimune 186
Tokyo 43, 47, 66, 83. *See also* Edo
Tokyo Imperial University 78
Tokyo Stock Exchange 78

Tosa domain 22, 92, 176, 189
Tōyama Shigeki 214 n.3
Toyotomi Hideyoshi 21, 206
transportation 39, 40, 68, 79
  railroads and 22, 46, 84, 101, 199
"Trend of the Times" (*Jiji taiseiron*; Fukuzawa Yukichi) 109-31
  commentary on 109-10, 127-31
Turgot, A.J.R. 4
Tytler, Alexander 14, 210 n.25

United States (U.S.) ix, 6, 66, 188
  Congress of 17, 98-9, 107, 196, 205
  Constitution of 17, 32, 38, 196-7, 205, 209 n.3
  Declaration of Independence of 17, 209 n.3
  politics in 32, 85
  president of 196, 205
  representative government in 17, 161
Utilitarianism (Mill) 160

Victoria, Queen (England) 162
vote of credit (vote of confidence; *seifu kaikaku no tōhyō*) 100

Watanabe Hiroshi 211 n.2
Weber, Max 159
West, the
  architecture of 39, 40
  civilization in 3-4, 79, 92, 101, 102
  colonialism of 80, 102
  Diet and 168, 172, 188, 198, 207
  education in 90, 129, 156
  elective assemblies in 32, 89, 190
  Fukuzawa and viii-ix, 16
  imperialism of 78, 80, 102, 203
  industrialization in ix, 5, 16, 167
  influence of viii, 50, 111, 167-8, 172, 188, 198, 207, 212(iv)
  Japanese missions to viii-ix
  learning from 56, 79, 90, 95, 111, 133, 160, 164, 187, 188
  majority rule in 140-1
  Meiji government and 23-4
  military of 3, 16, 21, 22, 90
  monarchy in 15, 17, 27, 143, 156, 160, 163, 164, 217 n.16
  religion in 12, 15, 135, 213(vi)

samurai and 11, 187
  technology of 22, 71, 90, 133
William and Mary (England) 16
William II (England) 14

Yamagata Aritomo 23
Yamaguchi Hiroe 29

Yang, Emperor (China; Sui dynasty) 173
Yanhui 50
yin yang and Five Elements 19–20
Yūbin hōchi shinbun (newspaper) 77
Yuri Kimimasa 111

Zhou dynasty (China) 7

www.ingramcontent.com/pod-product-compliance
Lightning Source LLC
Chambersburg PA
CBHW072149290426

44111CB00012B/2011